The Tradition of the Elders

The Tradition of the
Elders

The Way of the Oral Law

T. Hoogsteen

WIPF & STOCK · Eugene, Oregon

THE TRADITION OF THE ELDERS
The Way of the Oral Law

Wipf & Stock   DEC – – 2014
An Imprint of Wipf and Stock Publishers
199 W. 8th Ave., Suite 3
Eugene, OR 97401

www.wipfandstock.com

ISBN 13: 978-1-62564-905-8

Manufactured in the U.S.A.

Theodore John and Mary Ann:
For resolve

Contents

Preface

WHILE WORKING OUT THE structure of the covenant in its New Testament setting, I made a promise: to investigate the meaning and the significance of the Tradition of the Elders, Matt 15:1–20; Mark 7:1–23. Within that Tradition the agents of the Oral Law, that is, of the *paradosis,* figure prominently, throughout Matthew–Revelation always waylaying and attacking first the Christ, then the Gospel, the Church, and the coming of the Kingdom.

Slowly over the decades post-Ascension the Lord Jesus distinguished the Church from the Synagogue and the Gospel from the Oral Law, at times a painful process. Saul before he became Paul contributed to that pain, Acts 8:1–3. In contrast to the Church, the Oral Law legacy established both the origin and the destiny of Judaism, a major monotheistic religion.

Post-Pentecost the Lord Jesus drew the covenant line from the Old Testament through to the New, in the process constructing the New Israel, the Church, the present manifestation of the fullness of the Recreation.

I express appreciation to Matthew Wimer at Wipf and Stock for recognizing the merit of this book and for seeing to its publication process.

Introduction

BEFORE THE TIME THE Author of the Word inspired the New Testament documents, the Oral Law dominated the Church's social/political/ religious milieu. This Oral Law, given in the Gospels as the Tradition of the Elders, Matt 15:1–20; Mark 7:1–23, and in Pauline Letters as the written code, Rom 2:27; 2 Cor 3:6; etc., heavily decided *halakha*. This *halakha*, the comprehensive legal structure of life in Israel, the Pharisees based on Torah.[1] As much as Rome ruled in the Middle East and Hellenistic culture—religiously, morally, linguistically—permeated the Roman Empire, the Oral Law, or Oral Tradition, a path of divergence, constituted the more immediate historical environment for the writing of the Gospels, the Acts, and the Letters. Pharisaic movers and shakers had revolutionized the Church departing from the Old Testament dispensation.

Prior to the sun rising on the New Testament revelation, Mal 4:2, all commissioned Old Testament prophets solemnly inveighed against and dismissively condemned each impressionable idolatry the Church had adopted from surrounding nations and adapted for her own religiosity. After the prophetic era and in the Greco-Roman world, the people of the

1. Magonet, *The Explorer's Guide to Judaism*, 106, "Less well known outside of Judaism, but of extra-ordinary importance, is the huge body of what was to become rabbinic interpretation of the 'Torah' that spans a period from the second century BCE (Before the Common Era) right up to the tenth century, to be followed by as great a body of work of interpretation under the dominant societies of Christianity and Islam up to the modern period."

Ferguson, *Backgrounds of Early Christianity*, 375, "As a very broad generalization, subject to many qualifications, one can say that Palestinian Judaism is the most important background for the ministry of Jesus and the Gospels, and the Judaism of the Greek Diaspora is the most important background for the ministry of Paul and his Epistles and the Book of Acts."

covenant, notably the Pharisees, in subtle ways corrupted the substance of idolatry even more;[2] by John the Baptizer's time an idolatry of law brooded large in the Church, among Sadducees and Zealots as well. In the approximately 400 years between Malachi and the Baptizer's 26–27 AD ministry, the Pharisees installed and instilled the manacles of the law tradition: the Oral Law, which particularly the Pharisees defended with an unenlightened zeal for their monotheistic god, Rom 10:2. This Oral Tradition farmed out a more unsubmissive and deeper-reaching epoch of crisis in the Church than imposing Old Testament type idolatrous investments had. The Pharisees as the more resilient survivors out of the post-exilic era instigated the people of the covenant to believe an exploitive and sophisticated idolatry, the second teaching—distinct from the Written Torah, the Jewish Bible. Throughout particularly the last two pre-Christian centuries, turbulent and troublesome, Pharisaism thus fastened down the highly resistant historical and religious framework hindering, first, the work of the Christ and, a second, the inspiration of the New Testament.[3]

Now, then, *THE TRADITION OF THE ELDERS* registers and pries open the core ethic of the Oral Law, first, in its course, second, in its malice, third, in its eclipse, and fourth, in its design.

---

2. Schechter, *Studies In Judaism*, 80, "The evil inclination to worship idols was, as the Talmud expresses it allegorically, killed by the Men of the Great Synagogue, or, as we should put it, it was suppressed by the sufferings of the captivity in Babylon. This change of circumstances is marked by the following fact: — whilst the prophets mostly considered idolatry as the cause of all sin, the Rabbis show a strong tendency to ascribe sin to a defect in, or a want of, belief on the part of the sinner."

Bright, *The Kingdom of God*, 165, "The feeling was strong that Israel had purged itself, more than paid off its sin, in dire calamity. At the same time it was hard not to feel that the heathen powers were after all the true enemies of the people of God and the Kingdom of God."

Epstein, *Judaism*, 80, ". . . by the close of the exile the people was radically cured of all idolatrous taints and tendencies, and the monotheistic faith irrevocably established in Israel."

Ferguson, *Backgrounds of Early Christianity*, 378, "One problem that the postexilic community did not have, which had plagued its ancestors, was idolatry."

3. The New Testament is the final interpretation/application of Gen 3:14–19. Hence, Christianity never arose out of the vexed bowels of Pharisaism, not even out of Judaism.

Chapter 1

The Oral Law in its Course

THE DOMINATION OF THE Oral Torah gained momentum throughout the four centuries between the closing of the Old Testament canon and the opening of the New with the *Hasidim,* a movement of church members inside the post-exilic covenant community, redirecting the Lord's people, that is, they emerged in the prophetic silence of that four-century span, drifting away from covenant commitment into a human-scale rule of law. These Hasideans, the separated ones, reacted to the voracious Hellenism then sweeping also the Middle East. "A succession of Jewish leaders exhorted the Jews to resist the lure of the Hellenized . . . culture. They exposed the bait in Grecian hedonism, or philosophy of pleasure, and warned them against the folly of committing national suicide by exchanging their Jewish heritage for an 'ersatz' Greek culture."[1] With contempt for its gods, determined and questing *Hasidic* leaders actuated a corrective faction to Hellenism, but one not of the LORD God.

Rising in power, law-obsessed Hasideans, restless under Hellenism, unquestionably misread Ezra and Nehemiah as well as Haggai and Zechariah, thereby opening a giant drain sucking away faithfulness. "Almost instantaneously the whole of their religious life and outlook underwent a radical change. As they brooded over their tragic experiences which they recognized as the righteous judgment of God for their apostasy from Him, they gradually learnt to realize that their future depended on their obedience to God

---

1. Dimont, *Jews, God and History,* 77.

and entire submission to His will as communicated in the Torah."[2] Ostensibly, they concentrated on covenant law rather than promises; actually, for self-preservation, they started the Tradition of the Elders; thereby they then separated themselves from the world, the overwhelmingly invasive Hellenistic culture initially commanded by Alexander the Great (336–23 BC).[3] To this end, with divergent exegesis they laid all stress on Torah. "The Torah, which denotes 'the teaching' *par excellence,* includes doctrine and practice, religion, and morals."[4] Thus began the way of the Oral Tradition, for present purposes notably the *halakha,* the law-system of Judaism.

FACTIONS IN THE CHURCH

In BC 167, out of this defective response to Hellenism, or Greco-Romanism, sprang the Maccabees.[5] At the Maccabean decline, *c.* 63 BC, five singular groupings within the Church, Sadducees,[6] Pharisees,[7] Essenes,[8] and

---

2. Epstein, *Judaism,* 79.

3. Dimont, *Jews, God and History,* 79, "Alexander's ambition was not only to establish a Grecian empire but to extend Hellenic culture the world over. He wanted the people in his domain to speak Greek, act Greek, be Greek. This he hoped to accomplish by Hellenizing all conquered provinces."

Russell, *Between the Testaments,* 25, "It was when this policy of peaceful penetration was replaced by a policy of persecution, notably in the reign of Antiochus IV (175–63 B.C.), that a violent reaction set in which developed in time into a burning hatred of the whole Hellenistic way of life."

4. Epstein, *Judaism,* 23.

5. First Maccabees 2:42, 7:13; 2 Maccabees 14:6.

6. Russell, *Between the Testaments,* 25, "Long before the reign of Antiochus IV there had been a strong Hellenizing party among the Jews in Palestine whose ringleaders were to be found chiefly in the ranks of the wealthy and priestly aristocracy who, by reason of their social position, enjoyed the privileges of the royal court and curried the favour of the king."

7. Bronner, *Sects and Separatism During the Second Jewish Commonwealth,* 71, "It is possible that the term 'Pharisees' had its origin in a historical situation, rather than in a religious one. It is here conjectured that the title was originally applied to the 'Company of Hasidim' who, after religious freedom was attained, separated themselves from Judas Maccabeus and petitioned Alcimus for peace. The former leader and his followers contemptuously derided the group as 'separatists.'"

8. I leave the biblically unacknowledged Essenes aside.

Zealots[9]/Sicarii[10]—dissolved every sense of unity.[11] The overbearing Sadducees, preoccupied with the Temple for preserving their cult,[12] exerted power by shoring up the status quo; for this reason, they collaborated with the Roman authorities.[13] Secondly, according to their own revolutionary mindset, the Pharisees founded a self-containing life, a culture of law, the *halakic* way, an ideal of holiness. "In morals, holiness *negatively* demanded resistance to every urge of nature which made self-serving the essence of human life; and *positively,* submission to an ethic which placed service to others at the centre of the system."[14] By the well-prepared start of the Baptizer's ministry, the Pharisees had made this imposing Jewish thought-world constitutive of the Church then, contrary to the will of Yahweh,

9. Dimont, *Jews, God and History*, 98, "Politically, the composition of the Zealot party was closely akin to the earlier Hasidean party which had been responsible for the Maccabean rebellion."

Russell, *Between the Testaments*, 37, "Following the death of Herod in 4 B.C. tumults broke out in Galilee which from this time forward was known as the hot-bed of Jewish nationalism. Josephus tells us of one Judas the Galilean who, in association with Zadduk the Pharisee, rebelled against Rome and founded a new sect in A.D. 6. This is presumably the party later to be known as the Zealots (in Greek) or Cananeans (in Aramaic) or Sicarii (in Latin) which was to be a thorn in the flesh of the Romans for many years to come."

10. Flavius, *The Wars of the Jews*, II.xiii.3, "When the country was purged of [robbers], there sprang up another sort of robbers in Jerusalem, which were called Sicarii, who slew men in the daytime, and in the midst of the city; this they did chiefly at the festivals, when they mingled themselves among the multitude, and concealed daggers under their garments, with which they stabbed those that were their enemies; and when any fell down dead, the murderers became a part of those that had indignation against them; by which means they appeared persons of such reputation, that they could by no means be discovered."

11. Sanders, *Judaism*, 14, "In some respects party positions can be said to have originated during the biblical period, and especially during the exile, but the groups as we know them from Josephus, the New Testament, the Dead Sea Scrolls and rabbinic literature—the principal bodies of primary evidence—were shaped by the events of the Hasmonean uprising against the Seleucid kingdom and the period of Hasmonean rule."

12. Bickerman, *From Ezra to the Last of the Maccabees*, 139, ". . . Jonathan raised himself to the position of High Priest, despite the fact that he was not a member of the Zadokite family to which the office appertained. For the priest to obtain his position from the secular power was a Greek custom."

13. Dimont, *Jews, God and History*, 88, "With time, the political tension between Sadducees and Pharisees increased in intensity until it finally broke out into open conflict."

Bickerman, *From Ezra to the Last of the Maccabees*, 139, "Once again those who fought for the Torah accommodated the law to Gentile practices, while the legitimate High Priest (by right of descent) performed the service in a rump temple in Egypt."

14. Epstein, *Judaism*, 23.

which he had manifested in the aspiring ministries of Ezra and Nehemiah in concert with the prophetic labors of Haggai and Zechariah. Ezra 5:1. Thirdly, paroxysms of Zealotry rose and fell with the palpable pressures of Romanism within Palestine; the acuteness of each crisis made the living lash out again, implacably, even upon frightful loss of life. These three then, Sadduceism, Pharisaism, Zealotism, revolved about in the Church, the Pharisee dominating.

Persuasive only in the Church, Pharisees with roots in and the dominant spiritual heirs of the Hasidean movement enlarged the fabricated Oral Tradition. Ever brushing off the LORD God's faithfulness revealed through Ezra and Nehemiah, they ignored covenantal threats against unfaithfulness and with undisguised ambition this foremost faction in the covenant community seized upon their Torah-structured survival methodology; therewith they veered further away from the promises and the obligations into a legalization that conformed adhesively to native powers once generated by the *Hasidim*. Consciously enforcing a collective determination to separate themselves and Israel from pagan Hellenizing, the Pharisees distracted the post-exilic Church away from the covenant allegedly to live and die free of oppression by the feted ways of the Oral Law.[15]

The LORD God, however, had commanded the Church otherwise.

Post-exilic Israel's Way

Ezra, circa 458 BC, "bookman," "*Schriftgelehrter*" (rather than scribe) and priest (Ezra 7:6, 25; Neh 8:1–2, at assembled Israel's request read the law, possibly (part of) Deuteronomy.[16] Before the continuing Church, distinct then from all who remained in the Diaspora, this bookman and priest confronted the people of the Lord with the cause of the 587–39 BC exile.[17] By heart absorbing the hard facts of the Exile and acknowledging the LORD's anger for past sins, Ezra 5:12, 9:7, that generation gathered in Jerusalem sought again the way of the covenant. Similarly, Neh 8:7–8, 12,

---

15. Rivkin, *A Hidden Revolution*, 221, The Tradition of the Fathers, ". . . the *paradosis*, the laws not written down in the Law of Moses, would be the laws of the land."

16. Dimont, *Jews, God and History*, 70.

Everyone acquainted with Deuteronomy knows it conveys much more than legal information. Foremost, Moses' fifth book too reveals the LORD God's faithfulness through covenant reformation.

17. Levine, *The Aramaic Version of the Bible*, 3.

9:32. Ezra's colleague in rebuilding Jerusalem and the Temple too exposed Israel's unfaithfulness; all had forsaken the commandments by disbelieving the promises. In effect, their forefathers had broken faith. Ezra 10:2; Neh 1:8–9. Then through Ezra and Nehemiah, amidst Israel's social investments in covetousness[18] and subsequent heavy gloom of little faith, the LORD of the Church moved the biblically informed remnant to covenant faithfulness and bear unimpeachable witness before him to his glory and to Israel's crucial role in the world.

Skilled in the Law, Ezra taught the covenant people more than the impressive legalics the LORD God originally via Moses transmitted to Israel. If Ezra read (a part of) Deuteronomy, this document, no bare rulebook, clearly revealed the LORD's faithfulness through reformation, which constituted Israel's life with respect to the promises and the obligations. At an annual covenant feast, of Booths, i.e., initiation of harvest, Pentecost,[19] Ezra charged the people to gather in the right crop, covenant faithfulness. In a coordination of biblically-attuned heart and mind, with enviable stamina, Ezra 9:6–15, he in prayer remembered the Abrahamic covenant formation, in which he referenced redemptive acts of the indelible Exodus, Ezra 9:10–15, thereby to intercede for Israel's post-exilic ingratitude. The continuity between these two covenant formations, Abrahamic and Mosaic, carved open before the Church the way of the future.

One of the progressive responses the LORD's men insisted upon: the expulsion of all unbelievers[20] from the Church—Canaanite, Hittite, Perizzite, Jebusite, Ammonite, Moabite, Egyptian, and Amorite, Ezra 9:1–5. In this exacting way, rather than forcible conversions, the LORD God once more excommunicated the uncircumcised heart from out of his people and nation. This expulsion included wives of foreign descent who through idolatry scandalized the First Commandment, Ezra 9:1–5, 10:1–5; Neh 9:16–31, 10:28–31, 13:1–9, 13:23–27. Aiming at much more than mar-

18. Dimont, *Jews, God and History*, 65, "Many Jewish history books draw a picture of sorrow and desolation when writing the Jewish captivity in Babylon. Fortunately, this is an inaccurate picture. In the sixth century Babylonia was ruled by a series of enlightened kings who treated their captives with tolerance. Those Jews who 'wept by the rivers of Babylon' were but a handful of zealots; the rest of the Jews fell in love with the country, prospered, and became cultured."

19. Lev 23:34, 42.

20. A misinterpretation: Roth, *A Short History of the Jewish People*, 59, "... [Ezra] had done little beyond securing the appointment of a commission to enquire into the mixed marriages which had been made, and to enforce the severance of all extraneous family ties." Ezra 7:25–26.

riage reform, both Ezra and Nehemiah, backed by Haggai and Zechariah, commanded the covenantal marriage pattern common to the Church since the appealing events recorded in Gen 24:1–67; Abraham determined that Isaac's wife not be one out of the idolatrous uncircumcised. Hence, the purging of foreign-born wives fitted within the greathearted call to covenant faithfulness.

Another response in covenant faithfulness Ezra and Nehemiah tersely enforced: righteous sabbath observance, Neh 10:31, 13:15–22. As the LORD God had commanded through Moses, so again at this historic, post-exilic juncture, he willed upright remembrance and observation of the Sabbath joyfully grounded in the Fourth Commandment, not seductive habits acquired by traffic of assimilation.

With Haggai and Zechariah's support, Ezra and Nehemiah demanded marriage and sabbath reforms not because the Seventh and Fourth Commandments required more respect than the others, but because through vagrant sinning against these Commandments Israel still expressed unfaithfulness of heart, despite the Exile. By divine intervention, sins against the marriage and sabbath institutions at that time and in that place called for the elementary grasp on real amendment. Thus, through actually ongoing reformation, the vulnerable men of the Lord in royal service repurposed the glowing future given Abraham and ingrained for covenant living through Moses.

Israel, however, undefeated in idolatry, took control of an ideological course, renouncing the biblical plumb line of righteousness.

Post-exilic Israel's Deviation

1. In Israel, the *Hasidim* reacted negatively to the Hellenization then sweeping into the *civilized* world from Greece to India, from the Black Sea to far up the Nile; in response, the separated ones of the covenant community strove for a *kadosh*, a holiness, different from Abraham's. "Israel had thus to be apart *from* the world and yet remain *of* the world. Whilst keeping distinct from the surrounding nations, they had to throw the whole of their effort into the midst of current civilizations, seeking to raise human life to higher levels of existence. This was no easy task; yet they were to perform it because the Holy God[21] who had chosen them was to be observed in Holi-

---

21. To keep in mind: the *Hasidim* initiated Jewish monotheism, a divinity inconsistent

ness, and because their life could achieve its meaning only in the universal service to which they were summoned."[22] Except the *Hasidim* movement in its competitive process with Hellenism laid the basis for a contra-biblical enterprise; they collaborated to achieve in Israel a holiness adverse to covenant history. "The destruction of the temple and the Babylonian captivity had violently shocked the Jews. The God-fearing people among them realized that what had befallen them was the result of departure from Jehovah their God, and that their only hope of reconciliation and restoration was by returning to him with their whole heart (Jer. 29:13). God's law, as revealed in the Pentateuch, must be obeyed so that God's favor may again rest on his people."[23] Misinterpreting Ezra and Nehemiah, as well as Haggai and Zechariah, all imbued by the Hasidic ideal sought a social cohesion in *kadosh* less by covenant faithfulness and more by a natural hankering for legalism, which started off the Oral Law.[24]

---

with and, worse, in opposition to the Trinity.

Baeck, *The Essence of Judaism,* 59, "Monotheism is the result of a realization of the absolute character of the moral law; moral consciousness teaches about God." Ibid., 60, "Nothing like this birth of monotheism out of Israel's moral consciousness has ever occurred elsewhere in history. It is idle to speculate if and in what form it might have come into existence under different circumstances. Historically the fact remains that monotheism was given to mankind by Israel and by Israel alone."

Epstein, *Judaism,* 134, "They negate all embodiments and notions of the Deity which, however refined and sublimated, veil the one and only God of Israel more than they reveal Him. Thus are excluded, not only all dualistic no less than polytheistic creeds, but also the 'Trinity in Unity' of Christianity which, however much it may be explained away so as to make it compatible with the *one* God in the metaphysical sense, remains a direct denial of the *only* God who, from the beginning, had chosen Israel in His service."

22. Epstein, *Judaism,* 30–31. Ibid., 23, Epstein placed a more biblical definition, "The significance of this holiness is indicated in the meaning of its Hebrew equivalent, *kadosh,* which, whatever its etymology, expresses a quality consisting negatively in 'separation *from*' and positively in 'dedication *to*'. Applied to the charge laid upon Israel, holiness entails negatively a separation from all that is opposed to the will of God, and positively a dedication to His service."

23. Hendriksen, *Matthew,* 609.

24. Roth, *A Short History of the Jewish People,* 63, "In the traditional view, the memoirs of Nehemiah constituted the last of the canonical books of the Hebrew Bible. The subsequent period was, from the literary standpoint, an utter blank. . . . What was hitherto considered a period of intellectual quiescence now appears as one of unparalled literary activity. It is regarded as the period of the final redaction of the Pentateuch: of the composition of literary masterpieces . . ."

Later, as the Maccabean revolution disintegrated and its little known power-hungry leaders, the Hasmoneans, submitted to Hellenization,[25] the Church divided more determinately into bitterly clashing Pharisaism and Sadduceism, an early manifestation of denominationalism, with Zealotism operating on Israel's confrontational field of action from the sidelines. This costly denominationalism, hopelessly divided and divisive, broke the Church into complicated religious structures and movements.

2. The original *halakhah*—or *halakha*—foundation consisted of the Written Torah, at first, technically, the Pentateuch, to which later also belonged the Prophets and the Hagiographa, i.e., the Writings.[26] The Written Torah received canonized status by the ending of the first dispensation, thus constituting *Ta Nakh*,[27] the Hebrew Bible, which the Church later called the Old Testament. "The major product of the Jewish historical process was the Hebrew Bible, and this, in turn, produced its own dynamic: studying it, teaching it, and observing its *dicta* as elaborated and specified in the evolving Oral Tradition."[28] *Ta Nakh,* notably the Books of Moses,[29] presumptive Pharisees shared with temple-hugging Sadducees[30] and the (easily aroused

25. Bickerman, *From Ezra to the Last of the Maccabees,* 157, "This accommodation of new elements to the Bible, this consideration for native tradition, characterizes the Hellenization carried through under the Maccabees, and differentiates it from the rationalistic assimilation which had been the aim of the reform party."

26. Schechter, *Aspects of Rabbinic Theology,* 121, "For indeed 'the Torah is a *triad,* composed of Pentateuch, Prophets, and Hagiographa.'"

27. Ferguson, *Backgrounds of Early Christianity,* 505, "The modern Hebrew name for the complete Jewish Bible is Tanak, a word made up from the first letter of the name in Hebrew for each of the three parts (T = Torah [Law]; N = Nebiim [Prophets]; K = Kethubim [Writings])."

28. Levine, *The Aramaic Version of the Bible,* 5.

29. Kirsh, *We Christians and Jews,* 13, ". . . the books from Genesis through Deuteronomy contain much more than legislation; they contain narratives that we view as 'sacred history,' stories about heroes of faith like Abraham and Moses in which God is discerned as playing the decisive role."

30. Magonet, *The Explorer's Guide to Judaism,* 122, "The predecessors of the rabbis, the Pharisees (Hebrew: *perushim,* 'those separated', or 'separatists') stood in conflict with the descendants of the aristocratic priestly families, the Sadducees, whose power base was the Temple. The Pharisees transferred much of the ritual life from the Temple to the synagogue, placed great stress on study and personal religious observance and gradually played a greater and greater role in the civil and political life of Jewish society. By the first century CE they appear to have represented the beliefs and practices of most of the Jewish people."

Russell, *Between the Testaments,* 52, "Like the Pharisees they believed in the supremacy

to violence) Zealots/Sicarii. In the interminable frictions between these church groupings, exhaustive *halakha* burgeoned into a living law,[31] one modified and intensified to transcend disquieting times and crises of confidence by cultural adaption.

Aggressive Pharisees[32] assisted by scribes[33] to deform the Church and round out *halakha* boosted the Oral Law, a system of law symbiotic with the Written Torah. Down through the ages, the Written Torah and much more the Oral called for intensive study, teaching, and dissemination, ". . . since the repristination of the Law of God was one of the eschatological functions expected in late Judaism to occur in the End Time."[34] In this sense, the Law lived through drastic Persian, Greek, and Roman shifts into an eternal future. "In the broadest sense, however, the study of Torah refers not only to the Scriptures and the Oral Torah, but also to the entire body of rabbinic legislation and interpretation based upon the Torah that developed over the centuries."[35] The Pharisees thereby interpreted *halakha* according to two distinctive traditions of transmission, the Oral Torah systematically dominating the Written.[36] "By teaching and interpreting the Torah, both written and oral, and by applying it to every-day life they 'democratized religion', making it personal and operative in the experience of the common people. Their chief instrument in propagating the Torah was the Synagogue, which became a most powerful institution within Judaism

---

of the Torah, but unlike them they refused to acknowledge the binding authority of the oral law. They had, it is true, traditions and usages of their own both ritual and legal, but as these did not trace their origin back to Moses they were not regarded as being on a level with the Torah."

31. Russell, *Between the Testaments,* 50, "It is certainly true that, though the Pharisees were staunch supporters of 'tradition', to them it was no dead thing, and undoubtedly in certain of their doctrines (e.g. the Messianic Kingdom, the life beyond, belief in a multiplicity of demons and angels, etc.) they were influenced by Persian thought."

32. For balance, cf. Sanders, *Judaism,* 11–12, "Many scholars write in the assumption that Judaism was *divided* into parties; but the parties were quite small, and . . . none of them was able to coerce the general populace into adopting its platform."

33. Bickerman, *From Ezra to the Last of the Maccabees,* 69, "The scribe is not a lawyer acting in behalf of a client; but like the Roman *juris periti* of the same period, a person who has such knowledge of the laws and customs as to act as authority for the judge to follow in his decisions."

34. Kee, *Jesus in History,* 130.

35. Donin, *To Be a Jew,* 27.

36. Ibid., 27, "Torah is the embodiment of the Jewish faith. It contains the terms of his Covenant with God. It is what makes a Jew a Jew."

not only in Jerusalem, but also throughout the whole Dispersion."[37] With the twofold Law, conspicuous Pharisees controlled the LORD's Church,[38] leading her onto a historical off-ramp into a formidable opposition against, initially, the Incarnation.

In order to achieve this *halakha* and its holiness, the Pharisees as first perceived revelation in the sense of legal instruction. "Torah means more than law. It means 'instruction from God,' and as such has the force of the expressions 'revelation' and 'Word of God.'"[39] On shifting grounds of history they sought for order and stability, hence this deduction, ". . . *Torah* is the fountainhead of all wisdom, as broadly conceived."[40]

INSTRUCTIONS FROM THE WRITTEN LAW

Out of the original Torah,[41] the Pentateuch, the Hasidic circle of sages collected 613 *mitzvot (mitzvoth, mitzwoth)*,[42] wherein they included the

---

37. Russell, *Between the Testaments*, 51.

Bickerman, *From Ezra to the Last of the Maccabees*, 161, ". . . the Pharisees . . . wished to embrace the whole people, and in particular through education. It was their desire and intention that everyone in Israel achieve holiness through the study of the Torah, and their guiding principle was: 'Raise up many disciples.'"

Bronner, *Sects and Separatism During the Second Jewish Commonwealth*, 79, "The Pharisees, on the other hand, being essentially a religious party, drawing the majority of its members from the middle classes wished to see religion at work in all spheres of life. They wanted to deprive the priestly aristocracy of too much authority and wished to make the Torah the inheritance of each and every Jew."

38. Rivkin, *A Hidden Revolution*, 253, "The Pharisees were powerful, yet the very source of their power, the Unwritten Law, has effectively barred scholars from fully comprehending, or even acknowledging, it. The Pharisees wrote down neither their Oral Law nor their Oral Lore, since their commitment to oral transmission was a principled one. It was necessary to maintain this principle inviolate lest they, the Pharisees, be charged with violating the Pentateuchal commandment forbidding any addition to or subtraction from the laws which Moses had written down. To such charges, the Pharisees could plead innocent, for they had added nothing to the written laws; nor had they deleted any written laws."

39. Kirsh, *We Christians and Jews*, 13.

40. Levine, *The Aramaic Version of the Bible*, 135.

41. Schechter, *Aspects of Rabbinic Theology*, 117, "To the Jew the word *Torah* means a teaching or an instruction of any kind."

42. Taylor and Ricci, "Three Biblical Models of Liberty And Some Representative Laws," 123, ". . . Israel seems to cover all bases in terms of its supreme law insofar as it formulates the ultimate criterion both ways—positively and negatively. Interestingly, of the 613 laws of Rabbinical Judaism, 248 of them are positively formulated and 365 are negatively formulated."

Ten Commandments once dominically spelled out at the Sinai. "The chief paradigm of *revelation* for Jews is the event at Mount Sinai, when God gave Moses the law by which his people were to know how to do his will. The model-event of *redemption* for Jews is God's action in freeing his people from Egypt under the leadership of Moses."[43] Perceived and received as instruction, Torah and *mitzvot* followed touching but separate paths in Jewish religion. "Torah and Mitzvoth are a complement to each other, or, as a Rabbi expressed it, 'they borrow from each other, as wisdom and understanding—charity and loving-kindness—the moon and the stars,' but they are not identical. To use the modern phraseology, to the Rabbinic Jew, Torah was both an institution and a faith."[44] They, in effect, moved in perceptively concurrent and distinctive ways through the disintegration of pagan glory days, even in unstable environments; nevertheless, the Hebrew Bible and the *mitzvot* evolved always distinguishably different.[45]

Though these *mitzvot*, that is, the foundation of the Oral Law, regulated incremental changes and ever-expanding insights, yet under scrutiny their structural integrity remained amazingly standard. "Great rabbinic scholars-philosophers, therefore, found a greater measure of agreement among themselves in their *minyan hamitzvot*, the classification of the 613 religious duties which the Torah places upon the Jew, than in their attempts to present basic Jewish dogma in the forms of articles of faith."[46] This ingenuous "yoke of all 613 commandments"[47] characterized the Church's development (read: historic shift to deter the Incarnation) during the intertestamentary centuries, a prophet-less era[48] of complex challenges. A partial illustration of the *mitzvot*:

> 59. To honour father and mother (Ex. 20:12).
>
> 60. Not to smite a father or a mother (Ex. 21:15).
>
> 61. Not to curse a father or mother (Ex. 21:17).
>
> 62. To reverently fear father and mother (Lev. 19:3).[49]

43. Kirsch, *We Christians and Jews*, 98.

44. Schechter, *Aspects of Rabbinic Theology*, 117–18.

45. Kendall and Rosen, *The Christian and the Pharisee*, 127, "Judaism requires us to understand the written text through the prism of the Oral Tradition and exposition."

46. Donin, *To Be a Jew*, 28–29.

47. Freedman, *Jew vs. Jew*, 26.

48. Among the apocryphal writings, the author(s) of 1 Maccabees 4:46, 9:27, 14:41 awaited the recruitment of a true prophet.

49. Judaism 101, "A List of the 613 Mitzvot (Commandments)"—Webmaster@

Truth is, 60–62 reveal not separate, sagacious rules, but regulatory applications of the Fifth Commandment. Bridge building, the driver for the selection of these four appears below, relative to Matt 15:1–20; Mark 7:1–23.

The 613, individually *mitzvah*, drawn from Moses' Five Books,[50] hoary sages passed on from generation to generation in a relatively simple format—by word of mouth out of retentive memory—whatever grinding contingencies of time and place. By way of these baseline mitzvot, detached from the Written Torah, first the Hasidim, then the Pharisaic faction invoked a disruptive legacy: to superimpose the unwinding Oral Law upon the vulnerable Church. "Whilst the Decalogue indicated the substance and scope of Israel's 'priestly mission', it did not provide for the specific duties and obligations that devolved upon the people as a 'holy nation'. These were developed in a series of revelations to Moses which he transmitted to the people and which, incorporating the Decalogue, finally became the Torah commonly known as the Law, of which the Pentateuch is the written record."[51] In Judaism, the distance separating the twofold Law, however vague, vaguer, vaguest, always survived.

CLARIFICATIONS FOR THE ORAL LAW

The Oral Torah, allegedly contiguous with the Written, yet free moving, emanated outward exponentially in substance and authority. To legitimate their goal, Pharisaic Rabbis grew roots for the second teaching; they imposed the belief that a monotheistic Yahweh-substitute had granted Moses also this other tradition.

JewFAQ.Org

50. Epstein, *Judaism*, 23, "The Torah . . . is the direct consequence of the Sinaitic Covenant in its twofold implications—universal and national. While the Ten Commandments indicated the substance and the scope of Israel's universal 'priestly mission', the other Commandments were designed to train Israel for the holiness which they were to follow as a nation called upon to become 'holy unto God.'"

51. Epstein, *Judaism*, 22.

Magonet, *The Explorer's Guide to Judaism*, 106, "The important thing is that from the very earliest stages of the post-biblical period the Scriptures were examined for clues as to the meaning of contemporary events, as well as for expanding particular laws that operated within God's covenant with Israel."

The Origin of the Oral Law

1. By far the more popular interpretation for the birth force of the Oral Torah: the God of the Pharisees revealed this Tradition through Moses at the Sinai, that is, a revelation additional to the Pentateuch. The source of the second teaching therefore ran co-existential and co-constitutive with Moses' Five Books. "Side by side with the Five Books of Moses (Pentateuch), we believe that God's will was also made manifest in the Oral Tradition or Oral Torah which also had its source at Sinai, revealed to Moses and then orally taught by him to the religious heads of Israel."[52] At Sinai, in effect, this monotheistic deity granted Moses the optimal methodology for interpreting the Written Law, one not to be recorded, which second teaching Moses had to pass on unsullied. "This is how the Rabbinic tradition recorded its origins as the inheritors of the Torah: Moses to Joshua to the elders to the prophets. This is familiar biblical territory, though we might be surprised at the prominence given to the 'elders', who usually blend into the scenery in the biblical stories. The chain of tradition is passed through this line."[53] "The Rabbis however regarded it as equally ancient and equally important with the written Law. Both were received by Moses from (God on) Sinai, but the latter was committed to writing at once."[54] Transmitted verbally from generation to generation out of concern for essentially applying the baseline 613, the empirically minded second teaching proponents venerated a Pharisee-sensible strategy for order and stability in Judaism from its earliest day.

Specifically, this larger and overbearing twin to the Written Torah, the two locked symbiotically, initially clarified the *mitzvot,* many of which were worded (too) succinctly; the inheritors of the Written Torah in post-exilic Israel found these commandments, such as the Fourth, virtually unintelligible, lacking nuance, without the Oral Torah. Purportedly, then, before gaining its own life and religious impetus, the second teaching originated with Moses[55] to make the Written Torah logical and livable.

52. Donin, *To Be a Jew,* 24–25.
Barrett, *The New Testament Background,* 145.

53. Magonet, *The Explorer's Guide to Judaism,* 119.

54. Barrett, *The New Testament Background,* 139. Ibid., 145, "This oral Law (. . .) was believed equally with the written to have originated with Moses (. . .), and was consequently of equal authority."

55. Levine, *The Aramaic Version of the Bible,* 16, "According to legend, Moses had wanted to commit the Mishnah to writing but God made him desist. For God saw that

2. Others registered a second conventional way to explain the Oral Law's origins, one that anchored it early in post-exilic Israel, during the first century of the intertestamentary period. A paradigm shift had occurred, initially calming. "The peaceful existence enjoyed by the Jews under their Persian rulers enabled them to maintain and develop without any outside interference the work begun by Ezra. A succession of teachers known as *Soferim* (Scribes), generally identified with the Men of the Great Assembly, arose with the resolve to make the Torah the common possession of the people. With this aim in view they taught the Torah in Synagogue and school. They interpreted the biblical ordinances—civil, domestic, economic, and social—formulating their underlying principles, classifying their details, fixing their norms, regulating their usages, and adapted the laws to changes in conditions and circumstances. In their interpretation of the Holy Writ they were guided by the light of reason and the principles of righteousness, justice, and equity which were for them equally part of revealed Torah. They accordingly sought to mitigate the apparent severity of the law, bringing it more into harmony with life, and with the fundamental human wants."[56] The second teaching with its less rigorous rules thus had a post-exilic origin.

This other interpretation of the Oral Law's origins found its own believability in Jewish folk currents and religious disputes of the early post-exilic corporate community's existence.[57] "The first reinterpretations of Mosaic injunctions may have been based on nothing more than cleverness. But soon the interpreters were carried away by their own inventiveness. To outdo each other, they sought for profundity instead of mere ingenuity, and a new Biblical science was born, that of *Midrash,* or 'exposition.'"[58] This

---

the nations of the world would translate the Torah into Greek and then claim that they possessed the correct version."

56. Epstein, *Judaism,* 86.

Simon, *Jewish Sects at the Time of Jesus,* 37, "It should be added that both the movement which led them to enrich the unadorned biblical creed and their multiplication of commandments proceeded basically from the same tendency: in both cases they moved forward, beyond the written text."

57. Magonet, *The Explorer's Guide to Judaism,* 119, "Somewhere in this practice over the centuries evolved what was to become the 'oral Torah', itself an ever-growing body of material. Presumably that is why there is a repetition of the phrase 'handing on' . . . when we come to the 'Men of the Great Assembly.'"

58. Dimont, *Jews, God and History,* 164.

Magonet, *The Explorer's Guide to Judaism,* 106, "The key term we need to know is 'Midrash'. From a Hebrew root 'd-r-sh' meaning to 'search' or 'seek out', it means to explore

'new' science in a later epoch of conflict and fear of the unknown, that of the Hasmonean king-priests, gave contentious voice to the ideological mentality of the Pharisees caught up in its thought-world throughout post-exilic Israelite communities in Palestine and Babylonia.[59] In seeking applicatory meaning for the biblical laws conformable to the post-exilic paradigm, Rabbis therefore precipitated the Oral Torah,[60] an ever-growing body of overzealous exposition with slothful reliance on *mitzvot*. "Here we meet the *soferim*, 'scribes'—a word derived directly from *sefer*, 'a book'—whose task it was to instruct the people in their tradition."[61] Hence, these bookmen[62] out of a peculiar longing for ultimate unity coupled with a free moving logic added layers upon open-ended layers of complexity[63] to secure an ever-present life in death and a poise in undying hope for independence long centuries after Moses' death on Pisgah's top.[64]

---

in depth the different levels of meaning contained within a word, and in particular how that meaning can be affected by the context in which it is found."

59. Roth, *A Short History of the Jewish People*, 80, "Tradition had gradually broadened, from precedent to precedent; the decisions or practices of one Rabbi served as guidance for successive generations; a considerable body of oral tradition grew up to reinforce or supplement or clarify the Biblical text; fresh ideas were assimilated and given a Jewish tinge."

60. Ibid., 59, "The security of the capital once assured, Nehemiah threw himself, with the same zeal and organising ability, into the work of moral regeneration. In the long night of the Babylonian Exile, the conception of the 'Law of Moses' had gained a stronger, more intimate hold upon the consciousness of the Jewish people, but it was not yet observed in all its details by the masses."

61. Magonet, *The Explorer's Guide to Judaism*, 119.

62. Levine, *The Aramaic Version of the Bible*, 4, "Two centuries [after Ezra] there exists a class of 'bookmen' (Heb. *Soperim*, sing. *soper*). They are *not* primarily 'scribes', although the copying and transmission of texts was surely a concern they shared. Rather, their primary function was the study and interpretation of the sacred text in harmony with evolving uncodified tradition, enacting appropriate decrees, and instructing the populace."

63. Sanders, *Judaism*, 388, "The person who reads most scholarly accounts of the Judaism of our period finds lurking everywhere two ghostly figures, not only omnipresent but also all-controlling: the Pharisees and the Sanhedrin. In Josephus the reader discovers 'Mosaic' commandments that are not in fact in the Bible; the usual scholarly reconstruction is that he got them from the Pharisees, who singlehandedly created all extra-biblical laws. The priests had all sorts of rules governing sacrifice and temple procedure: at each step, they followed the Pharisees."

64. Kirsh, *We Christians and Jews*, 105, "Jews went on to identify Wisdom with the Torah, and attributes were exchanged between them. The Torah, too, was said to have been made before the foundation of the world, and to have assisted God in the creation (Ecclesiasticus 24:8–11, 23; Bar. 3:37—4:1)."

3. To legitimate authority in the Church Pharisees drew with abandon out of a variety of texts to prove a direct line from Moses over the *Soferim* to themselves. However, these biblical texts never even implied a continuous trajectory from the LORD-commissioned Moses for the Pharisees to establish their heterodox legal culture foisted upon the covenant community. Nor had the *Soferim* a visceral legacy in Ezra. Only, the *Soferim* and Pharisees disrupted the exegetical history of the Old Testament; by an ideological overpowering of the Hebrew Bible, they crossed a line to provide legitimacy for the post-exilic Tradition of the Elders. Passages they cited founded no *Moses-Soferim-Pharisee* easy road from a previous era into the world of the teachers of the Oral Torah.

- Exod 18:25–26, "Moses chose able men out of all Israel, and made them heads over the people, rulers of thousands, of hundreds, of fifties, and of tens. And they judged the people at all times; hard cases they brought to Moses, but any small matter they decided themselves."

- Deut 1:15–16, "So I took the heads of your tribes, wise and experienced men, and set them as heads over you, commanders of thousands, commanders of hundreds, commanders of fifties, commanders of tens, and officers, throughout your tribes. And I charged your judges at that time, 'Hear the cases between your brethren, and judge righteously between a man and his brother or the alien that is with him.'"

- Deut 17:8–9, "If any case arises requiring decision between one kind of homicide and another, one kind of legal right and another, or one kind of assault and another, any case within your towns which is too difficult for you, then you shall arise and go up to the place which the LORD your God will choose, and coming to the Levitical priests, and to the judge who is in office in those days, you shall consult them, and they shall declare to you the decision."

- Deut 31:19, "Now therefore write this song, and teach it to the people of Israel; put it in their mouths, that this song may be a witness for me against the people of Israel."

Stepping back: these passages point out formidable leaders and judges whom the LORD God had appointed to respective offices; they were no independent or separate class of bookmen, nor plausible lawmakers in an orderly ascent from and continuous with Moses. Basically, they were judges, never teachers, or makers, of the Law in the Pharisaical sense.

In contrast, seeking post-exilic powers of recovery during a moral low, Hasidim leadership constructed the foundation for the expanding mass of the Oral Law. With scant regard for the historical situation of the Church, these *Soferim*, proto-Pharisees, with inexplicable expository legerdemain also sought legitimacy from Nehemiah.

- Neh 8:6–8, "And Ezra blessed the LORD, the great God; and all the people answered, 'Amen, Amen,' lifting up their hands; and they bowed their heads and worshiped the LORD with their faces to the ground. Also Jeshua, Bani, Sherebiah, Jamin, Akkub, Shabbethai, Hodiah, Maaseiah, Kelita, Azariah, Jozabad, Hanan, Pelaiah, the Levites, helped the people to understand the law, while the people remained in their places. And they read from the book, from the law of God, clearly; and they gave the sense, so that the people understood the reading."[65] Such legerdemain never served the Church well.

These Levites, serving as willing couriers,[66] spread out and pressed home Ezra's reading. In part, the teaching consisted of instruction. Neh 8:9–10. In part, the Levites translated the reading into other languages; Neh 13:24, ". . . half of their children spoke the language of Ashdod, and they could not speak the language of Judah, but the language of each people." Here, the highly salient function of Ezra and the Levites consisted of teaching from the Word: a one-time effort, never an institution under compulsion to fabricate a secondary law system. Ezra with the assistance of (leading) Levites, therefore, clarified the plain sense of the Law.

However, supportive of Hasidic interpretation, Pharisees with equal elasticity predicated on the texts cited above, whereby they normalized and forwarded this improbable provocation of making laws always constitutive

65. Read with a care: Roth, *A Short History of the Jewish People*, 60, "On its conclusion, a special fast was ordained to express the general contrition. Immediately afterwards, the whole of the assembled people entered into a solemn League and Covenant. A formal contract was drawn up, binding on all who subscribed to observe certain fundamental prescriptions. To this, the chiefs of all the clans, from the governor himself downwards, affixed their seals. It was a memorable gathering, marking the beginning of the implicit reign of Law over the Jewish people, and it seems to have lived in the popular recollection as the Great Assembly, to which the last of the prophets were supposed to have handed on the torch of tradition."

66. Epstein, *Judaism*, 84, "On either side of Ezra stood professional expounders (*Mebinim*) who explained what was being read."

of the Oral Torah. Therefore, even a mediating connective between Moses and Ezra moved onto elusive terrain, terrain devoid of even a superficial basis anywhere in the Hebrew Bible, since not all agreed with this origination. "Rabbinic Judaism, though it claimed to have sprung directly from Moses, may be said to have begun with Ezra and contemporaries[67] and to have been handed down from them as the staple and official form of religion in Palestine in the time of our Lord."[68] Following through upon this manipulative way, such procedural mediation failed with respect to Old Testament historical givens.[69] In effect, Pharisaism broke with the hitherto normal administrative structure of the covenant community—kings, prophets, priests/Levites—in favor of Rabbis and scribes.

The Purpose of the Oral Law

Respectful of the 613's leading role, none specified "how" these ought to be worked out, applied specifically. Despite the clarity of the four *mitzvot* listed above to honor parents, none deduced rule(s) of application, teaching(s) on fearing and honoring parents, and much less method(s) of punishment.[70] Nor did these four clarify what constituted smiting and cursing. Similarly, the other *mitzvot* "revealed" no patterns for behavior or retribution, which permeated them according to Pharisaic intellectual forces with an ambiguous status. Hence application of the *mitzvot* became

67. Roth, *A Short History of the Jewish People*, 61, "Jewish tradition has tended to subordinate the name of Nehemiah to that of his colleague, notwithstanding the fact that the latter appears in the original sources as a personality less active, less authoritative, and less distinct. Later literature speaks of Ezra the Scribe almost as a second Moses, and numerous religious institutions of hoary antiquity are traced back to his initiative. There is in this something more than pure fancy. For the essential part of the work of resettlement in Palestine lay not so much in the political as in the literary and spiritual sphere."

68. Barrett, *The New Testament Background*, 139.

69. A misinterpretation: Roth, *A Short History of the Jewish People*, 62, "The modern critical school ascribes to Ezra, not merely the enforcement, but the redaction and even the authorship of a substantial portion of what subsequently became known as the *Torah*—the Law of Moses. Whether or not this is the case, it remains an indisputable fact that, with Ezra, the reign of the *Torah* over the Jewish people began—enforced, in the first instance, with the aid of civil authority. It is significant that the institution of the public reading and interpretation of the scriptures is associated traditionally with this period. Houses of prayer were now set up perhaps for the first time in localities distant from the Temple: a practice encouraged by the exigencies of the Babylonian exile."

70. Often, punishment happened by stoning, Lev 24:14; Num 14:10, 15:36; Deut 13:10; etc.

the core commitment, the *raison d' etre,* of the Oral Torah. "This was a body of material which in fact grew up as explanation and expansion of the written Law of the Old Testament."[71] In day-to-day response to this ambiguity, the proprietary Rabbis pursued the expansible limits of the *mitzvot* even into meaningless minutiae.

In its restless pursuit, the second teaching pushed the boundaries of Israel's Pharisaic holiness into more accessibility for public consumption, thereby generating increased social pressure to conform. "The Oral Torah included the finer points of the commandments, the details of the general principles contained in the Scriptures and the ways by which the commandments were to be applied. For example, the Torah forbids 'work' on the Sabbath. What constitutes 'work'? How shall 'work' be defined for purposes of the Sabbath? Except for several references to such tasks as gathering wood,[72] kindling fire, cooking and baking,[73] the Written Torah does not say. The Oral Torah does."[74] More. "The Written Torah prescribes capital punishment for various crimes. What legal rules and procedures had to be followed before such a verdict could be handed down? What were the limitations? The Written Torah does not say. The Oral Torah does."[75] These applicatory functions of the second teaching released fluidity into its adaptive temperament. ". . . the entire Jewish enterprise for two thousand years has been precisely to 'add to and subtract from' these words in the sense of interpreting and re-interpreting them for our own time, place and circumstances. Effectively by 'shutting down' the biblical record, by freezing these 'Five Books' and then the rest of the Hebrew Bible as unchangeable 'Scripture', the door has to be open to interpretation, and it is evident that the Judaism of the past two thousand years is that which was built up painstakingly by successive generations of rabbis, sometimes in quite clear contradiction to the biblical text itself."[76] Another il-

71. Barrett, *The New Testament Background,* 139.

Bronner, *Sects and Separatism During the Second Jewish Commonwealth,* 70, "It must also be borne in mind that the work of interpretation of the laws was carried out mainly by the teachers of the Pharisaic party and not by all the members."

72. Num 15:32–36.

73. Exod 16:23.

74. Donin, *To Be a Jew,* 25–26.

75. Ibid., p. 26.

76. Magonet, *The Explorer's Guide to Judaism,* 105. Also, "This should be neither surprising nor shocking, for such is the nature of all revealed Scriptures. They are fixed in time and space by the moment at which they are given, or at least committed to written form. However their very 'givenness' is the challenge they offer to present practices that

lustrative malleability: "The Scriptural injunction, 'And you shall teach them the statutes and the laws, and shall show them the way wherein they should walk and the deeds they should do (Ex. 18:20)' is accordingly paraphrased 'And you shall teach them the statutes and the *Torah,* and shall instruct them in the prayers they should pray in their synagogues, and the way they should visit the sick and bury the dead: how to perform lovingkindness and how to behave according to the strictures of the law and beyond the strictures of the law, even to the wicked."[77] Thus, to stand by the *mitzvot,* the second teaching allotted in many *explanatory gaps* specific applicatory insights and standard practices for the Jewish web of life.

These oral teachings once started and long transmitted by word of mouth, the Pharisees ceaselessly manipulated for living the code of interpretation relative to the 613, at least for themselves. "This Oral Torah—which clarifies and provides the details for many of the commandments contained in the Written Torah—was transmitted from generation to generation until finally recorded in the second century to become the cornerstone upon which the Talmud was built."[78] In other words, rephrased, the Second Law consisted originally of orally transmitted instruction, providing interpretive details for many Commandments, all the while laboriously acquiring its own existence. "Thus there had come into existence a body of teaching more modern, more pliable, more living, than that which the Temple priesthood could provide. The interpretation of the Bible, as the Rabbis conceived it, was less stereotyped; their legal decisions tended to be milder; and they did not scruple even to circumvent the strict letter of the *Torah* by transparent legal fictions."[79] Therefore, the Oral Tradition built a universe of meaning and living alternative to the Hebrew Bible, this to allay moral infirmities, settle endless conflicts in the Church, and prolong visible escapes from the forthright thankfulness the LORD God commanded by way of the Ten.

From its command position, then, this second teaching transmitted instructions for understanding and living the *mitzvot.* Effectively, the Oral Torah provided clarification for many of the commandments found in the Written Law, hedging about with verbiage the reliable directives of the Law. "The meaning of Scripture as set forth by the oral tradition takes its leave of the meaning gained from a naïve, literal reading . . . Scripture requires

are inevitably different."

77. Levine, *The Aramaic Version of the Bible,* 135.

78. Donin, *To Be a Jew,* 25.

79. Roth, *A Short History of the Jewish People,* 80.

decoding, which is what the rabbinic sages accomplish."[80] At heart, the Oral Law served to superintend Israel's over-all trends for stimulating individual as well as communal sanctification in holiness for the pious-seeming light of Pharisaic habits of thought. ". . . it is clear from the records that Pharisaism was at heart legalistic in character, and legalism can easily lead to formalism, and formalism to externalism and unreality, defects which revealed themselves in course of time in at least some phases of Pharisaism. But, in spite of this, the Pharisees created a spirit of true piety and devotion which affected the lives of the people and developed a religious individualism which gave a new relevance to the Torah of God."[81] This piety, whatever its warmth and emotional intensity, rolled around exclusively in the prevailing ethos of Torah-living,[82] befooled by legalism, formalism, and externalism, at best a pale reflection of the Decalogue.[83]

The Fencing of the Oral Law

Additional to categorically interpreting the *mitzvot,* throughout the first intertestamentary century newly uncommissioned-by-the-LORD book-men and later much more domineering Pharisees contrived a basic circle of protection about the Written Torah, inclusive the 613 commandments. This protective system its advocates later inscripturated as a segment of the Mishnah; from its *Pirkei Avos,* or *Aboth,* or *Avot* : "Moses received the

80. Neusner, *Judaism,* 56.

81. Russell, *Between the Testaments,* 51. Ibid., 83, ". . . legalism was not the only thing which Torah religion fostered. It encouraged in many *a deep personal piety* which found expression in *good works* and in service to others. All through the Book of Tobit, for example, there is a sense of reverence and respect shown to parents which indicates a true spirit of piety prevailing in many Jewish family circles at that time; in particular the prayers of Tobit and of Sara for deliverance from their troubles are no doubt typical of many prayers of their day. Ben Sira, too, breathes the spirit of prayer in several passages which closely resemble the Psalms in their devotional atmosphere (cf. 2.1–18; 17.24—18.14; 22.27—23.6)."

82. Dimont, *Jews, God and History,* 88–89, "The Pharisees stressed the new Oral Law, a series of reinterpretations of Mosaic law. They were responsible for introducing the elasticity into Judaism which made possible its survival in the times of stress ahead."

83. Schechter, *Aspects of Rabbinic Theology,* 70, "The Rabbis likewise looked upon the yoke of the Kingdom of God and the yoke of the Torah as the badge of real freedom." McBride, "The Yoke of Torah," 9, "What rabbinical tradition means by accepting 'the yoke of torah' is one's willing participation in the difficult and joyful, long-term and liberating vocation of holiness."

Law from Sinai and committed it to Joshua, and Joshua to the elders, and the elders to the Prophets; and the Prophets committed it to the men of the Great Synagogue.[84] They said three things: Be deliberate in judgments, raise up many disciples, *and make a fence around the Law.*"[85] This fencing prerogative protected the Written Law in several ways.

1. By constructing this protective barrier, Torah-sensitive builders sealed off the 613 against abuse, even unintentionally risky behavior. That is, ". . . to safeguard the original commandments; for example, certain acts should be avoided towards the approach of evening on Friday lest one should forget and inadvertently continue to do them on the Sabbath."[86] That is, ". . . to safeguard the Torah against any possible infringement, [the Rabbis] enacted cautionary rules, known as 'fences' which are designed, so to speak, to prevent any precipitate violation of the sacred enclosure of the Torah itself."[87] This protective property of the Oral Law, the whole of the evolving second teaching based on interpreting/applying the 613, involved surrounding the Written Tradition with a cohesive wall of rabbinic decrees, another unending task of the Oral Torah. "Moreover, it was logical to enlarge the scope of the Biblical precepts in certain cases a little further: to 'make a fence round the Law', as it was expressed, so as to prevent a person from infringing it unawares."[88] Encircling insurance about the *mitz-*

---

84. Barrett, *The New Testament Background*, 139n, "This was popularly interpreted as a body, 120 strong, of prophets and teachers in the time of Ezra; but the reference to Simeon suggests that the Mishnah referred to a succession of teachers of whom he was one of the latest." Great Synagogue = Great Assembly.

Magonet, *The Explorer's Guide to Judaism*, 119, "What precisely this body was is not certain, but it is clearly a significant transitional stage in the creating of what was to become 'Pharisaic' and later 'rabbinic' Judaism."

Bronner, *Sects and Separatism During the Second Jewish Commonwealth*, 38, "The aim of this body from the moment of its inception was to follow the course pursued by Ezra and Nehemiah, and to make Judaism and the Torah a matter of the very life and habit of the people. This organization is always referred to in the Talmud as 'The Men of the Great Assembly,' . . . rather than just 'Great Assembly,' . . . ."

85. Charlesworth, *Jesus within Judaism*, 104.

86. Barrett, *The New Testament Background*, quoting from *Aboth*, 140.

87. Epstein, *Judaism*, 87.

88. Roth, *A Short History of the Jewish People*, 126.

Bronner, *Sects and Separatism During the Second Jewish Commonwealth*, 80–81, "They also, sometimes, added new restrictions to Biblical law, following the Scribal dictum of making a fence around the Torah, in order to keep the people at safe distance from forbidden ground. For instance, they forbade the people to drink wine or eat with the heathen, in order to prevent associations which might lead to inter-marriage or idolatry.

vot, however, had more than a merely unwitting misinterpretation and/or misapplication of the Written Law as definable motive. It legitimated and liberalized disobedience.

By fencing off the *mitzvot,* the Pharisee faithful at a full-circled distance away from these commandments sought a freedom from the LORD God under the yoke of the Torah. "Instead of limiting the scope of canonical legislation it now extended its scope by hedging the rules of the Torah around with new regulations which protected the observance of the original rules. For instance, in order to ensure proper Sabbath observance they introduced many rules defining what constitutes work, even including under this head many harmless acts such as carrying a shawl or picking up a towel."[89] Manufacturing this ever-widening defensive perimeter to confine the Written Law brought about a siege mentality to intercept incitement to pharisaical evil and, on the other hand, to defuse decalogual life from intensifying gratitude.

2. Early on, as doctrinaire Rabbis encircled the 613 with the Oral Tradition, they with broad public support isolated the Commandments from active involvement in the life of the covenant community. Hence the Written Law functioned less and less and all the Church concentrated (exclusively) on the inexactitudes of the soft-edged and pliable Oral Torah. This arresting negation of the actual commandments by man-made laws freed the Pharisaic community to work heavily reliant on the Oral Tradition, even at the expense of the *mitzvot.*

Two instances. Does the Fifth command honoring fathers and mothers? With the Corban practice allegedly evocative of righteous behavior, every avaricious son who vowed his wealth to the God of the Jews released himself with Pharisaic approval from assisting needy parents financially; every such disobedient son imagined himself untouchable against punishment for breaking the Fifth. Hence, a secondary decree diffused the seriousness of violating a Yahweh-issued commandment. Similarly, does the Fourth drive converging interests of observing and remembering the

---

To the forbidden marriages of Mosaic law they added a number of others. After they had clearly enunciated what kinds of work were prohibited on the Sabbath, they also forbade even touching many things on the ground that it might lead to some prohibited labor. For example, one must not touch a pencil on the Sabbath, for it may lead to writing. However, they never went to excessive extremes, and always maintained that whenever there is even a doubt about a danger to human life this overrides the Sabbath."

89. Albright, *From the Stone Age to Christianity,* 355.

day of worship? The socially wide-spreading 'erub ordinance enabled impious neglect of the Fourth. "The Rabbis insisted upon the observance of the Sabbath, but all possible steps were taken to see that observance was reasonably possible. For example, the law against 'going out' (based on Ex. 16. 29 and interpreted as referring to 'going out' of one's domain [e.g. one's own residence) into another; . . .] was mitigated by means of the 'Erub (. . .). This word means literally 'interweaving', 'mixture', and was used to denote various means by which movement on the Sabbath might be liberated."[90] Such extended twisting of the Fourth allowed for remarkable engagement in labor and movement within the boundaries of one's own "home," a fictional space to include a neighborhood or even a village, which "legalized" breakage of the Fourth. Unfazed by the fact that Yahweh held sinners accountable, first all of the Church, the God of the Oral Torah fenced off any moral guilt caused by internal uprising against the Commandments.

Hence, the legal structure and living environment of the Oral Torah encircling the *mitzvot* disabled the order and stability of the Commandments, in essence setting the Pharisaic community at liberty to violate Yahweh's Decalogue, with the maximum leverage of Rabbinic authority, no less. Through the Oral Tradition, the Pharisees favored a much more flexible and resilient community of laws. In effect, they relegated the Commandments into the background and adored an alternative legal system.[91]

Flourishing, Torah leaders constantly sought and demanded respect for more shadowy ways to exonerate sins against the Written Torah, integrating extra precautions and protections, lest any one forswear a *mitzvah* or two. From the earliest Oral Law formulations, Rabbis scaled back obedience by miscalculating the seriousness of transgressions against the Decalogue. By unseen forces, then, this preemptive preoccupation for escaping actual Old Testament righteousness in every day living eliminated situations that purportedly stimulated deceits of the body, but which, in fact, and more to the point, *washed-away* guilt. To achieve this delicate balance at shrinking transgression and dispatching with repentance, rabbinic authorities perceived the Written Torah as a beautiful garden with every fence motif smothering willful as well as unintended damages; they thus preserved the suspended commandments from trespass, as well as disowned rabbinic followers and communities from actually indictable sins.

90. Barrett, *The New Testament Background*, 155n.

91. Demonstrably, every 'Christian' congregation and denomination to some degree engages in similar practices.

3. Fencing in, indicative of ownership, also endorsed fencing out,[92] another permanent impression that settled in deep under rabbinic weights of expectation. By way of Oral Torah, the framers of these intricate laws restricted always more access to their metaphysical garden, particularly by unbelievers, Gentiles. To contribute to this exacting framework, early Rabbis applied, for instance, Lev 18:3, "You shall not do as they do in the land of Egypt, where you dwelt, and you shall not do as they do in the land of Canaan, to which I am bringing you. You shall not walk in their statutes." Also Lev 18:30. Hence, allegedly, ". . . God says, 'What joy can I have in him?' but he who surrounds himself with a fence against anything unchaste is called holy, and he 'who shutteth his eyes from seeing evil' (in the sense of immorality) is worthy of receiving the very presence of the *Shechinah*."[93] That is, the glory of the Jewish deity. As much as this third fencing protocol applied to Egyptians and Canaanites, it also withheld Greeks and Romans, in fact, the powerful presence of woefully ignorant unbelievers[94] moving about, conquering, and settling in the Middle East from 400 BC onward, during and immediately after the intertestamentary period. Thus, rabbinic authorities disallowed passing through and resident aliens from prying into and befouling Israel's holiness, or casting even an innocuous shadow over the *mitzvot* and the Written Torah. To a fervent degree, the influence over the interpretation of the Written Torah had to remain inviolate; derisory outsiders owned no right by inadvertence to sully any of the 613 with acts of contempt and

92. McBride, "The Yoke of the Thora," 10, "Jews did not seek freedom from the law; they sought freedom from outside interference so that they could observe the law."

Bronner, *Sects and Separatism During the Second Jewish Commonwealth*, 39–40, "The safest way to avoid contamination by the Greek invaders and their Judean admirers was to separate oneself from them. They took the principle of the Scribes 'Make a fence around the Torah' to its extreme point, imposed upon themselves countless restrictions so as to keep at a safe distance from forbidden ground. Echoes of the severe separatist practices of the 'Early Hasidim' are found in the Talmud, and also in the Book of the Maccabees."

93. Schechter, *Aspects of Rabbinic Theology*, 206.

94. Bronner, *Sects and Separatism During the Second Jewish Commonwealth*, 39, "The Hellenistic onslaught disturbed and disrupted the religious life of the community. The alluring Greek culture began to attract many Jews, especially those of the upper strata of society and the commercial elements who came into continuous contact with the Greeks. The rich Judeans began to lose their equilibrium admired and aped the Greek customs and abandoned the native Judean virtues. Greek conviviality, with its riotous hilarity, with its sumptuous banqueting where wine flowed freely to the accompaniment of music, enthralled many Jews."

intimidation, much less the entire Jewish Bible.[95] Thus, the third fencing or circle of protection prohibited uninformed foreigners from profaning the Written Law.

Torah-true fool proofing by composite fencing constantly prompted more legislation. To intensify the Church's holiness, early on rabbinical forces built higher and thicker barriers to protect the *mitzvoth* in three ways, allegedly to ward off divine vengeance and, more compellingly, to smother any loss of security in self-righteousness. Therefore, with the triple constraint of inclusion and exclusion to create *halakah,* the leadership pressed home Jewish autosoterism upon a more than receptive people.

The Inscripturation of the Oral Law

1. One of the dynamics of the hoary Hasidic movement in its post-exilic survivor mood validated the unforced construction of synagogues, meeting places for skilled Torah studies. Synagogue from a Greek word meaning "'assembly" transmuted into the Hebraic "the house of (the) assembly." Synagogues eventually typified the Pharisees' masterminding bases of operation for extending and disseminating the Oral Law,[96] from which they hammered out its daunting inscripturation legacy.

From and within each synagogue structure the Pharisees formidably prescribed the Jewish way,[97] insulating themselves against the gluttonous pull of Gentile assimilation and earning holiness through *halakha*. As such, along this immensely ambitious axis, *halakha*'s comprehensive laws[98] en-

95. Epstein, *Judaism*, 30, "The separation which . . . is the negative aspect of holiness, included for Israel a separation from all contaminating contacts with the idolatrous civilizations and cultures of the surrounding nations."

96. Roth, *A Short History of the Jewish People*, 62, "This was the origin of what was afterwards to be known as the Synagogue, the prototype of the Church on the one hand and of the Mosque on the other—one of Israel's most important contributions to civilisation. There the *Torah* was not only read, but also expounded. The teacher thus acquired an increasing importance, at first rivaling and then surpassing that of the Priests and Levites who ministered in the Temple."

97. Simon, *Jewish Sects at the Time of Jesus*, 34, "Whereas the Sadducees held to the letter of the written text, the Pharisees, from the sole fact that they interpreted the text, were quite naturally led to go beyond it, to qualify it, to enrich it. In their eyes, the tradition that they invoked in doing this, far from opposing the Torah, was the natural prolongation and explication of it."

98. For balance: Sanders, *Judaism*, 11, "Rabbinic arguments are frequently only arguments, not laws, and in any case Pharisaic or rabbinic views did not *govern* first-century

visioned and escalated within a harsh environment a consistent culture of holiness[99] adrift from the Decalogue.

With respect to the evolution of the synagogue tradition, its unfolding pattern speaks from ground unrecoverable to memory. "The origin of the synagogue is understandably lost in the 'dark ages' that preceded Early Judaism (c. 250 B.C.E. to 200 C.E.). Yet, while it may ultimately antedate the time of Nehemiah and Ezra, when Jews gathered together in the forecourt of the Temple to hear the Torah read, the 'synagogue' was clearly an institution in Palestine before 70 C.E., as we know from reading Josephus and the New Testament documents."[100] Thus, in the legal evolution of Oral Torah, post-70 AD,[101] and even more post-135 AD, the synagogue-based Rabbis (The Tannaim of Palestine) taught the Oral Law as influenced by local situations, folk ways, and changing historical conditions; therewith they improvised divergent and contradictory doctrines of law[102] overrated as divine instruction.[103]

Jewish practice. The degree of Pharisaic influence varied from time to time and issue to issue."

99. McBride, "The Yoke of the Torah," 7, "Separation is an intrinsic, yet paradoxical aspect of Israel's sanctification."

100. Charlesworth, *Jesus Within Judaism*, 108.

May, "Synagogues in Palestine," 229, "The origins of the synagogue are shrouded in the mists of the past."

101. Roth, *A Short History of the Jewish People*, 52, "To comfort themselves for the loss of their country, they began to study this rich literature with increased affection, sifting it, arranging it, copying it, and perhaps reading it aloud when they came together. The Temple in Jerusalem, formerly the centre of their religious life, lay in ruins, and it was out of the question for them to construct a substitute in the land of their captivity. Worship, therefore, took the place of sacrifice, and prayer-meetings, at which the ancient literature was read and discussed, now became in all probability a regular institution."

102. Dimont, *Jews, God and History*, 165, "Two schools of Mishna developed about 35 B.C. One was that of Hillel, the other that of Shamai. Both men exerted great influence, but a wide humanistic gulf separated them."

Epstein, *Judaism*, 101, "The difference of attitude between Hillel and Shammai was not merely a question of temperament. In the last analysis it stemmed from divergent exegetical principles, which at times in fact worked in the opposite direction, Hillel holding a more rigorous view than Shammai." (Shammai = Shamai)

103. Epstein, *Judaism*, 84–85, "If, therefore, the Torah was to occupy the position which Ezra had intended to secure for it, its contents had not only to be explained literally, but also interpreted in a way which did not ignore the changes in the situation. Such were the requirements which the exposition which accompanied Ezra's reading was designed to satisfy. It was an exposition which meant more than simply an explanation of the written text. It also involved an interpretation flexible enough to cover new aspects and conditions of life not provided for in the text itself, and to include such enactments as the exigencies of the time demanded."

The synagogue tradition, buffeted by varying combative winds, commenced intervention processes to preserve the Oral Law in writing.

2. Starting circa 400 BC, enigmatic synagogue leaders—historically elusive progenitors of the Rabbis—shifted direction decisively; at a hinge moment they initiated the Oral Law, which from modest beginnings arbiters constantly refined and expanded. Then, under persistent pressures within infinitely complex tumults of blunt force—from the Persian to the Hellenic to the Roman and from constant changes within those pagan administrations of deadly ambition—the massively growing Oral Tradition had to be inscripturated to preserve its legal inheritances. In the course of the post-exilic centuries and especially after the fiery razing of the Second Temple,[104] with its deep-souled aftershocks,[105] Pharisaism's recentering intensified for hoarding immense toils of Torah-culture.[106]

---

104. Actually, the Third. Herod the Great's restoration/reconstruction of the Second Temple destroyed this structure in order to build the Third Temple. However, in conformity with current usage, I refer to the Third Temple as the Second.

Russell, *Between the Testaments*, 36, ". . . an indication of his desire to please the Jews as was, for example, his building of the new Temple at Jerusalem, begun in the year 20 B.C."

Flavius, *The Wars of the Jews*, I.xxi.1p, ". . . in the fifteenth year of his reign, Herod rebuilt the temple, and encompassed a piece of land about it with a wall; which land was twice as large as that before enclosed."

105. Roth, *A Short History of the Jewish People*, 111, "In the sphere of religion, the recent upheaval resulted in one new development of extraordinary importance. The stately ceremonial which had hitherto been carried on in the temple on Mount Moriah now became impossible; for . . . the Pentateuchal code forbade animal sacrifices anywhere but in the central sanctuary. The consideration formerly enjoyed by the Temple was henceforth inherited by the Synagogue, which during the six centuries since the return from Exile had become a feature of every town and village. Their importance, as 'lesser sanctuaries', prayer in which was no less dear to God than a heart poured out by the side of the Altar, was deliberately emphasised by the teachers of the period, no matter how eagerly they looked forward to the restoration of the conditions which prevailed before. The profoundest outcome of the apparent disaster was that it forced Judaism to exist—the first of the world's great religions to do so—without sacrificial worship."

106. Simon, *Jewish Sects at the Time of Jesus*, 35–36, "This oral tradition, running from generation to generation and from school to school, finally ended by being committed to writing, in the Mishnah and the Talmud. It was then fixed, as it were, and became the subject of the exegetical efforts of succeeding generations. But before arriving at this point, the idea of tradition had been a factor of development, of adaptation, and even, at least in certain cases, of progress in the religious life of Israel. It made Pharisaism the living element of official Judaism. It was the tradition that allowed the Pharisees to justify all the elaborations that they introduced regarding the scriptural precepts, on the level of observances as well as on the level of doctrine."

Due to the utilitarian power structure of the Oral Law, its originating force and old guard for a long time, with an iron hand, resisted writing its substance on scrolls; it was, note well, an oral tradition.

3. Overcoming often unsubtle Sadduceic resistance to inscripturation,[107] for retaining, remembering, and passing on the intricacies of masses of legislation, already long prior to the destruction of the Temple written forms of the second teaching appeared, impressive evidence of a fast-changing and combustible world, a storminess at enmity with Torah preservation. In that assimilationist historical arena, remnant Pharisaic fighting spirits against inscripturation receded into a vanishing past, for intractable pressures to write down the Oral Torah escalated. After Israel's disastrous defeats, again in 135 AD, particularly throughout the second century AD, for protecting the Oral Torah's rich depositories and the merits of the fathers, rabbinic leadership pushed harder for the steadying process of inscripturation with respect to hitherto formulated Jewish thought. This intensive care for survival in a sketchy outline:

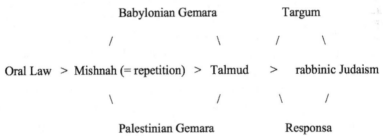

$$\text{Babylonian Gemara} \qquad \text{Targum}$$

$$/ \qquad\qquad \backslash \quad / \qquad \backslash$$

Oral Law > Mishnah (= repetition) > Talmud > rabbinic Judaism

$$\backslash \qquad\qquad / \qquad \backslash \qquad /$$

$$\text{Palestinian Gemara} \qquad \text{Responsa}$$

This unassuming oversimplification of an enduring pattern traces out an awesomely huge and fascinatingly complex legal system—living, breathing, ever expanding—to draw from its vast Jewish reservoir deeply rooted ethical meaning for every age. Because of this searching for meaning through developing the Oral Law, over the centuries the people of the Torah acquired a reputation. "The Jews were perhaps the most favoured

---

107. Dimont, *Jews, God and History*, 165, "The Mishnah, which originated independently in Babylonia and Palestine, began seeping into Jewish life about 200 B.C. It was not accepted with equanimity by all Jews. The Sadducees fought it vehemently, and the Pharisees defended it with equal vehemence."

Levine, *The Aramaic Version of the Bible*, 16, "Talmudic translation had elaborated legislation for the painstakingly careful copying of Hebrew Bible scrolls. And for centuries even the *writing* of the Oral Law involved strong opposition on the part of the Pharisaic leaders."

and the most hated race in the Roman Empire. Their peculiarities led to incessant friction with other races, yet they also, unlike other nations, were constantly active in commending their religious practices to others. Their self-defence and their zeal for their faith led to a fairly considerable literary output, of which little remains to us."[108] The remnant of that literary output the synagogual tradition passed on as the Oral Law.

Within the synagogue tradition, accepted wisdom built unquestioned support for a more permanent record than memorized findings of fact. To own the increasingly expansive Oral Tradition in terms of complexity as well as prevent loss of long-ago decisions and preserved pronouncements because of war-killed rabbis, inscripturation came with increased urgency. "Ultimately, this Oral Torah was reduced to writing. During the second century C.E., it was incorporated into the Mishnah, which in turn became the cornerstone for the Gemara which consists of the monumental records and minutes of the case discussions and legal debates conducted by the Sages."[109] Hence, in the turbulent course of Middle Eastern politics of empires, a thoroughly predatory environment, from BC to AD forward-thinking Rabbis inscripturated large parts of the second teaching. Further-more, as these leaders gained uncontested authority, they committed all *halakhah* to writing, initial Mishna precursors. Thus the Rabbis built up an awesomely large body of literature delivering the evolution of Jewish legalics as well as explaining the reasons for laws, regulations, and customs; this ever-growing collection of *halakhah* laid out the way of Rabbinic reli-gion. Through synagogue authority orally retained laws, regulations, and customs slowly acquired a stronger, i.e., written, legislative tightening up; thereby the Mishnah wrested the Oral Tradition away from falling into graveyards of extinction. "The Mishnah is a work of philosophy expressed through laws. That is to say, it is a set of rules, phrased in the present tense: 'one does this, one does not do that.' But when we look closely at the issues

108. Barrett, *The New Testament Background*, 200.

109. Donin, *To Be a Jew*, 26.

Neusner, *Scriptures of the Oral Torah,* 43, "Beyond Scripture, the written Torah, the Mishnah presents the entire topical program of the oral Torah. The sages who stand behind the document—authorities of the first and second centuries of the Common Era—worked out a complete and encompassing system for Israel's holy life. In the history of Judaism the Mishnah provides the single most extreme statement of the centrality of sanctification, the peripherality of the matter of salvation. The here and now of everyday life in the natural world forms the counterpart and opposite of the supernatural world of God in heaven, and the ordering and regularizing of the one in line with the main out-lines of the other constitutes, for the system of the Mishnah, the labor of sanctification."

worked out by those laws, time and again we find such profound essays on philosophical questions as being and becoming, the acorn and the oak, the potential and the actual."[110] Thus, foremost Rabbis laid stress on preserving and disciplining the shared consciousness and corporate memory stamped out in the lately founded 'Abrahamic' way of life.[111] In the process, despite all veneration for the Hebrew Bible, the Pentateuch, the Prophets, and the Writings lost out. "The fact of the matter is that the Hebrew Bible, for over two thousand years, has *not* been the central document that determines Jewish *actions* even if it is a constant source of Jewish *reflection*."[112]

4. Israel's citizens, stateless post-70 AD, through underlying convictions still considered themselves a nation, however dispersed. "Following upon the destruction of the First Temple in 586 B.C.E., and even more so after the destruction of the Second Temple in 70 C.E., the Jewish People evolved into a *textual community:* a largely diasporic nation-in-exile united *only* by a sacred text. The theocratic nation-state had ceased to exist, there was no territorial commonality, the temple cult no longer functioned, prophecy was no longer in vogue, and no single political, intellectual or religious hierarchy provided a *locus* for the traumatized fragments of Jewish civilization."[113]

110. Neusner, *Scriptures of the Oral Torah*, 7–8. Ibid., 10, "So the Mishnah, originally not a work of religion in a narrow sense, attained the status of revelation."

111. Magonet, *The Explorer's Guide to Judaism*, 49, ". . . the patriarchs as seen through the eyes of the rabbis . . . are to be our models, the written history of the Bible modified by its oral reworking."

Rivkin, *A Hidden Revolution*, 230, "Nor does the Mishnah hesitate to exclude from the world to come anyone who says that the resurrection of the dead is not derivable from the Torah (Sanh. 10:1). This, in effect, put the Sadducees, who rejected this belief because it was not articulated by Moses, on the same plane with those who asserted that the Torah was not from heaven. The Written Law is thus made utterly dependent on the Unwritten Law! God had revealed a twofold, not a onefold, Law. Those who, like the Sadducees, rejected this concept were not included within 'all Israel,' even though they believed that the Torah was from Heaven. Their flesh may have been the flesh of Israel, but their spirit was the spirit of unbelief." Of course, this was 'revealed' after the demise of Sadduceism and, also, to prevent a rebirth of this ideology.

112. Magonet, *The Explorer's Guide to Judaism*, 104. Ibid., "Instead the very nature of rabbinic Judaism depended upon a view that alongside the 'written Torah', given by God to Moses on Mt. Sinai, was an oral commentary to it, the 'oral Torah' or 'oral law', which enabled us to apply the teachings and legal precepts of the Hebrew Bible to new or changing circumstances."

113. Levine, *The Aramaic Version of the Bible*, 3.

Russell, *Between the Testaments*, 48 (from a Dr. H. Wheeler Robinson quote), "The institutions which it enjoined were, in large measure, brought to an end in A.D. 70; but

Despite an age of unstable beginnings marking the early first millennium, the Mishnah with its multitude of Torah-gendered factoids held the Jewish people in the bond of faithfulness to the (henceforth written) Oral Torah to categorize meaning. "In all these ways, therefore, the message of the Mishnah comes through: the holy Temple is destroyed, but holy Israel endures and will endure until, in God's time, the holy Temple is restored. That focus upon sanctification therefore imparts to the Mishnah remarkable relevance to the question on people's mind: if we have lost the Temple, have we also lost our tie to God? No, the Mishnah's authors reply, Israel remains God's holy people."[114] Even here, by most measures, ongoing agitation prevailed. "The first of the two stages of the formation of rabbinic Judaism therefore answered a single encompassing question: what, in the aftermath of the destruction of the Temple and the Temple rites, remained of the sanctity of the holy caste, the priesthood, the holy Land and, above all, the holy people and their holy way of life? The answer, that sanctity persists, indelibly, in Israel the people—in their way of life, in their Land, in their priesthood, in their food, in their mode of sustaining life, in their manner of procreating and so sustaining the nation—would endure."[115] By the inscripturation of

---

the Law showed its power by the creation of a new Judaism, able to endure without land, city or temple. Through the reading of the Law, supplemented by that of the prophets, in the scattered synagogues of the Dispersion, the knowledge of the one holy God and of His covenant with Israel was kept fresh in the hearts of all."

Hertzberg, *Judaism,* 154, ". . . as the exile wore on, especially the Second Exile after the year 70, . . . the most self-critical of peoples could not really believe that its sufferings was entirely the result of its own sins."

Schechter, *Studies in Judaism,* 44, "Indeed, during the age of the second Temple, men studied the Torah and the commandments, and performed works of charity, but they hated each other, a sin that outweighs all other sins, and for which the holy Temple was destroyed."

114. Neusner, *Scriptures of the Oral Torah,* 10.

Magonet, *The Explorer's Guide to Judaism,* 29, "Israel's hope was always the hope of redemption that God would one day bring for this people, this special treasure, God's own stiff-necked, stubborn, disobedient but beloved children."

115. Neusner, *Judaism,* 69.

Bickerman, *From Ezra to the Last of the Maccabees,* 18, "From now on, the superiority of learned argument over authoritative decree prevailed."

Simon, *Jewish Sects at the Time of Jesus,* 29, "The events of A.D. 70 definitively removed the Sadducees from the scene. The other sects had disappeared, having died or been absorbed either into the church or into the Pharisaic synagogue itself. Thus the Pharisees remained practically alone, until new schisms would arise. They no longer had any reason, therefore, to call themselves Pharisees, since this title denoted being set apart. There no longer existed any group from which to be set apart. They were quite

the Oral Law and its consoling myths the Jews, scattered worldwide, owned a communal bond, looming large. "To be God's chosen people is a merit and a distinction. It is also the explanation for Jewry's tragedies. The Babylonian captivity after the destruction of the First Temple in 589 B.C.E.[116] and the Exile of the Jews from the Holy Land after the razing of the Second Temple by the Romans in the year 70 were both great crises of faith. Had God put the Jews aside? No. They had sinned, perhaps no more than other peoples, but it was their duty to be more obedient."[117] Obedience in this sense, of course, pushed continuing Jewry[118] in its wider community further away from covenant reformation. In other words, Pharisaism as a movement died, its spirit to rise Phoenix-like[119] for shape-shifting into Rabbinism for greater self-preservation under pressures of Roman persecution, Christianization of the Empire, and later Islamic conquests.

Upon the 135 AD destruction of Jerusalem, as rabbinic authority in the synagogual tradition increased, step by calculated step, the compensating and resilient Rabbis replaced in Jewish hearts the Temple with adaptive Torah-living. ". . . rabbinic Judaism responded to this second destruction of the Temple by maintaining that the holiness of the life of Israel the people, a holiness that had formerly centred on the Temple, still endured. Israel's

---

simply Jews, or rather, they were *the* Jews. Pharisaism and Judaism were now coextensive." Ibid., 24, "When the temple was destroyed, they disappeared with it. Even before A.D. 70, the center of gravity of the religious life had shifted from the single sanctuary to the synagogues, scattered everywhere throughout Palestine and the diaspora. For the most part, the synagogues gave expression to the Pharisaic ideal."

116. On p. 44 above appears the date, 586 B.C.E.

117. Hertzberg, *Judaism*, 32.

118. Epstein, *Judaism*, 112, "The Pharisees were indeed the party eminently suitable for coping with the needs of the times. For some time the Pharisees has been moving away from the national unit and the territorial state in the direction of individualism and universalism—the only foundations on which a reconstruction of Jewish life was now possible."

119. Neusner, *Scriptures of the Oral Torah*, 24–25, "The ancient rabbis looked out upon a world destroyed and still smoking in the aftermath of calamity, but they speak of rebirth and renewal. The holy Temple lay in ruins, but they asked about sanctification. The old history was over, but they look forward to future history. For their purposes they appealed to the truth of the written Torah, but they also wrote down and preserved as Torah from Sinai the truth their own day had received—from Sinai too. The task of holding together sanctification in the here and now and salvation at the end of time, the enormous challenge of finding warrant in the written Torah for the truth revealed in the oral Torah—these two challenges produced the response before us: the vast canon of the oral Torah worked out in relationship to the written one."

sanctification thus transcended the physical destruction of the building and the cessation of sacrifices. Israel the people was holy, was the medium and the instrument of God's sanctification."[120] This irreversible refocusing from the Temple to the people the Rabbis, openly bold and thinking big, moved relentlessly along,[121] in slow rhythms fueled by energies of revolution into every near tomorrow.

5. Certainly upon the burning and razing of the Temple internal Jewish determination overtook and cut through common-core resistance within rising Pharisaism/Judaism to systematize the hugely unwieldy Oral Law hitherto memorized and for the most part passed on by word of mouth. Within this stricken and scattered nation, Rabbi Akiba[122] and associates studiously initiated the first major compilation of the second teaching; these exhaustive scholars and compelling teachers found it necessary to re-dact in an orderly fashion the masses of interpretation,[123] thus formulating the fused elements of the official Mishnah version,[124] its authority settled by consensus.

120. Neusner, *Judaism*, 65.

121. Russell, *Between the Testaments*, 44, "The ritual of the Temple had been replaced by reverence for the Torah; the priest had given way to the Rabbi; the Temple was supplemented by the Synagogue. Judaism thereafter was to be essentially a religion of the Book."

122. Barrett, *The New Testament Background*, 143, "R. Akiba b. Joseph was born *c.* A.D. 50 and died a martyr in the revolt of Bar Cocheba . . . in A.D. 135. Ibid., "His great literary achievement was the first redaction of the oral Law in systematic written form. His 'Mishnah' was developed by R. Meir, and finally used by R. Judah himself . . .."

Dimont, *Jews, God and History*, 152–53, "In the third rebellion against Rome, when the Christians were unable to accept bar Kochba as their messiah, they declared that their kingdom was of the other world, and withdrew themselves completely from Juda-ism and everything Jewish. The alienation process was completed. Judaism and Christi-anity became strangers to each other."

123. Barrett, *The New Testament Background*, 163, "The social and religious com-mandments by which the written and oral Law regulated Jewish life were so numerous and far-reaching as to produce marked social distinctions between the scrupulous and the careless."

124. Roth, *A Short History of the Jewish People*, 127, ". . . he was the first scholar to arrange the accumulated tradition according to subject matter. His pupil, Rabbi Meir, re-vised and elaborated the body of teaching which his master had assembled. It is possible that these scholars continued to rely on oral instruction without committing anything to writing. The prodigious Oriental memory might have made it feasible for this method of transmission to continue indefinitely, granted tranquil conditions. But conditions in Palestine were far from tranquil, and, by the end of the second century, the living tradi-tion appeared to be dwindling with startling rapidity."

In the Mishnah compilation processes, at first scribes wrote out many *mishnayot*, short thematic collections belonging to the second teaching, that is, various parts and pieces of the Oral Law, for entirely valid reasons. A) To remove the differences of biblical interpretation advocated by diverse factions and schools. B) To lay claim to uniformity in doctrine. C) To produce a shorter, more definitive Oral Law tradition cleansed of everything worthy of ridicule. D) To enforce a norm for textbook discourses as well as further legal decisions. The presiding genius of the Mishnah legacy healed a common wound, the *diaspora,* and groomed Judaism's fundamental constituents,[125] forming the ethical foundation for the continuing Jewish nation.

Before systematizing officially the Oral Torah, early Mishnah-compilations orchestrated another clear-eyed aspiration: to counteract the *diaspora,* the scattering of the Jewish people. Extensive communities after Ezra and Nehemiah's covenant-renewing labors remained settled in hospitable zones throughout Babylonia, Egypt, and elsewhere. Portable Mishnah-collections from these various centers, inclusive Judea, with ripple effects bound the Jews together by the defining marks of a common language, law, and system of meaning.

Final Mishnah compilation, of course, underscored as fact the previous works at organization. "For a compilation presupposes the existence of other works, of which the compiler makes use. Thus there must have been some Rabbinic work or works composed long before our Mishnah, and perhaps as early as 39 C.E.[126] This work, or collection, would clearly have provided a better means for a true understanding of the period when Rabbinism was still in an earlier stage of its formation, than our present Mishnah of 200 C.E."[127] Later, gifted Rabbi Judah (= Rabbi Judah Ha-Nasi = Judah ha-Kadosh = Rabbi Judah the Prince = the Patriarch = Rabbi[128]), *b.* 135 AD, compiled

---

125. Neusner, *Judaism,* 183, "The Mishnah is organized by subject area and imposes upon the laws a coherent structure that joins one fact to another in a systematic presentation of generative principles illustrated by particular rules." Ibid., 184, ". . . the framers of the Mishnah chose to adhere to a highly disciplined, logical, thematic organization."

126. These the Apostle Paul identified as the written code.

127. Schechter, *Aspects of Rabbinic Theology,* 3–4.
Neusner, *Judaism,* 69, "Rabbinic Judaism as put forth by the Mishnah, *c.* 200, ignored Christianity and its emphases."

128. Barrett, *The New Testament Background,* 141, "*Rabbi* refers to R. Judah the Prince (or Patriarch; . . .) who on the basis of earlier collections compiled the Mishnah (. . .). He . . . probably lived till after the end of the century."
Neusner, *Judaism,* 179, "The other part of the Torah of Sinai, its principles and details, was transmitted orally, via the memories of masters and disciples from generation to

and redacted the authoritative Mishnah. Hence, the final Mishnah-redaction compiled from reliable traditions the Rabbis adopted[129] by constructive consensus for the official text containing the *halakah*-governing rules. The influential backing of Rabbi Judah's Mishnah, of course, consolidated evolving Jewish identity even more. This Mishnah-processing completed by Rabbi Judah[130] presented a highpoint and a life-defining witness designed to fight for the Judaism always engaged at the apprehensive forefront, a generational event and stabilizing influence.

Thus, under the deliberate redaction leadership of Rabbi occurred the premier codification of the Oral Law, a sweeping overhaul, which included Israel's political and civil laws. This regimented compilation and distinguished redaction placed the stamp of uniformity to regulate sustained advancement upon a previously uncontrollable and unmanageable Oral Tradition. Hence, for practical purposes, the ascendancy of the Mishnah provided comprehensive enough authority for deciding religious and legal questions. As such, this restatement of uniformity in halakic doctrine through the preservation of "old Jewish thought,"[131] stimulated the operational search on a secure basis for more contemporary and existential meaning, thereby unfolding further Torah amplitude.[132]

---

generation until it was ultimately collected and organized as the Mishnah, a law code that was completed *c.* 200 C.E. under the sponsorship of Rabbi Judah the Patriarch, the recognized ruler, under the Romans, of the Jews of the Land of Israel."

129. Schechter, *Studies in Judaism,* 36–37, "The great literary production of this period was the Mishnah, which, through the high authority of its compiler, R. Judah the Patriarch, his saintliness and popularity, soon superseded all the collections of a similar kind, and became the official textbook of the Oral Law."

130. Epstein, *Judaism,* 122, "As a digest, [this Mishnah] includes all that 'Rabbi' considered worthy of preservation, even divergences of opinion that had originated either among earlier generations or among his own contemporaries. In this way 'Rabbi's' Mishnah contributed towards the standardization of the Law, whilst leaving, at the same time, ample scope for further research and study, investigation and development."

Neusner, *Scriptures of the Oral Torah,* 3, "What Moses and the prophets and sages . . . formulated and transmitted only in memory, orally, now reaches us in written form. The authorities, circumstances, and substance hardly conform to those of the first, the written Torah."

131. Schechter, *Aspects of Judaism,* 1.

132. Rivkin, *A Hidden Revolution,* 232, "The Mishnah is thus a repository exclusively of the teachings of a scholar class. And since these teachings are set forth authoritative and binding, and since they are teachings which, for the most part, are not written down in the Pentateuch, they testify to a system of authority that is self-assumed, self-asserted, and self-validated. Such a self-generated, self-validating system—a system nowhere acknowledged or mandated in Scripture—could have emerged only in the wake of a deep

The large Mishnah turned to key advantage the uniformity of the written Oral Torah, unlocking its authority for deciding more sensitively religious and legal questions. By design, this restating and preserving of the expansion in *halakic* doctrine through preserving the cumbersome teachings of the ancients stimulated unbroken research into the cultural transmission of Jewishness.

6. Synagogue leadership, grounded in and confirmed by Mishnah authority, brought in line impressive formulations to appease Judaism's continuing legal appetite, more regulations and rules of equal value for the stateless and scattered Jewish nation. "The Torah, [the Pharisees] contended, had not been given to the priests exclusively; it had been given to everybody. The priests had been elected by man to perform Temple ritual, not appointed by God to be the exclusive distributors of His word."[133] Because of trust-building distribution of Torah, all of the Jewish nation had to benefit and conform, thus raising the Mishnah to the admirable heights of its unfolding visions. "The philosophical law code of the Mishnah constitutes the first and most important document of the halakhah after Scripture. It set out categories under which the law was organized, yielding coherent principles that transformed cases into laws, and laws into jurisprudence. Over the next four centuries, *c.* 200–600, the Mishnah's authoritative organization and articulation of halakhah was supplemented and systematically criticized."[134] Inveterate Rabbis carried the inscripturated Oral Law elaborations into the onward-moving present of widely dispersed Jewish centers for equity of access and uninterrupted study. In effect, the Mishnah rode the gratifying crest of the oldest official post-biblical codification of the Oral Tradition. It gathered into itself the broad consensus for further instruction as well as storing up the stable teaching base for waiting generations.[135]

---

and profound revolution, a revolution that transferred ultimate authority over the Law from the Aaronide-Zadokite priesthood to the scholar class of the twofold Law." Ibid., 233, ". . . the Mishnah testifies to a revolution led by a scholar class, proclaiming the twofold Law as the true and authentic revelation, and it also testifies to the fact that this scholar class was none other than the Pharisees."

133. Dimont, *Jews, God and History,* 165.

134. Neusner, *Judaism,* 180.

135. Neusner, *Scriptures of the Oral Torah,* 11, "What happened beyond 200 and before 400? Two processes, one of which generated the other. The first of the two was that the Mishnah was extensively stated, line by line, word by word. The modes of study were mainly three. First, sages asked about the meaning of words and phrases. Then they worked on the comparison of one set of laws with another, finding the underlying principles of each,

Therefore, post-135 AD, after facing down volatile resistance to commit the Oral Law to writing, Jewish-rabbinic leadership owned the Mishnah.[136] This compilation, organized and forwarded independently of the Written Torah, received its emboldened status: the unstoppable authority of Oral Torah. This slow-phased collection, elephantine in size, included virtually the entire extant oral doctrine—judicial, political,[137] and religious—from the earliest *halakic* exegesis to, at the latest, the early third century AD.

7. At the same time as the Mishnah's inscripturation process took place, another, similar document, equally enormous in scope, gained ascendancy, the *Tosefta*, or *Tosephta*, less celebrative, allegedly a vehicle to carry left over materials.[138] This running parallel-to-the-Mishnah compilation of legal and religious discourse served to supplement the Mishnah. "The first document after the Mishnah was a complementary compilation of halakhah, the *Tosefta* ('Supplements') of *c*. 300."[139] "The Tosefta is a corpus of complementary or supplementary materials for the Mishnah, following the plan and order of the Mishnah and citing the same authorities as occur in the Mishnah, in the language and syntax of the Mishnah. Since the Tosefta contains numerous verbatim citations of the Mishnah, the document as a whole certainly comes later than the Mishnah, ca. 200 C.E., and since its materials, for their part, are cited in the Talmud of the Land of Israel, ca.

---

and comparing and harmonizing, those principles. So they formed of the rather episodic rules a tight and large fabric. Third, they moved beyond the narrow limits of the Mishnah into still broader and more speculative areas of thought. So, in all, the sages responsible to administer the law also expounded, and, willy-nilly, expanded the law."

136. Ibid., 71–72, "What makes the chain a statement of an extreme position is the compositors' inclusion of names, within the tradition of Sinai, of authorities of the Mishnah itself. That fact indicates the whole of their polemic: the Mishnah's rules derive from authorities who stand in a direct line to Sinai. Then the Mishnah enjoins the standing and authority of God's revelation to Moses at Sinai and forms part of the Torah of Sinai. Later on, as we shall see, in the Talmud of the Land of Israel or the Yerushalmi, the process by which this component of the Torah reached the sages of the first and second centuries would be spelled out. It would be described as a process of oral formulation and oral transmission through the memories of sages, hence the oral Torah."

137. The Roman Empire absorbed Israel's political authority and reduced his judicial powers.

138. Barrett, *The New Testament Background*, 145.

139. Neusner, *Judaism*, 180.

Barrett, *The New Testament Background*, 124–25, "The Sadducees were too closely bound up with the political life of their nation to survive the disaster of A.D. 70, and the Rabbinic literature, which was written down after that date, presents a consistently Pharisaic point of view."

400 C.E., the closure of the Tosefta should fall sometime between those two estimated dates. A guess of ca. 300 seems justified."[140] As the Jews in the history of their worldwide community strove for relevant Torah-style meaning, the literary transmission of the rabbinic *Tosefta* too motivated and structured tireless *halakhic* growth in Judaism.[141]

8. After the authoritative redactions of the Mishnah and the *Tosefta*, newer spreading literary pools reshaped Judaism further. "No sooner was the work completed than fresh discussion began to centre round it. It was no more possible for it than for the Pentateuch to be so comprehensive as to meet all conceivable cases. Fresh problems of a religious or legal nature were always arising, and were brought to the schools for decision. In addition, eager students raised theoretical points (sometime more remarkable for ingenuity than plausibility) which were taken into consideration no less seriously than the practical issues. They would be examined carefully from all sides, in the light of the Mishnah or of less authoritative independent compilations—such as the *Tosephta* ('supplement') or *Baraita* ('outside statements'), which stood in much the same relation to the former as the Apocrypha does to the Bible."[142] Throughout arduous centuries of Jewish learning, debate, and discussion, Rabbis in both Palestine and Babylonia recorded monumental documents, overlarge minutes of case histories, and intricate commentaries on the already voluminous Mishnah and *Tosefta*. As times changed and the Roman Empire collapsed, Jewish scholars faced first the Christianization of the Roman Empire after Constantine the Great (306–37

---

140. Neusner, *Scriptures of the Oral Torah*, 63. Ibid., 25–26, "The Talmud of the Land of Israel is a document that reached closure approximately a century after the political triumph of Christianity. In the aftermath of the conversion of the Roman Empire to Christianity and the confirmation of the triumph of Christianity in the generation beyond Julian 'the apostate,' sages worked out in the pages of the Talmud of the Land of Israel and in the exegetical compilations of the age a Judaism intersecting with the Mishnah's but essentially asymmetrical with it. It was a system for salvation, focused on the salvific power of the sanctification of the holy people."

141. Ibid., 5–6, "The canon of rabbinical writings consists of exegeses of two principal documents, the Scriptures (the written Torah) and the Mishnah, a law code, ca. 200 C.E., which is the first document of the oral Torah. The explanations of the Mishnah begin with the Tosefta, a corpus of supplementary sayings, and continues with the Talmud of the Land of Israel, ca. 400 C.E., a systematic exegesis of the Mishnah, and the Talmud of Babylonia, also a systematic explanation of the Mishnah, ca. 500–600 C.E. A separate body of exegesis concentrates on Scriptures, first of all, books of the Pentateuch, of Five Books attributed to Moses."

142. Roth, *A Short History of the Jewish People*, 128.

AD), then the Islamization throughout much of that same world. All the while, the Rabbis, or sages, under duress formulated additional ranges of legal enactments, collected in the *Gemara* of Babylon and Palestine.

Later, for controlling and transmitting the Mishnah, *Tosefta,* and *Gemara*, the Rabbis through inventive editing compiled Talmuds (*Talmudim*), the Palestinian[143] *c.* 400 AD and the Babylonian *c.* 600 AD. "Mishna and Gemara together make up the Talmud."[144] Each Talmud more purposefully assisted the Jews to own the Jewish discourse, a habitat of flexible legal decisions and instructional doctrines for a universality of application. Thus, these Talmuds with the Mishnah as cornerstone[145] reconstructed what once consisted as the unwritten Oral Torah. However, note: "The Babylonian Talmud, considerably larger, became the 'second Scripture' of Judaism, to the study of which Jewish men dedicated themselves for a lifetime."[146] Nevertheless, the whole structure the Rabbis with abiding commitment, capturing its energies, still named the Oral Torah, distinct from the original Written Torah.

143. Epstein, *Judaism,* 126, "In its present shape, the Palestine Talmud is a product of the middle of the fourth century. By that time Christianity had already, as a result of the conversion of Constantine (306–37), been established as the official religion of the Empire, and Jerusalem converted into a capital of Christendom. Judaism was now a political as well as a religious heresy, and a militant Church backed by the power of the state was making life for the Jews in Palestine unbearable."

Neusner, *Scriptures of the Oral Torah,* 30–31, "The Talmud of the Land of Israel's Judaism is a scarcely choate cathedral in process, the labor of many generations, each of its parts the conception of diverse moments of devotion, all of them the culmination of an ongoing and evolving process of revelation in the here and now."

144 Donin, *To Be a Jew,* 26.

145. Ibid., 25.

Neusner, *Scriptures of the Oral Torah,* 6, "The oral Torah reached written form in two stages, the one marked in ca. 200 by the framing of the Mishnah and its closely associated documents, the Tosefta and tractate Avot, the other defined in ca. 400 by the Talmud of the Land of Israel and its friends, Genesis Rabbah and Levitical Rabbah."

146. Magonet, *The Explorer's Guide to Judaism,* 124. Also, "The Babylonian Talmud is an extraordinary, highly complex work, edited with great literary finesse. In it the rabbis debate the relationship between the laws of the Mishnah and other compilations and the Hebrew Bible. But they also explore in exacting detail and with rigorous logic the application of these laws to everyday life and experience, incorporating and debating the different traditions, opinions and circumstances that surround any given subject."

Neusner, *Scriptures of the Oral Torah,* 20, "The success of the Judaism shaped in this place, in this time, is clear. Refined and vastly restated in the Talmud of Babylonia, two hundred years later, the system of Judaism worked out here and now enjoyed the status of self-evidence among Jews confronted with Christian governments and Christian populations over the next fifteen hundred years."

The Oral Torah, compiled,[147] proved the invaluable basis for labor-intensive study and teaching as well as legal enactments. "The final redaction was due to the industry and logical analysis of the *Saboraim,* or 'Reasoners', who lived in the following obscure generations. Thus the so-called Babylonian Talmud came into being."[148] Through this immemorial tradition, the Rabbis built up and strengthened the foundation of Judaism. "[Judaism] desired rather to evolve a corpus of practices, a code of religious acts, which would establish a mode of religious living."[149] Hence, the Oral Tradition, adaptable legal system always under way for stress-tested theological and moral concepts, dominated and centered Judaism.

9. Upon recognition of the Jewish foundational milieu, the *Talmudim,* Rabbis evolved other types of literature to meet lavish demands and malleable expectations of the times: *Targum* (commentaries)[150] and *Responsa,*[151] the latter connecting and binding the various and separated Jewish communities in Palestine, Babylonia, Egypt, and Europe through a constant conversation of questions and answers, adding flavor to the era. "The practice goes back to the Talmudic period, and flourished through the Middle Ages, of addressing halakhic questions to rabbis who were deemed to be authorities

147. Ibid., 5, "The sages of the Mishnah and the Talmud and Midrash compilations present what they, and all Israel from then for a long time with them, maintained were teachings that, in the language of their own place and time, contained the truth of Sinai. Writing down many of these teachings in the Mishnah, Talmuds, and Midrash compilations, sages shifted the oral part of the one whole Torah from one medium to the other, and that is why we can read them here."

148. Roth, *A Short History of the Jewish People,* 131. Ibid., "In form the Talmud—whether that of Babylon or that of Palestine—is a running commentary on the *Mishnah,* written in racy Aramaic, alternating with Hebrew. That code, indeed, serves simply as a point of departure."

149. Donin, *To Be a Jew,* 28.

150. Levine, *The Aramaic Version of the Bible,* 9, "Increasingly, the public reading of the Hebrew Bible was accompanied by a translation, or 'targum,' a term which originally signified the translation of Hebrew into any other language. In time, the generic term 'targum' evolved into a specific designation for biblical passages either originally written in Aramaic (Ezra, Daniel, and fragments of Genesis and Jeremiah) or translated into Aramaic."

151. Dimont, *Jews, God and History,* 120, "The laws which they formulated over a thousand-year span, many of them becoming part of the Talmudic code, were disseminated to the Jews through a unique 'courier service' known as *Responsa,* which did not need any political power for enforcement."

in Jewish law."[152] Thus, the old framework of the Oral Torah evolved, a source of wonderment at rabbinic ingenuity.

This multiplying, changing, modifying system of law served post-70 AD as food for life in the Jewish stronghold and substitute for the Temple, the synagogual people themselves. As much as the Oral Tradition solidified at length in the Babylonian Talmud, the Rabbis constantly honed this legal code for pivotal Jewish identity,[153] driven by the memorable search for meaning amidst fragmenting forces of history.

Out of steadfast loyalty to the building blocks of *Talmudic* studies, unflagging scholars and inquisitive sages wrote commentaries on the texts of the Mishnah-Talmud, *midrashim*, rabbinic teachings attached to the inherited treasures of the Oral Tradition. "Parallel with the attention given . . . to Mishnah went its cultivation of Midrash. . . . there emanated these series of Midrashim in which the centuries-long process of Biblical interpretation reached a high point never since surpassed."[154] This rabbinic manner of interpretation, written within and for the worldwide Jewish community of letters, exhibited powers of subsequent growth in the Oral Tradition ever under way.

Overall, the foundational drive and bedrock conviction of the centerpiece Babylonian Talmud to validate the Oral Torah in its policy of stabilization cannot be overestimated. "The Talmud was the instrument for Jewish survival and exercised a decisive influence in directing the course of Jewish history for fifteen hundred years, as it meandered through the Sassanid, Islamic, and feudal civilizations. It was the drawbridge which connected the Jewish past in the East to the Jewish future in the West. One end of this bridge was anchored in the Written Law, and the other end lowered into the Oral Law."[155] As a result, reverential praise for the Talmud abounded. "For the [Talmud] is a work which can never be used without proper discretion. Like many another great book of an encyclopaedic character, the Talmud has been aptly described as a work 'full of the seeds of all things.' But not

---

152. Magonet, *The Explorer's Guide to Judaism*, 131. Ibid., "The Responsa literature is a mine of information on the state of Jewish life and the kind of questions that arose within the communities."

153. Ibid., 17, "By the time the biblical books became canonized and Judaism began its different evolutionary phases, the issue of the 'oneness' of God was quite resolved. The rabbis, the successors of the Pharisees who created 'Judaism' as we know it, had no doubts about the revolutionary nature of this belief in One God and that Abraham was the founding figure."

154. Epstein, *Judaism*, 116.

155. Dimont, *Jews, God and History,* 162.

all things are religion, nor is all religion Judaism. Certainly ideas of foreign religions have found their way into this fenceless work, but they have never become an integral part of Jewish thought."[156] "What cannot be doubted, however, is that it is the rich legal tradition of the Talmud that has determined Jewish character and culture down to modern times."[157] With the acutely sensitive stuff to survive through centuries-long sustained transmission, the latest Jewish base of operations earned unreserved praises, its enduring values receptive to and productive of widespread activity.

For a preliminary summation: "There is no end to the depths of meaning to be found in studying the Torah; there is no limit to the new facets of understanding to be discovered as one carefully examines this extraordinary gem."[158] Herein lays the Jewish mystique, the impressive code of ethics for a deeply ingrained life. "In the course of its history Judaism has had periods when it heard those questions which are the questions of all ages, the questions of the miracle of the glory of God with which the world is filled. Then again there were lengthy periods when men heard the admonishing answers, which are the answers for every hour of life, proclaiming the power of the commandments of God."[159] Always expanding and adapting its basic thoughts, Rabbis on Jewish frontlines movingly recomposed the Oral Torah.[160]

156. Schechter, *Aspects of Rabbinic Theology*, 9.

157. Kirsch, *We Christians and Jews*, 52.

158. Donin, *To Be a Jew*, viii.

159. Baeck, *The Essence of Judaism*, 93.

Neusner, *Scriptures of the Oral Torah*, 26, "Given the political changes of the age, with their implications for the meaning and end of history as Israel would experience it, the fresh emphasis on salvation, the introduction of the figure of the Messiah as a principal teleological force, the statement of an eschatological teleology for the system as a whole—these constitute answers to questions. The questions were raised by Christian theologians, the answers provided by the Judaic sages. The former held that the Christian triumph confirmed the Christhood of Jesus, the rejection of Israel, the end of Israel's hope for salvation at the end of time. The latter offered the Torah in its dual media, the affirmation of Israel as children of Abraham, Isaac, and Jacob, the coming of the Messiah at the end of time. The questions and answers fit the challenge of the age."

160. Schechter, *Studies in Judaism*, 13, "Jewish Tradition, or, as it is commonly called, the Oral Law, or, as we may term it (in consideration of its claims to represent an interpretation of the Bible), the Secondary Meaning of the Scriptures, is mainly embodied in the works of the Rabbis and their subsequent followers during the Middle Ages."

Baeck, *The Essence of Judaism*, 25–26, "The Holy Scripture is the most stable element of Judaism and at the same time its most dynamic force. Much the same can be said of the Oral Law, which is a development of the presuppositions implicit in the Bible. The

The Tradition of the Elders

10. In effect, then, through Torah, from the first manifestation of the Oral Tradition into post-*Talmudic* studies, Jewish leaders sought *halakha*, the comprehensive teaching that directs all this work into the synchronous Jewish way of a life. "*Halakha* is the overall term for Jewish law; it refers also to the final authoritative decision on any specific question. It rests first and foremost upon the Biblical statutes and commandments in the Written and the Oral Torah, then upon all the rabbinic legislation and enactments, including religious-judicial decisions that were handed down through the ages in the form of Responsa and Commentaries by great rabbinic scholars. All this serves as the authoritative basis and provides legal precedents for the ever-continuing process of religious-legal decision making in our own day. The word halakha itself means 'the way on which one goes.'"[161] Always practical, in faith Jewish *halakha*[162] calls forth deeds. Thus, *halakic* statutes and regulations in a complex way concentrate on and release an expansive range of personal/private, familial, and social behavior, often minutely.

Halakha rests firmly and finally upon the Written and (originally) Oral Torahs, and, in the internal functions of Jewish history, upon all rabbinic legislation and enactments, specifically on religious-judicial decisions handed down over centuries. "Halakha asks for a commitment in behavior. It deals with ethical *obligations* and religious *duties*."[163] Torah studies, therefore, cover an unmatched range of behavior, the entirety of rabbinic literature—legal and interpretive—based on the unchanging *mitzvot* and the constantly growing, evolving body of statutes and regulations of Judaism, the haggadic,[164] apocryphal, apocalyptic, targumic, halakic, midrash.[165]

---

very notion of an Oral Law implies . . . that it can never be brought to a conclusion; it is a permanent quest. Even it it were recorded in writing, no definite limits could be set to it. The Oral Law has served as an important stimulant to the development and freedom of the Judaic tradition."

161. Donin, *To Be a Jew*, 29. Also, "Halakha is concerned with the proper application of the commandments (*mitzvot*) to every situation and circumstance."

162. Epstein, *Judaism*, 30, "All the common ways of life, all human interests, come under its rule. Thus, the Torah becomes a means for strengthening the supremacy of the divine holy will as the measure of all strivings of the human heart, and for bringing all the details of life, individual and corporate, into relation with the service of God."

163. Donin, *To Be a Jew*, 29.

164. Or: Aggadah.
Magonet, *The Explorer's Guide to Judaism*, 111, "*Aggadah* is the expression of man's ceaseless striving, which often defies all limitations." Ibid., "*Aggadah* deals with man's ineffable relations with God, to other men, and to the world."

165. Kendall and Rosen, *The Christian and the Pharisee*, 178, "Midrash: the Jewish

"The Torah, whether Written or Oral, is the teaching that directs man how to live. Although it speaks primarily to Israel, it also has directives for all men. It is concerned with every aspect of human life."[166] Polycentric Torah embodied all. "Sanctifying the life of Israel now will lead to the salvation of Israel in time to come: sanctification and salvation, the natural world and the supernatural, the rules of society and the rules of history all become one in the life of Israel."[167] In its own energetic manner, this ". . . allows us to characterize the Pharisaic system as at least a Judaism of sanctification,"[168] which paved the way for the later Rabbinism.

Halakha,[169] shaped by the Talmudic Code as the overall designation for the Jewish spirit, tended to flexibility, with constant potential for innovation, never a narrow legalistic patterning. "*Halakhah* revolves around two poles: the legal, that is, specified and detailed rules of behavior, and the relational, that is, the yearning to given expression to the intimate covenantal relationship between God and Israel. Both these poles have shaped *halakhic* thought and practice."[170] Through malleable interpretation of the Talmudic Code, Judaism asks for commitment in behavior in every situation and circumstance, covering all aspects and relationships of human life, often with a universal scope: Torah is valid and commendable for all people. Therefore, in its broad-

---

homiletical exposition of biblical texts. The classical period of Midrashic works is parallel to the period of the TALMUD."

Dimont, *Jews, God and History,* 160, "Unofficial interpretations of Mosaic law and Biblical exegesis, in Hebrew."

166. Donin, *To Be a Jew,* 26.

167. Neusner, *Scriptures of the Oral Torah,* 14.

168. Neusner, *Judaism,* 64. Also, "No wonder Pharisees, by all accounts, affirmed the eternity of the soul (as the first-century Jewish historian Josephus says) and the resurrection of the dead (as Luke's picture of the Pharisee Paul in Acts maintains). For the way of sanctification led past the uncleanness of the grave to the renewed purity of the living person, purification out of the most unclean of all sources of uncleanness, the realm of death itself."

169. Magonet, T*he Explorer's Guide to Judaism,* 111, "*Halakhah* represents the strength to shape one's life according to a fixed pattern; it is a form-giving force." Ibid., "*Halakhah* is the rationalisation and schematisation of living; it defines, specifies, sets measure and limit, placing life into an exact system."

Taylor and Ricci, "Three Models of Biblical Liberty," 122, "This performance as legal process was called by the Rabbis *halakhah,* the making of a way or path."

Shearer, *The Sermon on the Mount,* 45, "Any attempt to complete that law after fifteen hundred years, by giving it a 'broader and deeper meaning,' is certainly an attempt to modify the law just to that extent, and the modifier is really a law-giver."

170. Magonet, *The Explorer's Guide to Judaism,* 222, quoting A.J. Heschel.

est meaning, all Torah-studies refer not only to its Bible, Genesis-Malachi; these also incorporate the Oral Law inscripturated through long processes in order to open up more *halakhic* living,[171] based on upgraded Torah interpretation and legislation, the whole inundated by an aura of right ordering.

Hence, Judaism never became a set of beliefs about God, the origin of man, and the foundation of the universe. It is a comprehensive way of life with numerous rules and practices, the right doing of which constitutes Jewishness, a Jewishness always Torah-based. "It is the Torah as the sum total of the contents of revelation, without special regard to any particular element in it, the Torah as a faith, that is so dear to the Rabbi. It is the Torah in this abstract sense, as a revelation and a promise, the expression of the will of God, which is identified with the wisdom of Prov. 8, thus gaining, in the course of history, a pre-mundane existence, which, so to speak, formed the design according to which God mapped out the world."[172] *Halakha* in its broadest sense molds every phase of life. At the heart of this way of life shone the 613 *mitzvot*, fenced off. More general, *Halakha* represents in tight kinship all laws, practices, and customs channeled through and shaped by Talmudic studies.[173] That is, studies without end.[174] "For the Torah was always a living law, constantly applied by a living people to real conditions that were often changing."[175] Similarly, from a century earlier: "The belief that study of the Torah is one of the Deity's main concerns, and that God Himself is each day expanding the scope and insight of Torah, engaging in this labor in association with the souls of the saints who have departed mortal life, is a theological metaphor; but for the Rabbinic scholars the metaphor represents reality—the profoundest of all realities."[176] Torah-

---

171. Roth, *A Short History of the Jewish People*, 127, "The general issue was not what a man must do and what a man must not. It was, rather, what a man should do and should not, if he desired to carry out the *Torah* in its every detail. It was a code of life rather than one of law."

172 Schechter, *Aspects of Rabbinic Theology*, 127.

173 Ibid., xx, "The study of Torah, as conceived by most Rabbis of the Talmud, is such a labor; and whatever else one may be willing to abandon, that study must be recognized as of paramount importance."

Dimont, *Jews, God and History*, 117, "They built their Judaism by searching the Torah for new meanings."

174. Schechter, *Studies in Judaism*, 64, "The Torah is not in heaven. Its interpretation is left to the conscience of Catholic Israel."

175. Donin, *To Be a Jew*, 27.

176. Schechter, *Aspects of Rabbinic Theology*, xix.

Kirsch, *We Christians and Jews*, 113, "In such a world, to grow up a Jew was to grow

knowledge now shaped in the post-Enlightenment era constitutes the Jewish judicial system and its way of life, *halakha*, which covers the entirety of Jewish law,[177] in control of every aspect of life and relation—between man and man, and between man and God.

Thus far the Oral Law on its historical course.

---

up in so thoroughly Jewish a religious environment that there was only one religious option—Talmudic Judaism. Peoplehood perpetuated the religion. But even more, Judaic religion, which was not merely doctrine but the *complete* definition of the Jewish way of life, perpetuated peoplehood."

177. Baeck, *The Essence of Judaism*, 263, "In accordance with the severity and duration of the struggle which Judaism had to conduct, these duties were exceedingly numerous. They include the manifold statutes, forms, customs, and institutions—e.g., the dietary laws and Sabbath rules, elaborated in the Talmud and usually given the erroneous name of the ritual Law. These serve not the religious idea itself but mainly the protection it needs—a security for its existence through the existence of the religious community. This, and only this, is the primary measure of their value."

Albright, *From the Stone Age to Christianity*, 391, ". . . the teaching of the Pharisees was not at all suited to become the vehicle of a great evangelistic movement, which was to embrace all mankind in its parish and was to transform the Jewish doctrines of man's relation to God into a new religion of incomparable vitality."

Chapter 2

The Oral Law in its Malice

A T THE APPROACH TO the Incarnation, Roman dreams of empire surrounded and penetrated the Church, at times a silently brooding fear,
at times a violently injurious immediacy; the successive authorities of that
behemoth world power craved a substitute kingdom strange to the sovereignty of the Lord God. In its way, however, the Empire constrained the
competitive Pharisees and Sadducees, two dominant schools in Israel, from
civil war and internecine savagery, even while these same honorless furies
helped deflate the Pax Romana[1] with exhausting strife. More than Matthew,
Luke forcefully noted the Roman presence and pressure, Luke 1:5, "In the
days of Herod, king of Judea . . ." Matthew mentioned kingpin Herod the
Great only after the fact of the Incarnation, in connection with the Magi,
Matt 2:1–12. Despite limited references initially in the Gospels, throughout
the dominion of the Torah Caesarian short swords enforced an expansive
foreign rule of law.

Laying now a timely finger on the palpable pulse of history limited to
this domain of inquiry: in the ever-memorable onrush of events overseen

---

1. Russell, *Between the Testaments*, 47, "The Torah was uncompromising in its prohibition of idolatry in any shape or form; hence the bitter hatred of the Jews for anything
that savoured of the cult of the Emperor; hence also their violent opposition to those
buildings in the Greek style decorated with the idolatrous figures of animals and men;
even the trophies which adorned the theatres were looked upon by many as images and
so were *anathema* to the Jews who worshipped a 'jealous God' who would brook no rival
to his throne."

by Matthew, Mark, Luke, and John,[2] i.e., from the Incarnation to the Ascension, the fierce power of the Oral Law strained for its zenith, which it achieved in the Crucifixion.

At the outset of this often tense instability, unruly Pharisees besieged the Christ within the massive Torah-environment[3] to discredit his integrity as the Messiah and prevent him from achieving the Crucifixion and the Resurrection. In short, they unsubtly thwarted the Son of God/Son of man's itinerary to prevent him from the Ascension and omnipotent rule over all created reality for the sake of the ongoing church. Slowly, they planned to kill him by the one legitimate means at their disposal, the Roman death for insurrectionists.

MALICE IN REALITY

For orientation: a summary of the historical course from before the time in which the Christ (= Messiah[4]) entered the Church incarnate. Despite hostile turnings and twistings on contested ground by Canaanites, Hittites, Perizzites, Jebusites, Ammonites, Moabites, Egyptians, and Amorites earlier translocated to the Land of Promise, Ezra 9:1, the LORD God led the Church for her post-exilic emergence to Jerusalem, the summit of Zion. In that setting of sensitivity to place and time, he, unimpaired by adversarial winds of human malice and spite, or ancient enemies, disturbed with

---

2. Simon, *Jewish Sects at the Time of Jesus,* 23, "The evangelists were sympathetic neither to the Pharisees nor to the Sadducees, and were especially keen on pointing out their faults."

3. Rivkin, *A Hidden Revolution,* 69, "The laws the Pharisees championed were the unwritten laws, the laws handed down from the 'Fathers,' transmitted orally and not committed to writing. These laws differed *radically* from the laws recorded in the Pentateuch, and for this reason they were rejected by the Sadducees. That these unwritten laws of the Pharisees were radically different is evident from the agitated reaction to their abrogation and their replacement by the Written Law alone. The Pharisees did not deny the authority of the Pentateuch, but they most emphatically insisted that the unwritten laws were binding, and they were willing to fight to the death for their belief."

Bowker, *Jesus and the Pharisees,* 21, "The movement was not intended to be a party within Israel. It was intended to be Israel itself."

4. Russell, *Between the Testaments,* 119–20, ". . . in the Old Testament the word 'Messiah' is not a technical expression signifying the name or title of the ideal leader of the future kingdom. It is simply an adjective, meaning 'anointed,' descriptive of one who has been set apart by God for a special purpose." First Kings 19:16; Ps 105:15; etc.

foresight the jostling and yielding nations, on the right day to reveal all covenantal freedom of life, food, and space for an eternity among his own.

Unfolding Transition

Relishing in hope,[5] princely Zerubbabel, with stirring Ezra and Nehemiah, the latter two supported by prodding Haggai and Zechariah, worked within the Davidic covenant formation to rebuilt the covenant community. Decade upon demanding decade, centering about the time-bound Temple these outstanding office bearers at the LORD's command faithfully reconstructed the ongoing church. Mercifully, the LORD God had released a remnant from Babylonian captivity in an unprecedented way for life, food, and space in his durable kingdom.

Upon dying Babylon's disruption and defeat, Cyrus the Mede, a shepherd and anointed of the LORD, Isa 44:28, 45:1, among his many reorganizational rulings for a conventional Persian world also issued in 539 BC a political proclamation with respect to Israel-in-Exile. Hereby he unknowingly unpacked Jer 25:12, 29:10, "For thus says the LORD: When seventy years are completed for Babylon, I will visit you, and I will fulfill my promise and bring you back to his place." Effectively, the majestic Lord of the Church, upon prophesying the return of his own to the ancestral soil of their unsavory forefathers, open-heartedly accomplished this redemptive advance.

This was unwitting Cyrus' forthright public statement sensitive with royal homage. Second Chronicles 36:22–23; Ezra 1:2–4, "Thus says Cyrus king of Persia: The LORD, the God of heaven, has given me all the kingdoms of the earth, and he has charged me to build him a house at Jerusalem, which is in Judah. Whoever is among you of all his people, may his God be with him, and let him go up to Jerusalem, which is in Judah, and rebuild the house of the LORD, the God of Israel—he is the God who is in Jerusalem; and let each survivor, in whatever place he sojourns, be assisted by the men of his place with silver and gold, with goods and with beasts, besides freewill offerings for the house of God which is in Jerusalem." Well-regarded Cyrus[6]

---

5. Bright, *The Kingdom of God*, 165–66, "A purge of monstrous proportions had occurred, leaving but a cut-down stump of David's house and a pitifully few chastened people. The purge is past; we are the Remnant! And for our leader we have none other than Zerubbabel, grandson of Jehoiachin, prince of the line of David!"

6. Kirsch, *We Christians and Jews*, 30, "Cyrus is therefore no accident. He is the

with this persuasive proclamation commissioned Davidide Zerubbabel (= Sheshbazzar, Ezra 1:11, 5:16), to reform the Church.[7]

For a reference framework: the pertinent rulers of the Persian Empire during a long century, which succession list of authority figures helpfully lays out the broader historical context.

> Cyrus II (550–529 BC)
>
> Cambyses I (529–22 BC)
>
> Darius I, the Mede (522–486 BC)
>
> Ahasuerus, or Xerxes (486–65 BC)
>
> Artaxerxes (465–23 BC)

These imposing world rulers occupied and controlled the hurting territories of the Middle East throughout the tough times of Israel's resettlement. In that cultural history, they from a geographic distance unknowingly helped prepare the Church to ready herself for the approaching Incarnation, the coming in the flesh of the Messiah.

In response to Cyrus' proclamation, with Zerubbabel traveled forty two thousand, three hundred and sixty vanguard Israelites, responsive church members, Ezra 2:64–65, seven thousand and thirty–seven servants, as well as two hundred singers. Later, in Artaxerxes' reign, 458 BC, Ezra led a considerable company of men, plus women and children, approximately ten thousand in all, of the Church to the renewed covenant community, Ezra 8:1–14; at the same time, Ezra 8:15–20, he included thirty–eight aspirants with respective families. Then Nehemiah also added a small contingent. The remnant[8] as a whole living on covenantal bedrock with global portent had praiseworthy and prolonged cause to sing Pss 85:8–9, 126:1–6,

---

appointed agent of the God of Israel to effect the end of the compulsory exile and to make possible the restoration of Jerusalem."

7. Dimont, *Jews, God and History*, 65, "Many Jewish history books draw a picture of sorrow and desolation when writing of the Jewish captivity in Babylon. Fortunately, this is an inaccurate picture. In the sixth century Babylonia was ruled by a series of enlightened kings who treated their captives with tolerance. Those Jews who 'wept by the rivers of Babylon' were but a handful of zealots; the rest of the Jews fell in love with the country, prospered, and became cultured."

8. Ibid., 67, "The Jews had not only prospered in Babylonian exile and become refined, they had also multiplied. Whereas at the beginning of the exile there had been hardly 125,000 Jews in the entire world, there were now 150,000 Jews in Babylonia itself. About a fourth decided to take advantage of Cyrus's edict and return to Jerusalem. Here they joined the small number of Jews who had managed to survive the debris and ruin of those devastating three wars which had led to exile in Babylonia fifty years earlier."

"When the LORD restored the fortunes of Zion,
we were like those who dream.
Then our mouth was filled with laughter,
and our tongue with shouts of joy;
then they said among the nations,
'The LORD had done great things for them.'
The Lord had done great things for us;
we are glad."

To validate his still poorly defined Church, the Almighty mobilized mighty Cyrus, a world conqueror, to proclaim political liberty to all of Israel in captivity. However, the God of Israel dislodged only a remnant to make the journey through inhospitable regions[9] for bonding with those of the covenant who had continued in and about Jerusalem at the behest of power-tripping Nebuchadnezzar. Quietly, then, the LORD God elected out of all Israel these action members and bonded them to those who had remained in the Land of Promise, 2 Kings 24:14, 25:12; Jer 40:7; etc.; these he constituted the ongoing covenant community, the new Israel for that time. This divinely cut bifurcation revealed the actuality of the post-exilic church. The relatively insignificant number of returnees as well as the small indigenous community[10] of Israel he fused with sustainable design as his people, Israel in truth. All others of Israel,[11] numerically far superior but slumbering under and beguiled by layers of distracting unbelief, the LORD God severed from the buoyant community of the promises and the obligations to face the other future.

---

9. Ezra 8:22, the office bearer's refusal to ask for protective troops.

10. Bronner, *Sects and Separatism During the Second Jewish Commonwealth*, 35, "The first factor to consider is that the Book of Kings tells us that the intellectuals, the leaders and the worth of the nation were exiled to Babylon. Only the poorest and humblest of people were left behind in Judah to be vine-dressers and husbandmen. With no spiritual leaders left to guide them, this remnant of rustics gradually amalgamated and intermarried with the Samaritans, the Edomites and Ammonites who occupied the deserted areas of Judah. It appears that the returned exiles took little or no interest in these Jews, but concentrated on maintaining the purity of the returned community." 2 Kings 24:4.

11. Dimont, *Jews, God and History*, 119, "The Jewish stay in Babylonia after their liberation was *voluntary*. Before they had lived in 'exile'; now they lived in 'Diaspora.'"

Brooding Malice

1. During the political and cultural sovereignty of Hadassah/Esther's Artaxerxes, the LORD God tested the transitioning church in the Land of Promise and Jerusalem for faithfulness in worshiping him according to the Levitical rites relative to the Second Temple. However, shortly after Haggai and Zechariah, another prophet of lasting memory exposed an evil spirit with rippling distortions comfortably at home in the revolutionary-minded covenant community. Mal 3:6–12,

> "For I the LORD do not change; therefore you, O sons of Jacob, are not consumed. From the days of your fathers you have turned aside from my statutes and have not kept them. Return to me, and I will return to you, says the LORD of hosts. But you say, 'How shall we return?' Will man rob God? Yet you are robbing me. But you say, 'How are we robbing thee?' In your tithes and offerings. You are cursed with a curse, for you are robbing me; the whole nation of you. Bring the full tithes into the storehouse, that there may be food in my house; and thereby put me to the test, says the LORD of hosts, if I will not open the windows of heaven for you and pour down for you an overflowing blessing. I will rebuke the devourer for you, so that it will not destroy the fruits of your soil; and your vine in the field shall not fail to bear, says the LORD of hosts. Then all the nations will call you blessed, for you will be a land of delight, says the LORD of hosts."

Post-Malachi, this multi-pronged indifference to covenant reformation manifested itself in the Church and among the Jews in Babylonia through the *Soferic* School[12] and then by the *Hassidim*. In this overriding process of bargaining with disobedience to hearten demagogic malice,[13] the reconstructed covenant community centering about Jerusalem fused with all of the old *diaspora*,[14] other than the Pentateuch-bound Sadducees, in the combative synagogue movement.[15] Therewith the dividing-line be-

---

12. Epstein, *Judaism*, 87.

13. Albright, *From the Stone Age to Christianity*, 119, "In general, it may perhaps be said that a homogeneous, evenly balanced evolution is just as likely in disturbed areas, as in ancient Palestine, where a given society is more open to outside influences and to equalizing currents, as in a relatively isolated land like Egypt."

14. Apostle Peter wrote letters to the later dispersion, the church members rooted out of Jerusalem and Judah because of persecution.

15. Finkel, *The Pharisees and the Teacher of Nazareth*, 39, "The law and the religion

tween the Church and what Apostle John called the world fell into disrepute, fading away. Too soon, with absence of humility before the LORD God, the master narrative of malice structured by the ominously obligatory dimensions of the Oral Law took hold to incite another life, the broadly ranging Pharisaic world of meaning.[16]

2. Throughout the intertestamentary age, encroaching Hellenism moved into Jerusalem and environs, contaminating the LORD's domain with one more ideology, laced with polytheism. The then Syrian ruler, who also dominated Jerusalem, ramped up and enforced his parochial tyranny with military force. Many Jews among the rich and aristocratic,[17] while seeking to

---

need teachers to further their study and interpretation, in order to comply with changes of times and conditions and to introduce new doctrines, legislations and instruction. The heirs to the Scribes-teachers all came from the lower priestly classes, Levitical families and the plebeians. These teachers introduced new regulations and explained minutely the laws as recorded in the Books of Moses. Because these teachers insisted on a strict code of separation and cleanliness and formed closed circles composed of strict observers, the opposition nicknamed them 'The Pharisees', i.e., the ones who are separated."

16. Bright, *The Kingdom of God*, 170, "In and after the Exile a succession of godly, yet very practical men took hold of Israel's faith and made it into Judaism. Their ideal was a community whose major business would be to become the holy people of God by the scrupulous observance of the law. If the Apocalyptic hoped for a Kingdom that only God could produce, it might be said that the Holy Commonwealth envisioned a Kingdom which man's righteousness could, if not produce, at least precipitate."

Finkel, *The Pharisees and the Teacher of Nazareth*, 106, "With termination of the era of prophecy the teachers and scribes of the succeeding periods were responsible for the interpretation of the divine Law and the words of the prophets. Revelation now assumed another character: the conservation of the inspired words through tradition and interpretation. The introduction of new norms to guide the daily life of the people was considered by the Pharisees a link with the true law, the law of Moses on Sinai. The examination of the Scriptures in the form of midrash (exposition) or pesher (uncovering the meaning of a text) was the revelation of the teachers."

Neusner, *Scriptures of the Oral Torah*, 1–2, "The oral Torah serves to complement and complete the written one—and vice versa. If we wish to understand Judaism, therefore, we first of all must ask how the Torah in two media, written, memorized, forms a single and cogent statement. Given the standing and authority of the Torah in Judaism, that is, God's full and exhaustive statement of God's will for the world and for holy Israel, God's first love, the issues are considerable. For the Judaism of the dual Torah, written and memorized, encompasses in its vision not Israel alone, but all of creation, to the outer reaches of uncharted space, and the entirety of humanity, traveling companions of all times on earth. All nations, all creatures through the revelation of the Torah come into relationship with God, creator of heaven and earth, ruler of the world, redeemer and savior of all being."

17. Albright, *From the Stone Age to Christianity*, 353, ". . . the Hellenizing high priests Jason and Menelaus (cir. 175–65) went so far in their efforts to win the support of the

retain Jewish fundamentals, favored a measure of Hellenism. However, the majority[18] opposed the Syrian's heavy-handed dictates. ". . . the ill-advised repressive measures of Antiochus Epiphanes drove Jews of every religious gradation and economic class under the one banner of the Hasideans as a protest not against Hellenism, but against the denial of religious liberty."[19] Out of the Hasidean movement arose the Maccabees, whose liberating war against Antiochus IV Ephiphanes wrought actual freedom from foreign domination. "It was . . . notably in the reign of Antiochus IV (175–63 BC), that a violent reaction set in which developed in time into a burning hatred of the whole Hellenistic way of life."[20] Spasms of destruction under this unbearable Syrian tyrant[21] and his authoritarian regime may not suffer underestimation for its brutality in Israel: ruthless suppression of all who practiced circumcision, celebrated the Sabbath, and owned Torah copies. "Curiously, the Maccabean War for independence against the tyranny of Antiochus Epiphanes in the second century B.C. produced no surviving texts that invoked the Messiah. For the war against Antiochus was not only a war for independence but a religious war, for it aimed at freedom from the oppression of an emperor who had determined to stamp out Jewish religion. Antiochus believed that the security of his empire required all his

---

new Seleucid overlords of Palestine that they actually proposed or accepted the reorganization of Judaism as a Syro-Hellenic religion."

18. Bronner, *Sects and Separatism During the Second Jewish Commonwealth*, 39, ". . . eager pursual after the Greek values by the influential and wealthy Judeans evoked an ardent reaction in the Jewish community. The pious men, who had followed the Scribes, were horror-stricken at the assimilation that began to make unprecedented inroads into the Jewish religious life. They decided to defend their beloved and sacred heritage by hedging themselves in entirely and completely within the four ells of the law."

19. Dimont, *Jews, God and History*, 87.

20. Russell, *Between the Testaments*, 25.
Albright, *From the Stone Age to Christianity*, 353, "All pious Jews, regardless of party and creed, now rallied to the support of the Maccabaean patriots, who struggled with an energy and a zeal seldom approached and perhaps never surpassed in history, until under Simon (143–35 B.C.) they attained their goal, the autonomy of Judaea and the purification of Jerusalem."

21. Russell, *Between the Testaments*, 25, "Long before the reign of Antiochus IV there had been a strong Hellenizing party among the Jews in Palestine whose ringleaders were to be found chiefly in the ranks of the wealthy and priestly aristocracy who, by reason of their social position, enjoyed the privileges of the royal court and curried the favour of the king."
Bright, *The Kingdom of God*, 181, "Matters came to a head when Antiochus IV (Epiphanes: 175–64) came to the throne in Antioch. This king was an able, devious, and complex character. A more fanatical Hellenizer there never was."

subjects to conform to one religion—of his choice—a Hellenistic version of Greek polytheism in which Antiochus himself was to be revered as a manifestation of Zeus."[22] Nevertheless, the hard-agitating Maccabees, the later Hasmoneans, won. In a bloody way, they with fidelity to place secured Jerusalem's independence.[23]

During the harsh historical and inner turmoil of the period, differences between the covenant community centered in Jerusalem and the more numerous Jews from the *diaspora* fell away, vanishing, and the two peoples united on the basis of the Oral Torah. "Outside Judea in the places of dispersion, with their main centres in Babylon and Egypt, the Jewish communities in close relation with the Judean community in Jerusalem developed a spiritual unity, founded on the Torah and a common body of traditions, ideals, hopes, and aspirations."[24] This contrary blending of those whom the LORD God had left behind, the ones who formed the *diaspora,* with the covenant community replaced the frame of reference of the final Old Testament covenant community with another centerpiece, the Jewish people as a whole. "It is surely very significant indeed that, despite the fact that the Temple had been desecrated only a short time before (I Macc. 1.54), it was not the Temple but the Torah to whose defence and support the people were summoned. An appeal to the Temple would have rallied a section of the people; but an appeal to the Torah had a greater chance of rallying the whole people; and, even if not all responded, all were involved, for the whole nation reverenced the Torah as the declared will and revelation of God."[25] That is, the Oral Torah. With this suppression of the promises and

22. Kirsch, *We Christians and Jews,* 31.

23. Whereas at heart Jews fought for religious liberty to live the Torah, a commercial interpretation of the events exists: Crossan, *The Birth of Christianity,* 159, "Rural commercialization, land expropriation, and peasant dispossession are more or less synonymous. And as they increase, so also does the incidences of peasant resistance, rebellion, or revolt."

24. Epstein, *Judaism,* 86.
Schechter, *Studies in Judaism,* 16–17, "Liberty was always given to the great teachers of every generation to make modifications in harmony with the spirit of existing institutions. Hence a return to Mosaism would be illegal, pernicious, and indeed impossible. The norm as well as the sanction of Judaism is the practice actually in vogue. Its consecration is the consecration of general use—or, in other words, of Catholic Israel."
Simon, *Jewish Sects at the Time of Jesus,* 6, "Beyond their differences of opinion, the priesthood, the Sanhedrin, and the rabbinical schools at least had in common that they were preoccupied with practice and conduct more than with doctrine: observance was at the center of their thought and discussion."

25. Russell, *Between the Testaments,* 45. Ibid., "To attack the Torah was to attack

the obligations, the covenant community clearly signaled its revolutionary inner sanctum,[26] intending to earn whatever salvation they perceived for entering the world to come.[27] As they pulled back the communal veil of secrets, all Jews pitted themselves against the Head of the Church, mocking thereby also the history of the promises and the obligations.

Hardening Malice

Pivotally, Matthew confirmed Jesus' genealogical lineage from Mary over David to Abraham. Upon this procession of forebears, the first listed of the Synoptic writers revealed the Christ entering uninvited the Church for his omnipotent works of covenant reformation. Despite great messianic agitation,[28] he followed the eschatological time-line, arriving at his Bethlehem destination at the precisely appointed hour. With quiet dignity and solemn purpose the Son of God/Son of man[29] strode amidst misrepresented and misguided end-time yearnings towards his time-consuming

---

Judaism itself; to defend the Torah was to defend the faith of their fathers."

26. Achtemeier and Achtemeier, *The Old Testament Roots of Our Faith,* 75, "No longer was membership in Israel a gift of God, given by his gracious acts in history. No longer was the Israelite one who had been redeemed from Egypt or settled in the promised land or born into a nation ruled by the Davidic king. No longer was it God's initiative which made the Israelite a member of the chosen race. Now each Hebrew had to earn his place in Israel by following the law."

27. Simon, *Jewish Sects at the Time of Jesus,* 36, ". . . this supererogation often seems withering and deadening. Yet to the Pharisees it was the condition and the very source of all authentic religious life. The multiplicity of commandments, far from being resented as an intolerable yoke, on the contrary both revealed and called forth the multiplicity of divine blessings. Indeed, it was the inflexible rigor of observance that assured the survival of Judaism."

28. Bultmann, *Primitive Christianity,* 83, "The course of this world is divided into two ages, this age and the age to come."

Bright, *The Kingdom of God,* 165, "The hope of the imminently coming Kingdom flamed early in the Restoration community, only to meet cruel disappointment."

Klinghoffer, *Why the Jews Rejected Jesus,* 62, "The first century was a time when Jews habitually thought in terms of the fulfillment of scriptural prophecies. Contemporary happenings were instinctively run through such an analysis, the question being: Does this event, does this person, match those scriptural passages where the prophets describe the coming of the promised Davidic king?"

29. Kee, *Jesus in History,* 131, ". . . the fact remains that Mark presents Jesus as one whose ministry among men was characterized by the work of interpreting anew God's Law, and doing so not in continuity with rabbinic methods of interpretation (1:22) but with his own unprecedented authority."

and labor-intensive goal, instructively teaching,[30] healing, and prophesying throughout the whole of his Father-ordained mission. Infused with and nurtured by the almighty authority of the Holy Spirit, he reached forward to the Crucifixion and its purposeful beyond.

Josephus (Joseph ben Matthias, AD 37–100?) recounted this history dismissively, a phase in Israel's history hardly worth Pharisee opposition:

> "Now, there was about this time, Jesus, a wise man, if it be lawful to call him a man, for he was a doer of wonderful works,—a teacher of such men as receive the truth with pleasure. He drew over to him both many of the Jews, and many of the Gentiles. He was [the] Christ; and when Pilate, at the suggestion of the principal men amongst us, had condemned him to the cross, those that loved him at the first did not forsake him, for he appeared to them alive again the third day, as the divine prophets had foretold these and ten thousand other wonderful things concerning him; and the tribe of Christians, so named from him, are not extinct at this day."[31]

According to this flair for historical appraisal, the Word little impressed Israel and/or Josephus.

1. Following in general Matthew's process of structuring the First Gospel: for disturbing the inner darkness of the Church, the indefatigable Baptizer[32] on the offensive to prepare the way for Christ called a glowering cluster of intermingling Pharisees and Sadducees a brood of vipers.[33] Matt

---

30. In contrast to the Lord Jesus: Simcox, *The First Gospel,* 78, "The scribes of the people were men who knew well the scriptures but who made it a point not to give out bold, original interpretations. They stuck cautiously to the opinions of acknowledged authorities. They could tell you what one learned rabbi or another had said about some moot subject. This was the safe course. Jesus made no pretense of following it."

31. Flavius, *Antiquities of the Jews,* XVIII.iii.3.

Kee, *Jesus in History,* 32, "It is incredible that Josephus could have written this account of Jesus exactly as it stands, since he would have had to be a Christian believer to have affirmed unequivocally that Jesus was the Messiah. The recognition of Jesus as the Messiah is doubtless a Christian interpolation."

Bruce, *Jesus & Christian Origins Outside the New Testament,* 38, for similar sentiments.

32. Major, et al., *The Mission and Message of Jesus,* 439, "John the Baptist is the last and greatest representative of the prophetic order: and John's preaching is all within the framework of the old Covenant."

33. Simon, *Jewish Sects at the Time of Jesus,* 13, "Everything was still in a state of flux in this infinitely complex phenomenon that was Judaism around the beginning of the Christian era. To be sure, the party of the Pharisees already held the key positions and

3:7; Luke 3:7. These divisive pretenders to lordship in and over the Church on an investigative journey from Jerusalem gave early signs of the malice coming. "They did not wish to lose their hold on the multitudes who were flocking to John to be baptized. If this was the place where the action was they wanted to be part of it, in order, if possible, to assume leadership."[34] John the Apostle, John 1:19–20, pointedly, without a trace of accommodation, also opened up this sizeable conflict.[35] "And this is the testimony of [the Baptizer], when the Jews sent priests and Levites from Jerusalem to ask him, 'Who are you?' He confessed, he did not deny, but confessed, 'I am not the Christ.'" From hereon, surging waves of malice struck at Jesus' feet, to dislodge him from the foundational way to the Cross.[36]

2. The first to confront Jesus? The Satan. Matt 4:1–11, Mark 1:12–13, Luke 4:1–13. Full of diabolical determination and demonic cunning, the Enemy with a thousand beguiling ruses, but without lasting gains, had moved heaven and earth to imperil and banish the Incarnation from the course of the ages; now, by malicious twistings of the covenant promises he plotted the impelling shape of battles to come: by seeking to kill him and forestall the covenant Lord from gaining his Father-ordained mission. Therefore, the Enemy, insatiably hateful, sought perversion of the covenant promises, in the case of Matthew: food, life, and space; in the case of Luke: food, space, and life. Luke's sequencing of these acerbic temptations made clearer than Matthew's that had Jesus thrown himself off the Temple pinnacle, he caused his own death, which was Satan's intent in order to amass a blaze of glory. At defeating Satan and these poorly packaged allures of festering

---

tended to impose their norms. However, its supremacy was not yet uncontested."

34. Hendriksen, *Matthew*, 203.

35. Simon, *Jewish Sects at the Time of Jesus*, 91–92, "Such preaching collided headlong with the accepted ideas. It struck directly at the easy conscience of the parties in power, the Pharisees and the Sadducees. According to the Gospel of Matthew, it was against these men that the diatribe quoted . . . was addressed. John's preaching, like all messianic preaching, raised public unrest among the crowds which flocked to the Jordan. This unrest was alarming to those in high places."

Luke 7:30, these Pharisees and lawyers John did not baptize.

36. Bowker, *Jesus and the Pharisees*, 42, "What, then, *was* the offense of Jesus, and why did anybody wish to take action against him? Fundamentally, the offence of Jesus, so far as *jurisdiction* was concerned, lay in his attitude to the various sources of authority, since in many different ways he claimed and exemplified direct authority, and power, from God."

hatreds, the first signs of his decline, the Lord Jesus preserved the covenant promises in the unyielding pursuit of reforming the three forever.

3. Upon this, for him, embarrassingly debilitating failure, plastic Satan commandeered his secondary lines of attack, the confrontational Pharisaic and uncompromising Sadduceic communions of interest; he had trained these Thora-thinkers and -movers with deep-hearted motivation over portentous intertestamentary centuries for escalating spirits of revolt within the Church against the Christ. Alarming schemers, armed with the discriminatory Oral Law, initially Pharisees and supportive scribes,[37] contemptuously dogged Jesus over the years of his ministry for self-serving gain, to kill him when feasible. These non-commissioned leaders within the Church aflame with a collective sense of planned prejudice, lured the members[38] of Christ away from faithfulness into dark mazes of unfaithfulness, blindly optimistic; they wanted all to pressure for the death of the Son of God/Son of man by murder. This distasteful and scornful plotting flared into the open on the long-awaited day he entered publicly upon the impressive range of his winnable ministry.

From the Kingdom-minded start of his ministry, Jesus Christ, the Messiah, suffered brutalities from both Pharisees and Sadducees,[39] sometimes alternated, sometimes coordinated. Over the approximately three years, insulting waves of malice each comprised of jealousy heaved against the Lord of the Church. With increasing malignancy, Satan's malnourished troops sought Jesus' public shaming in the devastated-by-ideology covenant community; with self-soiling intrigue they hatched extermination plots to fasten him onto the Cross and tighten their overreaching hold on the Church. Nevertheless, the Lord and Savior, free moving amidst his unwelcoming and unbelieving own, planned to re-impose covenant faithfulness as the solid ground for the tomorrow-bound Church.

37. Major, et al., *The Mission and Message of Jesus*, 389, "The interpretation of the Law and the working out of the theology and morals of Judaism they left to experts, the scribes. These belonged largely, though not entirely, to the Pharisaic party, and were its intellectual leaders. The scribes are thus a group within the much larger body of Pharisees."

38. Simon, *Jewish Sects at the Time of Jesus*, 15, "The religion of this undifferentiated mass presented no distinctive characteristics, although it was appreciably less demanding and undoubtedly more luke-warm than that of the organized religious parties."

39. Dimont, *Jews, God and History*, 88, "When Jesus preached in Galilee and Jerusalem, the Sadducees did not regard him as a radical, but as a zealot—in other words, as a Pharisee."

Therefore, the Son of God/Son of man, assimilating the ripening signs of the age, divinely authoritative strode with calm demeanor into the work of the Church—without consultation, without permission from his rivals, *Pharisaioi* and *Saddoukaioi*. The Church was his creation and with dominical authority, he interpreted prophecy, taught parables, disseminated wisdom, healed illnesses, exorcised demonic powers, raised to life several who had deceased, even summoned and lawfully commissioned 12 men for the new apostolic leadership, always without malice. Among the numerous of the Church, sizing-up Nicodemus gave a hopeful sign, John 3:1–15. More to the issue at hand, gathering multitudes listened willingly, hungrily at times, but without the necessary heart comprehension, the indwelling of the Spirit still absent.

Jesus initiated his gracious ministry in Gentile-overrun Galilee, at a remove from heartland Jerusalem, there opening future-knowing Isa 9:1–7. In the ideology-ridden landscape of Palestine, he exercised his sovereign judgeship in and over the Church by the awesome wisdom sayings collected as Matt 5:1—7:28/Luke 6:17–38. According to Spirit-indwelled and articulate Matthew, this teaching within the time constraints of the First Gospel offensively directed against ingrate Pharisees, the Lord followed up by an enemy-unsettling series of healing miracles. Christ's mission, castigated by Thora-heavy Pharisee interferences, forthrightly established his credibility as the Messiah, because in distinction from the Pharisees, he taught with authority.[40]

Soon a disarming wave of malice, discrete, lapped at Jesus' feet, testing. Matt 8:18–22; Luke 9:57–62. A scribe, a bookman, a teacher of the Oral Law, edging in, declared, "Teacher, I will follow you wherever you go." This expert in the Oral Law perceived the glory bursting out of uplifted crowds at the astounding miracles, which moved him, full of presumption, to aspire for discipleship. However, Jesus had not issued *help-wanted* solicitations, thereby seeking employable volunteers for this office with its high exposure to harsh action and violence of Pharisaic resistance; he called only those whom he had chosen. To this intrusive teacher of the Oral Law the Lord of the Church pointed out the rootless existence he and the Twelve

---

40. Bultmann, *Primitive Christianity,* 64, "The only kind of progress they recognized was the accumulation of possible interpretations. There was therefore no attempt to work out a particular thesis, or to abandon it in the light of further criticism. New interpretations were simply recorded side by side with the old, and no attempt was made to decide which was the true one. It was the function of learning to preserve as many existing interpretations as possible."

faced for evangelizing the covenant community as well as Gentile worlds, whereupon this bookman faded back into non-compliant demographics of Pharisaism. The serving Christ had come to cleanse the Church of the Oral Law, not draw one of its vocal proponents into his immediate company, thereby then topsy-turvy compromising the integrity of his redemptive ministry as well as the progressive bonds of the covenant. He then discomfited this notional teacher of the Oral Law from following him with a less hospitable farewell than to Nicodemus.

Early on, Spirit-driven Apostle John recounted that Jesus walked to rural remote Galilee, John 4:1–6; he withdrew temporarily from Pharisee animosity and confrontation, since his time of messianic revelation had not yet come. However, unfaithfulness with its intolerable license never succumbs obediently to the Word. For the Galilean Pharisees, querulously remembering unfinished business, and unrelenting, still plotted his downfall.

In the well-disciplined labors of his ministry, Jesus administered other imposing miracles, stilling a raging storm and exorcising resistant demons, both with pronounced decision. Then the instructive Synoptic writers unfolded a thematic account, Matt 9:1–8; Mark 2:1–12/Luke 5:17–26. Jesus[41] forgave a paralytic's sins and as lasting proof of this authority healed him physically. Scorning teachers of the Oral Law present at the occasion, taken aback, accused the Christ of blasphemy.[42] Mark and Luke added to this quarrelsome accusation the dispiriting, "Who can forgive sins but God alone?" Luke also included the observation that these Pharisees and teachers of the Oral Law, boiling over with resentment, had come from every village in Galilee and from Judea and from Jerusalem to sit in judgment upon the Son of God/Son of man. All the same, healed and forgiven, the paralytic took up his pallet and walked away. Thus, the Lord of the Church revealed his power to forgive sins. "Did the scribes admit their defeat? Did they at least acknowledge that Jesus had justified his claim? On this point Matthew is silent. So are also Mark and Luke. The sequel would seem to indicate that they admitted nothing and became more and more hostile (Matt. 9:11, 34; 12:2, 14, 24; Mark 2:16, 24; 3:2, 5; 3:22; 7:1ff.; Luke 5:30; 6:2, 7, 11)."[43] Then, as this brimming wave of malice slid back into the grating undertow

41. Matt 1:21.

42. Hendriksen, *Matthew*, 419, "Here again the scribes were right. But now their thinking arrives at the fork in the road, and they make the wrong turn. Either: *a.* Jesus is what by implication he claims to be, namely, God; or *b.* he blasphemes, in the sense that he unjustly claims the attributes and prerogatives of deity."

43. Ibid., 420.

of undisciplined hatred, other blunt instruments of evil multiplied from beneath the surface of mistrust and covetousness, according to Matthew, immediately. The Pharisee faction still found Jesus easy prey.

At table in Levi's house, other apparently welcome tax collectors and sinners reclined and ate with Jesus and the Twelve. Matt 9:10–13/Mark 2:15–17/Luke 5:29–32. Observing Pharisees (and teachers of the Oral Law too, Luke 5:30) descended upon the apostles-in-training; they asked, "Why do you eat and drink with tax collectors and sinners?" Members of the Church labeled as tax collectors and sinners habitually discounted the priority of the Oral Law:[44] often only indispensably ritual hand washing before mealtimes. "'Publicans *and sinners*' had at least this in common that none of them paid much attention to the rules and regulations which by the rabbis had been superimposed upon the law of God. Of these 'traditions' Pharisees and scribes made everything."[45] Jesus himself responded to this wave of malice with extra energy, denouncing this Oral Law stipulation: its enforcement strategy made ritual purification sharply supersede the larger ways of mercy, in this case, compassion for normally shunned tax collectors and sinners. Proud, self-righteous, exclusionary, the Pharisees punctuated this attack with an unbiblical sense of urgency.[46] Noteworthy: Luke, 15:1–2, recounted another such inner compulsion at controversy. "Now the tax collectors and sinners were all drawing near to hear him. And the Pharisees and the scribes murmured, saying, 'This man receives sinners and eats with them.'" Obviously, Jesus transgressed a hard line of the Oral Law. Still, nothing warranted the indescribable hatred brewing, except the Person of the Christ and the nature of the Gospel.[47] Pharisees insisted upon self-manifested righteousness for present privileges and future glories.[48]

44. Achtemeier and Achtemeier, *The Old Testament Roots of our Faith*, 77, "In Jesus' day . . . scribes and Pharisees could consider that they were God's elect, because they followed the law, while tax collectors and sinners had no place in the community because they broke the legal requirements."

45. Hendriksen, *Matthew*, 423.

46. Hendriksen, *Luke*, 304 on this item of the Oral Law, ". . . the disciples of the learned shall not recline at table in the company of the people of the soil (the rabble, the disreputable ones)."

47. Kirsch minimized the offense, *We Christians and Jews*, 49, "They differed with Jesus chiefly with regard to the divine law."

48. Epstein, *Judaism*, 142, "Man can . . . achieve his own redemption by penitence, being assured that God himself is ever-ready in His abundance of loving-kindness to receive the penitent sinner and purge him of all iniquity."

4. Thereupon, Jesus marred the Pharisaic fasting practice, Matt 9:14–17; Mark 2:18–22; Luke 5:33–38, and executed more miracles, including a resurrection from the dead. After an exorcism, Matt 9:22–37; Luke 11:14–23; Mark 3:20–30, the Lord's ecclesial opponents launched a first demonization, "He casts out demons by the prince of demons." Mark fleshed out this act of defamation with retentive detail, "He is possessed by Beelzebul,[49] and by the prince of demons he casts out demons." Equally, Luke recounted, "He casts out demons by Beelzebul, the prince of demons." This coarse and grimy wave of malice struck harder, with unrelenting intent to harm, to turn wondering multitudes away from listening to and following the Christ. Jesus had already pointed out the necessity of harvesting in the Church. Matt 9:35–38; Luke 10:1–12. As discomfited Pharisees and teachers of the Oral Law, fearing the unknown and with dawning recognition of dissolving influence, perceived synagogue members slipping away to hear the Teacher, snappish, they spat inordinate venom.[50] Satan's troops, disqualified to lead into the future but deeply entrenched, remobilized and unwound another imperious wave of malice laden with palpable rage. Be it observed: these explosive fusions of powers to injure crested arythmically, always at opportunely calculated hours.

5. In the foreknowledge of worse malice, real and pressing, the Lord Jesus dispersed the Twelve for hard training into enemy territory, his Church at that time. Matt 10:1–42; Mark 6:7–13; Luke 9:1–6. Matt 10:16–20, "Behold, I send you out as sheep in the midst of wolves; so be wise as serpents and innocent as doves. Beware of men; for they will deliver you up to councils, and flog you in their synagogues, and you will be dragged before governors and kings for my sake, to bear testimony before them and the Gentiles. When they deliver you up, do not be anxious how you are to speak or what you are to say; for what you are to say will be given to you in that hour; for it is not you who speak, but the Spirit of your Father speaking through you." Luke 10:1–12. Hereby, the Lord pointed up front to the reputable

49. Second Kings 1:2, re: Baalzebub, detested god of Philistine Ekron.

50. Hendriksen, *Matthew*, 438, "The hostility revealed already in verses 3 and 11 reaches a very high point here in verse 34."

Epstein, *Judaism*, 102, "The opposing views of these two schools stretched themselves practically along the whole gamut of Jewish life—ritual, domestic, social, and economic. Yet, despite their manifold differences, their basic allegiance to the written and oral Torah prevented them from degenerating into separate sects, and the two schools would often meet in conference in order to discuss their respective opinions and reach a decision by a majority vote."

necessity of missionaries in the Church at that time; he commissioned the Twelve and for the purpose given granted them unfailing powers of speech, healing, and exorcism amidst widespread distress—with a frank sense of urgency pertinent to this ministry, a ministry with its inherent risks and potentially sorrows of persecution.

Matthew's Spirit-informed account of Jesus' first mission charge to the Twelve in the Church opened up increasingly the intensity of perverse devotion they incited on the edge of the transitory unknown. Therefore, they had to be sufficiently acquainted with and sensitive to the multiple layers of the corrosive crises rising. Without compunction, to gain an edge along the baleful line of attack, coiling foes with renewed rounds of ferocity equated Jesus and Satan, the latter that strange hybrid of unfiltered covetousness and shocking hatred. Again, emphatic, Matt 12:24; Mark. 3:22; Luke 11:15, "It is only by Beelzebul, the prince of demons, that this man casts out demons." Thus, untroubled by violence to the Ninth Commandment and desperate for a sustained presence in the Church, to be the Church, they sought to persuade themselves and mutable throngs following the Christ, whom Pharisees labeled "the devil in person,"[51] of the Pharisaic righteousness that propelled them carnally back and forth against the Lord and Savior. Matthew, in his twenty-third chapter, closing in on the Church-unsettling approach to the Crucifixion, further unfolded the death wish Satan's troops displayed, the sort of belief fairly gauging reprobation. To drive home this pulsating point of fact, the Lord Jesus called these indelibly marked members of the Church intolerable Devil's brood, John 8:34–47.

In duly preparing the Twelve for astute apostleship, Jesus instructed these men for multi-purpose servanthood also with a sharp awareness of the scatology into which they had to make headway to establish the Church and extend the Kingdom's boundaries. Therefore, he implanted a comparison between himself and the Baptizer, which he concluded sharply. Luke 7:31–35; Matt 11:16–19, "For John came neither eating nor drinking, and they say, 'He has a demon'; the Son of man came eating and drinking, and they say, 'Behold, a glutton and a drunkard, a friend of tax collectors and sinners!'" As his own people betrayed him with slander, the Lord and Savior hereby demonstrated Gospel delaying perils the Twelve faced. For in a shared fantasy with respect to earning eternal life in the general resurrection at the end of the age, Pharisee-persuaded members of the Church

---

51. Hendriksen, *Matthew*, 468.

never intended to take Jesus' words to heart, much less repent and reform. Israel's multitudes determined to achieve eschatological redemption in the world to come on their own terms. Thereto, they planned, even on the edge of hopelessness, to pester and humiliate first the Lord himself, then the Twelve, with immensely provocative opposition.

As Jesus hereafter strode onwards through bitterness of conflict, quietly, authoritatively, in terms of Matthew's Gospel, he thematically declared with prophetic confidence another dominant depth in his church work. Luke 10:21–22; Matt 11:25–30, "I thank thee, Father, Lord of heaven and earth, that thou hast hidden these things from the wise and understanding and revealed them to babes; yea, Father, for such was thy gracious will. All things have been delivered to me by my Father; and no one knows the Son except the Father, and no one knows the Father except the Son and any one to whom the Son chooses to reveal him." This influential declaration the omnipotent and self-sacrificing Lord and Savior addressed to the partisan crowds following him, listening to his teachings. Such a thematic revelation obviously separated Jesus and the Father from the axiomatically impossible monotheism perpetuated by the adherents of the Oral Law. Sharply, Jesus poised the impregnable dividing-line between himself and aggressively moving opponents of the Gospel in the covenant community straying from antiquity deeper into wayward undercurrents of dark vengeance.

Again, opportune Pharisees,[52] barricaded behind iron conventions and inherited customs, regrouped and rose to the attack, accusing Jesus' disciples of harvesting on a Sabbath. Matt 12:1–8; Mark 2:23–28; Luke 6:1–5. The men, hungry, plucked ripe heads of grain and ate the kernels, as permissible, Deut 23:25. The Pharisees, ironically, failed to see a beam in their own eyes; they themselves broke the Fourth Commandment with their 'erub convention.

---

52. Hendriksen, *Matthew*, 511, "Filled with envy they were always watching Jesus to see whether something he said or did could be used as a charge against him, so as to destroy him. As to the Pharisees here referred to, whether they had come a great distance—having traveled on his heels, perhaps from Judea back to Galilee, as some think—or were from nearby, one thing is certain: their intentions were not honorable. There was murder in their hearts."

Major, et al., *The Mission and Message of Jesus*, 479, "Jesus claims that something more important than the Temple and its ritual has come into the world. That something is the Kingdom of God. He does not break through the traditions of the scribes merely in order to be different, but in obedience to a higher obligation, the claims of the Kingdom."

This Pharisaic charge of unlawfulness[53] rested on the Oral Law, which through a distorted perspective surrounded Sabbath observance with numerous prohibitions allegedly to protect the Fourth; these layered *halackhic* criteria intended to guard Seventh Days from moral disgrace, thereby to enhance with utmost precision the sanctity of each Sabbath. In fact, however, with the Oral Law they eased the Fourth into much easier rules as, for instance, with the *'erub*.[54] Attuned to the *'erub*, or *'eruv*, they refuted and revised Fourth applications as Jer 17:19–23, and developed troubling trends of Sabbath disobedience, permitting them to carry on with every day sorts of work. Neh 13:15–18. To curb Sabbath desecration according to the Oral Law standards, they placed the rabbinical tradition above the Law; in effect, they found dedication to the Oral Law with what was left of the Sabbath weightier than hearing and obeying the Lord of the Sabbath. The original institution of the life-affirming Sabbath they buried with inflexible obstinacy under morally binding forces. With reference to 1 Sam 21:6 and Num 28:9–10, Jesus sovereignly repulsed also that harsh wave of malice . . . only to face in that devious culture of opposition more irreconcilable hostility.

On a subsequent Sabbath,[55] Jesus with a conquering word executed a healing, which synagogue authorities peering through flexible codes and cases of the Thora-filter considered unnecessary,[56] if not rigorously enforceable forbidden labor. On this cynical occasion, Jesus beat back Satan's mercenaries afoul of their own pliable practice: a Seventh Day readiness to

53. Kirsch, *We Christians and Jews*, 49, "When Jesus' disciples plucked grain as they walked on the Sabbath, 'threshed' it in their hands, and ate it, it was Pharisees who challenged Jesus' permissiveness (Mark 2:24). The disciples were seen as in violation of the Pharisees' strict interpretation of the biblical prohibition of work on the Sabbath."

54. Neusner, *Judaism*, 51, "Private property is commingled; everybody shares in everybody's. The result is, private property takes on a new meaning, different from the secular one. In contemporary Judaism, an *eruv* or symbolic fence joining private properties over a considerable area allows people to carry things outside their own homes."

55. Major, et al., *The Mission and Message of Jesus*, 481, "Jesus cannot have been unaware of the great price which had been paid by His people for the right to keep the Sabbath. He cannot have been insensitive to the sacred associations of the observance in Jewish homes and in every department of Jewish life. Why then does He deal so drastically with the thing that was so sacred to His people, a thing which He had doubtless been taught in childhood to regard as sacred?"

56. Kirsch, *We Christians and Jews*, 49, "The Pharisees took offense when Jesus healed the man. For the Pharisees it was lawful to expend effort such as was normally prohibited on the Sabbath provided it was necessary to save life; but presumably the man with the withered arm was not in danger of death and could have waited for treatment until the Sabbath was ended."

rescue a sheep fallen into a pit.[57] Matt 12:9–14; Mark 3:1–6; Luke 6:6–11. Mark perceptively added that the Lord dispersed his churchly adversaries' finger pointing with justifiable indignation.[58] Certainly, any human being exceeded an animal in value.

John recorded an otherwise unknown account in which Jesus refused to go openly about in Judea because glum Jewish governing officials craved more inflexibly to kill him. John 7:14–36. However, God the Father had omnisciently appointed the historic hour and the method of death, not contentious Jews even if of high standing. To frustrate precipitate action, for primary functionaries of the synagogue and the Temple sought his death, the Lord and Savior at a feast of Tabernacles merged into countless celebrants flocking into overcrowded Jerusalem. Among the numerous many from Judea, Galilee, and distant *diaspora* homelands, he disintegrated the identifiable evil of that surging wave.

Often, Jesus healed on Sabbaths, thereby revealing the passionate power of the life-giving first covenant promise. Luke 13:10–17, 14:1–6; John 5:2–9, 5:15–18, 7:14–24; etc. Always, however, indignant Jews/Pharisees/teachers of the Oral Law with self-generated authority displayed hate-drenched readiness to do away with him physically.

Matthew recorded: venting Pharisees took counsel, how in those revolutionary times to destroy Jesus by force. Mark also, with due diligence, identified the fact that harsh rulers held this highly charged political process coupled with competing authorities, Herodians. Mark 3:6. Matthew and Luke in a different way laid out this surging malice. Matt 12:14; Luke 6:11, "But [the Pharisees] were filled with fury and discussed with one another what they might to do Jesus." As the pounding of the rowdy surf gathered in emboldening ferocity, the rough and tumble waves of malice grew fiercer. Around this time, the Pharisees and the chief priests sent officers to seize him, John 7:30, 45–52), a politically advantageous stunt that dissolved into idle talk, the Sanhedrin officers however berating the arresting party.

---

57. Major, et al., *The Mission and Message of Jesus*, 480, "Opinions were still divided in the Rabbinical schools at a much later time. Some said that if an animal fell into a pit on the Sabbath, it was lawful to bring food to it there. Others held that is was further permissible to place mattresses and cushions under it, so that it might get out by its own exertions."

58. Hendriksen, *Matthew*, 517, "It was Jesus himself who was about to do good to this man. Christ's critics, on the other hand, were harboring thoughts of murder, the murder of the Benefactor (verse 14)."

Following Matthew's account, the Lord Jesus with noble distinction accomplished more of Isa 42:1–4; he healed all the infirm who flocked to him for this charitable purpose.

After Jesus restored physically a blind and dumb demoniac, increasingly antagonistic Pharisees hurled at him a second time a painfully cruel dagger, lusting for the defamation of his character. Matt 12:22–32; Mark 3:20–27.[59]/Luke 11:14–22. Matt 12:24, "It is only by Beelzebul, the prince of demons, that this man casts out demons." Jesus' conjuration of an evil spirit aroused the Pharisees,[60] who once more demonized the Lord of the Church, the only source of life. The Christ countered this presumptuous absurdity with the parabolic statement of a kingdom divided against itself, in this case Satan against Satan. The disruptive hostility of the religious authorities, plotting the Savior's too early demise, cast this cheerless wave of malice hard to the surface, deep from within raging depths of covetousness.

Leading forces, initially the Pharisees, painfully aware of losing followers and even more of the stressful undermining of Oral Torah prominence, willed a hard reverse of events, whatever unthinkable costs, with or without social approval. At that time, free in the narrowness of the present and cognizant of his enemies' petty limitations, the Incarnate addressed with unforgettable warnings all burdened by rearing coils of transgression. Matt 12:31–32, "Therefore I tell you, every sin and blasphemy will be forgiven men, but the blasphemy against the Spirit will not be forgiven. And whoever says a word against the Son of man will be forgiven; but whoever speaks against the Holy Spirit will not be forgiven, either in this age or in the age to come." Matt 12:36–37, "I tell you, on the day of judgment men will render account for every careless word they utter; for by your words you will be justified, and by your words you will be condemned." For another phrasing, Mark 3:28–30, "'Truly, I say to you, all sins will be forgiven the sons of men, and whatever blasphemies they utter; but whoever blasphemes against the Holy Spirit never has forgiveness, but is guilty of an eternal sin'—for they had said, 'He has an unclean spirit.'" Jesus' parabolic and prophetic recourse against this Pharisaic allegation had impact.[61] John 7:20.

59. Mark's context differed from Matthew and Luke's, also by the fact that teachers of the Oral Law from Jerusalem, that is, spies delegated by the Sanhedrin, made the accusation. The involvement of the meddlesome Sanhedrin by all counts dragged the Sadducees compoundingly into the throes of the fray.

60. Hendriksen, *Matthew*, 524, "This time, unlike in 12:2, 10, the opponents do not address Jesus directly, but slander him behind his back."

61. During this time, teachers of the Oral Law and Pharisees also sought to entrap

John, 8:12–59, recorded a moral evasion in which Pharisees[62] tested the Lord and Savior on the basis of the Deut 17:6, 19:15 double-witness teaching, credible evidence for a foundational norm of justice. When Jesus revealed himself the Light of the world, his enemies countered with the exasperated accusation and vitriolic affront that he bore invalid witness to himself, a single witness, predictably unacceptable in terms of the Written Law. Within the obstructive agitation of this insensitive confrontation, the Lord and Savior accosted his opponents' unalterable heart, "You are of your father the devil, and your will is to do your father's desires." Once more, from innermost recesses, dark thinkers[63] demonized him, twice; according to John 10:19–21, they repeated this bedevilment of the Messiah.

Along this forward line of attack, the Jews equated Jesus and Satan, with urgent tones to persuade themselves and shifting throngs about the Christ to promote Pharisaic righteousness. They craved to outmaneuver the Son of God/Son of man with repeated eruptions of malice and dominate the hapless circle of misery called Israel solely by means of the Tradition of the Elders.

Through growing levels of high-profile confrontation, fully functioning teachers of the Oral Law and Pharisees had suffered unflattering public humiliation with disastrous repercussions. Hence, from beguiling margins, the next wave of malice hit with a deferential insistence, nothing coincidental, faking it with a 'polite' request for a sign; they tempted Jesus to make sense of and 'prove' his messiahship. The sign they sought?[64]

Jesus with a woman caught in adultery. John 8:2–11; Deut 22:22–24.

62. Rivkin, *A Hidden Revolution*, 99, "In this passage the Pharisees are linked to the authorities in general. They determine the beliefs that are legitimate. They are contrasted with the crowds who do not know the Law and who are accursed for defying the Law. And even when in his account of Jesus' healing on the sabbath day (chapter 9) John seems to refer to the Pharisees as though they and all the Jews were one and the same, the Pharisees nonetheless are pictured as legal authorities."

63. Ibid., 98, "The Gospel of John offers us Pharisees who do not possess the distinguishing features ascribed to them by the Synoptics and Acts. The Pharisees in John seem to have no distinguishing features at all. They seem to be a name, not a reality. They appear as hardly more than a synonym for *Jews*. They are not even differentiated from the Sadducees! They never challenge Jesus on points of the Law but only on his claims to having been sent by God. The only tangible datum that John reveals about them is that they were leaders whose authority with the people was great."

64. Neusner, *Scriptures of the Oral Torah*, 18, "Specifically, in the canonical documents of the period at hand for the first time we find clear reference to the notion that when God revealed the Torah to Moses at Sinai, part of the Torah was in the medium of writing, the other part, in the medium of memory, hence oral. And, it would later

For the almighty Messiah to create a rock too heavy for him to lift? Better! In a sudden burst of energy, the arrival of the Pharisee-tempered messiah, Rome's physical defeat, the inauguration of the world to come, the general resurrection of the dead, eschatological redemption, the arrival of the Kingdom,[65] and they in charge. Absent that collective sign,[66] Jesus lost, in their estimation. "[This] idea of fulfilment is associated in Jewish teaching with a vision of the Kingdom of God. But this kingdom is not relegated to the celestial stage of another existence, unconnected with the struggles, problems, hopes, and aspirations of the present. It is a kingdom to be built *here* on earth, under divine guidance, by the hands of man. Human endeavour, which determines the whole complexity of human destiny along the high road of fulfilment, is none other than that which is translated in terms of personal and social righteousness; and the universal realization of these ideals of righteousness in all human relations constitutes the quintessence and distinctive element of the Jewish conception of the Kingdom."[67] As the

---

be explained, the Mishnah (and much else) enjoyed the status of the oral Torah. They explain the Messiah-claim of Israel in very simple terms. Israel indeed will receive the Messiah, but salvation at the end of time awaits the sanctification of Israel in the here and now. And that will take place through humble and obedient loyalty to the Torah."

Major, et al., *The Mission and Message of Jesus*, 596, "The form of the Pharisees' question shows that they are thinking of the Kingdom as something still future. They believe that it will come; and they ask 'when?' That is, they ask the question which so many of the Apocalypses ask and attempt to answer. The answer of Jesus may mean that it is idle to ask *when* the Kingdom will come, since it is already present; or that the question cannot be answered, since the answer is known to God alone."

65. Epstein, *Judaism*, 139, "The kingdom of God, in its terrestrial and social setting, provides the key to the understanding of Judaism in all its varied manifestations, and, indeed, the solution to the riddle of the existence of the Jewish people."

66. Klinghoffer, *Why the Jews Rejected Jesus*, 71, "You can easily imagine his contemporaries dismissing him with characteristic Jewish irony: So Jesus gathered crowds of five thousand. So he performed magical feats like producing food for a multitude from a few loaves or fishes. So he performed faith healings. So he's even reported to have revived two individuals thought to have died. Very nice! But let him do what the 'son of man,' the promised Messiah, had been advertised as being destined to do from Daniel back through Ezekiel and Isaiah and the rest of the prophets. Let him rule as a monarch, his kingship extending over 'all peoples, nations and languages.' Let him return the exiles and rebuild the Temple and defeat the oppressors and establish universal peace, as the prophets also said."

67. Epstein, *Judaism*, 139. Ibid., 140, "The belief in the fulfilment of divine purpose in the supra-historical and supranatural is shared by other religions; but what is distinctive in Judaism is its insistence that the consummation in the Beyond is conditioned by the fulfilment in the historical and social context of daily life. Simon, *Jewish Sects at the Time of Jesus*, 43, "Suffice it to say that the Pharisees seemed to have awaited, with complete

hard-edged Pharisees and scribes strove to accomplish their entrenched belief regarding the finality of history, with the assistance of a messiah, they, in fact, poised themselves to achieve this restoration of order. "The Pharisees (and Mt. adds 'and Sadducees') are now on the track of Jesus and demand from Him, in order to prove Him a deceiver, a sign from heaven. The word 'tempting' has the sinister meaning of putting to the test in order to prove that something is not what it seems to be. They were sure He could not give them a sign from heaven."[68] Thus, they treated the Messiah, the Son of Man, and Israel's Savior.

The Lord, however, easily reading the reflecting pool of morally corrupt minds and hearts consumed by mad dreams, promised that evil[69] and adulterous,[70] that is, idolatrous, generation only the perplexing sign of Jonah. Matt 12:38–42; Luke 11:29–32. Mark, 8:11–13, however, ignored this Jonah sign, three punishing days and nights in the belly of a fish. Jesus, contrary to the expectations, answered forthrightly, following out the uninterrupted movement of Old Testament history: the Resurrection as the deliverable evidence of the Kingdom in time and history, the beginning of the end, his new creation here and now. In effect, Jesus overruled his rivals in the Church.

---

and unanimous (although short-lived) optimism, the return of the exiles to the Holy Land, the crumbling of foreign domination, the extermination of the impious, in short, the advent of the kingdom of the Messiah—the peaceful and prosperous prelude to the final events and to the establishing of the 'world to come.'"

68. Major, et al., *The Mission and Message of Jesus,* 106.

Mark 8:11–13; Matt 12:38–42, 16:1–4; Luke 11:14–23.

69. Major, et al., *The Mission and Message of Jesus,* 106, "In Mt. those who seek a sign from Jesus are described by Him as evil and adulterous. By 'evil' is probably meant, so hardened as to be lacking in moral and spiritual perception; by 'adulterous' is meant 'disloyal to God.' Ever since the days of the prophet Hosea, adultery had had this second sense of spiritual infidelity."

70. Ibid., 381, "'Adulterous' is used, as often in Old Testament prophecy, in the sense of 'unfaithful to God,' 'apostate.' This meaning would be unfamiliar to Gentile readers, and Lk. may have dropped the word for that reason."

Hendriksen, *Matthew,* 533, "It has to be thrilling, exciting, sensational. Well, what *did* they want? Did they want Jesus to cause the heavenly constellations to change places in the zodiac? Did they want him to make the Bull (Taurus) catch up with the Giant Hunter (Orion)? Must he perhaps blaze his name across the sky in enormous letters of gold? Is he expected to produce in the sky above them a vision of Michael suddenly leaving his celestial abode and coming forth to deliver the Jews from the galling yoke of the Romans? Their demand was wicked, for in addition to being insulting and impudent it was also hypocritical, for they felt sure that what they so politely asked Jesus to do he could not do anyway."

The teachers of the Oral Law and the Pharisees, maddened by ambition and desperate to hold onto control over the Church, with sudden acceleration needed to block Jesus in his messianic mission by way of an all-annihilating victory. Therefore, they insisted that Jesus institute, immediately, inclusive the overthrow of the Roman yoke, the Jewish ideal of the Kingdom,[71] or abandon his messiahship. Had they persuaded him to execute the sign they concocted, he compromised with shame and eschatological disaster the timeliness of the Incarnation, tabulating impoverished glory points for his own person, while tossing away the Father's will and purpose. The disrespectful opponents with ingrained disregard for the Gospel also failed miserably with this pseudo-deferential wave of malice.[72]

In the rising levels of these shortsighted attacks, wave upon wave with rapidly shifting breathing spaces, Matthew confirmed the tighter focus in the forbidding tide of malice. Throughout this unanimity in unfriendliness, however, the irreversible Son of God/Son of man responded with riveting parables; publicly targeting the Church, willing to listen or not, He pointed out without pain relief the choke point of unbelief, a ceaseless hunger for self-righteousness. Seizing then the fertile sense of the moment, the Spirit-incited Synoptics insisted inside the dense physicality of the Old Church the beginning of the New. Only all who responded from the heart to Jesus' summons, motivated solely by grace, constituted the true, ongoing covenant community, the revelation of grace the Spirit promised for Pentecost Day. Nevertheless, to those Old Church members, inclusive the leadership, Jesus addressed with respect to the Father's will the knowledge of the New Church. But scandalized, all balked at believing him, the Messiah. Matt 12:46–50; Mark 3:31–35; Luke 8:19–21.

To depict the disorientating intensity of hatred the common foe provoked, John 11:8, the Twelve at hearing notice of Lazarus' illness immediately invoked risk management; they cautioned Jesus against the silently waiting evil, "Rabbi, the Jews were but now seeking to stone you, and are you going there again?" That is, to Judea. Each of the disciples in the face of death much preferred survival, thereby bringing into doubt their sincerity of commitment to Jesus.

71. Bright, *The Kingdom of God*, 164, "The Kingdom of God is then vindicated and established before all the world. It is the final victory of God over all the pagan, evil powers of the earth."

72. Bultmann, *Primitive Christianity*, 82, "In the last analysis, the Messiah would really be no more than a figurehead. The real king would be God himself." That is, the Jewish monotheistic deity.

Inspiring the first Father-given members for the New Church, Jesus issued more parables, also the purpose of these incisive stories: to separate eternally the Old Church into the reprobate and the elect. Matt 13:10–17/ Mark 4:10–13/Luke 8:9–10. For this parabolic teaching, Pharisee-corrupted Nazareth's good inhabitants (measured according to the Oral Law) murderously rejected the Lord of life. Matt 13:34–35.

Slowly, blinding and deafening, for undermining Jesus' ministry the leaven of the Pharisees had leached deep down into the covenant community's constricted consciousness. Mark 6:1–6; Matt 13:53–58, ". . . coming to his own country he taught them in their synagogue, so that they were astonished, and said, 'Where did this man get this wisdom and these mighty works? Is not this the carpenter's son? Is not his mother called Mary? And are not his brothers James and Joseph and Simon and Judas? And are not all his sisters with us? Where then did this man get all this?' And they took offense at him." Slanderously, the covenant people among whom (Joseph and) Mary had raised him questioned the basic integrity of his Person and work. Better an inglorious ending to life in the Church than submission to the Christ.

Matthew, remembering the Baptizer, memorialized his martyr death, a beheading, that other leading Roman execution method.

Thereupon the Gospel's writers, quietly marveling, documented the hospitable feeding of five thousand, Matt 14:13–21; Mark 6:30–44; Luke 9:10–17; John 6:1–14. Plus, he preserved the credible account of the Twelve caught by a lashing storm on the Sea of Galilee/Lake Gennesaret/Sea of Tiberius, John 6:16–21, a providentially planned preparation for the soon to follow swirling wave of malice. Seeing Jesus, the Lord of heaven and earth, walking on storm-tossed waves strengthened the fear-saturated Twelve for the next crisis, which started provocatively enough, with an accusatory appraisal, to unleash radicalizing depths of malevolence.

In Matt 15:1–20; Mark 7:1–23, Pharisees and teachers of the Oral Law specifically referred to the tradition of the elders; all along and up close with diminishing patience they had measured Jesus by the righteousness of these unwritten building blocks of Judaism. Starting deep, they tossed this chilling wave of malice high. "For [your disciples] do not wash their hand when they eat."[73] Thus, these meddling representatives of the Oral

---

73. Bultmann, *Primitive Christianity*, 65, "The Pharisees, in their zeal, imposed upon the laity the laws of purity which had originally applied only to the priesthood, thus giving the whole of life the character of ritual holiness."

Law raised their undependable holiness against that of the Son of God/ Son of man, Lord and Savior, stellar Judge of heaven and earth. Jesus, however, targeted the Corban, an escape clause from justice and an ingenuous manipulation for greed, to condemn the Pharisees as well as all teachers of the Oral Law with an appropriate quotation from Isaiah, 29:13, an ancient prophecy.

Thereafter, Jesus, steadily striding unarmed towards the First Judgment, displayed more miracles, inclusive the communal feeding of four thousand.

Noteworthy: from the beginning of his ministry and throughout, Jesus restructured the ongoing history of and in the covenant community, an appraisal applicable equally from Matthew, Mark, Luke, and John. "The Markan Jesus refuses to become identified with Jewish national or racial exclusiveness. He is willing to perform healings and exorcisms among and in behalf of Gentiles (5:1–20; 7:24–30); he refuses to arouse Jewish national hopes by encouraging disobedience to Roman law (12:17). He will not engage in typical rabbinic debate about the interpretation of the Law; instead, he confronts [the Church] directly with God's radical demand (10:1–12; 10:17–27; 12:28–34)."[74] The Lord worked labor-intensively to reform Israel's covenantal faithfulness, never intending even to validate Pharisaism and emerging Judaism. He drew the covenant's historical line from Genesis past the Incarnation to the Crucifixion, apart from diversionary Pharisaism and its misleading developments in time.

Upon the second miraculous feeding, colluding Pharisees and Sadducees[75] conspiring to find a contemporary power balance, launched a bunching-up wave of hostility more malevolent. Matt 16:1–4; Mark 8:11–13. Mark, let it be noted, specified this as a Pharisee assault only. These

---

74. Kee, *Jesus in History*, 142–43.

75. Simon, *Jewish Sects at the Time of Jesus*, 24, "The Sadducees indeed came mostly from the priestly class, although the two groups were never identical. They represented an aristocracy that seems to have been haughty and exclusive. They had little contact with the people and little influence over them. At the beginning of the Christian era their authority, primarily cultic, seems scarcely to have gone beyond the confines of the temple."

Major, et al., *The Mission and Message of Jesus*, 161, "It had become clear to the High Priestly clan in Jerusalem that they must somehow get rid of Jesus. His teaching was too popular and too provocative to allow its continuance. Yet every attempt to stop it had ended in failure. Action must be swift and secret: swift because things were rapidly approaching a crisis; secret because any disturbance of public order caused by the open arrest of Jesus would bring the High Priest into conflict with the Roman authorities—a result to be avoided at all costs."

impudent leaders of the tradition of the elders asked, indeed, demanded a sign from heaven whereby Jesus had opportunity to demonstrate his credentials—after the countless miracles he had given! "This time (contrast 12:38, 39) we are told specifically that the purpose of the enemy was *to tempt* Jesus, to put him to the test, in the hope and with the expectation that he would fail, and would thus be publicly discredited."[76] They looked fervently for a military majesty to reign as the enemy-overpowering king; all hoped to witness the epoch of conflict turning the world upside down, a plenary panacea constitutive of the age to come.[77] However, Jesus, the Lord of heaven and earth, rebuked both subversive ideological factions in the Church: they lacked the ability to interpret the signs of the times, even less the culminating signs of the age he revealed.[78] "An evil and adulterous generation seeks for a sign, but no sign shall be given it except the sign of Jonah." Hereupon, he turned his back to them, walking away. He had sufficiently proven his messiahship. All the while miffed unbelievers adrift in the Church refused to believe everything with respect to his ministry, Luke 17:20–21.

Subsequently, Jesus warned the Twelve against the collective teaching of the far off-course Pharisees and Sadducees. Matt 16:5–12; Mark 8:14–21; Luke 12:1–3. In Mark's account, the Lord alerted his disciples to both the poisoning leaven of the Pharisees and the decaying leaven of the Herodians, in this case Sadducees closely allied with the Roman occupiers. The Twelve first had to perceive the inner darkness of the Oral Law and the specter of loss in the Judaic way of life as they walked on-course with Jesus into the acutely contemporary and compelling evidence of covenant reformation.

Peter's confession, Matt 16:13–20; Mark 8:27–30; Luke 9:18–22, marked out a high point on the Lord Jesus' life-defining *via dolorosa* to the Cross, "You are the Christ, the Son of the living God." Next, with the revelation of the Church's foundation and the keys of the Kingdom, Jesus

---

76. Hendriksen, *Matthew*, 636.

77 Neusner, *Judaism*, 60, "The Messiah's kingship would resolve the issues of Israel's subordinated relationship to other nations and empires, establishing once and for all time the correct context for priest and sage alike."

78. Hendriksen, *Matthew*, 637, #594p, "Note *kairwn*. Jesus is speaking about epoch-making periods in history, not about time viewed as a change from the past into the present into the future, mere duration."

Bultmann, *Primitive Christianity*, 60, "By binding herself to her past history, Israel loosened her ties with the present and her responsibility for it. Loyalty to the past became loyalty to a book which was all about the past. God was no longer really the God of history, and therefore always the God who was about to come."

charged the Twelve to tell no one that he was the Christ. At that time, too, Jesus with solemn commitment foretold his crucifixion and resurrection, Matt 16:21–23; Mark 8:31–33; Luke 9:22, the critical reality that failed to register with the Twelve.[79] When Peter rashly voiced refusal to believe, Jesus denounced the man as a hindrance to the progress of the Gospel. "Get behind me, Satan." At that visionary turning point, Jesus taught the Twelve a more heartening grasp of apostolic discipleship, inclusive pain-racked martyrdom.

John, 10:22–30, publicized an otherwise unknown, coarsening wave of malice. Jesus under intense scrutiny at a Feast of Dedication[80] taught on Temple precincts also to gathering Jews who questioned him. "How long will you keep us in suspense? If you are the Christ, tell us plainly." This jarring intrusion, to shore up impossible to manage unbelief, affirmed the reality of smoldering hatred. These slanderous Jews in that uneasy tension again picked up ready stones, therewith to kill him and thereby undermine Sadducee powers of justice.[81]

After the distinctive statement of the Transfiguration and another healing miracle, Jesus prophesied a second time the coming of his crucifixion and resurrection. Matt 17:22–23; Mark 9:30–32; Luke 9:43b–45. His prophetic interpretation and structuring of history confounded the Judaic eschatological expectation, a general resurrection of the dead at the end of time and therewith the inauguration of the Kingdom, the manifestation of the Jewish world to come.[82]

---

79. Hendriksen, *Matthew,* 655–56, "From the human point of view the concepts *Messiah* and *suffering* were wholly incompatible. Peter, allowing himself to be influenced by Satan, was speaking from the foolish human point of view when he said, 'Mercy on thee, Lord, this shall never happen to thee.'"

80. Bultmann, *Primitive Christianity,* 59--60, "Devout Jews made pilgrimages to the Temple for the great feasts, even from the Diaspora. These feasts acted both as a demonstration of national solidarity and loyalty to law, and also as an anticipation of the eschatological joy."

81. Rivkin, *A Hidden Revolution,* 99–100, "John clearly conveys the notion that the Pharisees were the leaders to whom the people would go to get things done. They were those who had the authority to evaluate Jesus' acts and to put a stop to them. They have such influence that they, along with the chief priests, have the authority to convoke the council and take steps to silence Jesus. Thus John testifies to the *power* of the Pharisees, though he does not communicate to us any doctrine that would *differentiate* them from the chief priests or from any other grouping in Judaism."

82. Ibid., 230, "This non-Pentateuchal dogma of the world to come and resurrection is a core teaching of the Mishnah. Indeed, this belief is the cornerstone of the entire *halakhah* system. It was only because the true believer and true devotee of the twofold Law

Collectors of the annual temple tax, probing morbidly in the line of duty, held out a hand for Jesus' half-shekel. Matt 17:24–27; Exod 30:11–16. Sadducee employed, they too hoped to find the Lord afoul not only of the Oral Law, specifically of the Mosaic.

Matthew followed this undercutting confrontation with a life-sustaining discourse on humility, the sobering parable of the lost sheep, vestigial bearings for New Testament Church Discipline, and the growing pains for overcoming the perpetual sticking point of seventy-times-seven forgiveness.

Somewhere in Galilee, manipulating Pharisees with convoluted stubbornness tested Jesus on the permanency of a fundamental of marriage law; Mark 10:2–12, Matt 19:3–12, "Is it lawful for a man to divorce his wife for any and every reason?" Maliciously, they probed for a weakness, any area of discord in collision with Judaism's unwritten laws, in this case, adaptations over time to subvert the Seventh with evasive actions. "If Jesus endorsed the more strict interpretation, favored by Shammai, he would be displeasing the followers of Hillel. Moreover, there seem to have been very many who agreed with Hillel's 'liberal' opinion. . . . Besides, if the Lord sided with Shammai the Pharisees might have accused him, though not justly, of being inconsistent when he nevertheless consorted with sinners and ate with them."[83] Rather than side with either of these long-standing and inflammatory factions within the broader Judaic movement, the Lord of the Church projected the biblical marriage line from Genesis into the eschatological future.

After Jesus called malodorous Lazarus from a dank sepulcher, John 11:1–44, the Jews, brimming with violence, plotted more unflinchingly the death of the Lord and Savior. John 11:53, "So from that day on they took counsel how to put him to death." Therewith they widened floodgates of hostility to legitimate hateful messianic misinterpretations; in an unforgiving environment and with reckless folly, Pharisees and Sadducees galvanized a powerful dissolvent against the Gospel without grasping the consequence, the frightening future of unbelief.

Before turning decisively towards Jerusalem and the Cross, Jesus across the growing gulf validated by his dividing-line pointed out Pharisaic

---

could hope for the immortality of his soul and the resurrection of his body that he was ready, willing, and able to yoke himself to the twofold Law and abide by its discipline."

83. Hendriksen, *Matthew*, 714.

covetousness for luxurious lifestyles.[84] Luke 16:14–15, "The Pharisees, who were lovers of money, heard all this, and they scoffed at him. But he said to them, 'You are those who justify yourselves before men, but God knows your hearts; for what is exalted among men is an abomination in the sight of God.'" Shortly thereafter, Luke, 18:9–14, who communicated constant in all care for historical factuality, skillfully related soaring Pharisaic self-righteousness in terms of a parable, the distinctive identities of two men praying in the Temple, one impenitent.

In the expectant Synoptic setting, Matthew, Mark, and Luke confirmed Jesus' sustained turning towards Jerusalem. Matt 19:1–2; Mark 10:1; Luke 17:11. In this continuum of motivation to suffer the Cross, he gave highly integrated instruction on marriage, blessed children, opened up inheriting eternal life, laid out the duly chosen parable of a householder, and more impressively, for the third time, prophesied his crucifixion and resurrection. Mark 10:32–34; Luke 18:31–34; Matt 20:17–19, "Behold, we are going up to Jerusalem; and the Son of man will be delivered to the chief priests and scribes, and they will condemn him to death, and deliver him to the Gentiles to be mocked and scourged and crucified, and he will be raised on the third day." As God, Jesus foreknew precisely—into the appalling details—the clear pattern in which and the primary goal for which he ministered in the Church.

Lacking appreciation for as well as understanding of Jesus' reformation of the Kingdom, James and John with covetous maternal assistance exercised untoward ambition: a preferment in seating arrangement in the Kingdom. Responding to this odious covetousness, Jesus healed two blind men and proceeded upon his *triumphal* way[85] into the City of David. With the Incarnation, he had not come to satisfy subversive centers of misplaced pride, much less doubly dubious ideologies contrived by children of revolution, the Pharisee and Sadducee. Therefore, on this Day of Separation and amidst the mistaken throngs of the Church, with pastoral empathy he spoke

---

84. To assert the contrary, Major, et al., *The Mission and Message of Jesus*, 587, "That charge would have fitted the Sadducees or the publicans very much better. The Pharisees certainly did not despise worldly possessions; but it was not they who held the great vested interests but the Sadducees; and it was not they who sold their country and their own souls for gain but the publicans."

85. Major, et al., *The Mission and Message of Jesus*, 610, "Why do the Pharisees object to the demonstration? The answer to this question is that in accordance with their principles they could do no other. If Jesus was hailed as king that seemed to involve at once political rebellion against Rome; and it was a settled principle with the Pharisees that the only thing that justified revolt was interference with their religion."

the immediate future for the covenant community, his own people. Luke 19:41–44, "And when he drew near and saw the city he wept over it, saying, 'Would that even today you knew the things that make for peace! But now they are hid from your eyes. For the days shall come upon you, when your enemies will cast up a bank about you and surround you, and hem you in on every side, and dash you to the ground, you and your children within you, and they will not leave one stone upon another in you; because you did not know the time of your visitation.'"

In Jerusalem, to the consternation of poorly prepared Temple authorities, he cleansed the holy precincts of buyers and sellers who made the House a den of thieves.[86] Isa 56:7; Jer 7:11; Matt 21:12–13; Mark 11:15–19; Luke 19:45–46; John 2:13–22.[87] In addition to this judgment and with a surge of compassion, he healed numerous covenant members of life-eating illnesses. Moreover, children sang timely Hosannas to the Son of David.[88] These healing miracles and ringing Hosannas roused the brazen ire of the chief priests and teachers of the Oral Law; but that imminent hatemongering torrent of malice broke too soon,[89] Matt 21:14–16; Luke 19:37–40, ebbing away with the muttering and grumbling of worse-to-come savaging revenge.[90]

Returning from nearby Bethany one morning, the Lord denounced a fruit-less fig tree, a troubling image representative of revolutionary Israel,

86. Kirsch, *We Christians and Jews*, 56, ". . . the opening for corruption is obvious when one considers that to have one's animal rejected was to be compelled to purchase a fit animal from the priests, which gave the temple a monopoly and the price structure that goes with monopoly. The temple operated another monopoly. In order to purchase an animal, a pilgrim had to pay with temple currency. That meant purchasing temple money, again at monopolistic prices, from the temple money changers."

87. Ibid., 56, ". . . when Jesus expressed his judgment as strongly and publicly as he did, given his prestige and popularity, the temple administration was bound to be threatened and shaken. This alone could have motivated some chief priests to seek 'a way to destroy him' (Mark 11:18)."

88. Hendriksen, *Matthew*, 766, "As to 'Hosanna to the Son of David,' it should be noted that 'Hosanna' means 'save now,' or 'save, pray.'"

89. Ibid., 760, "Jesus forces the members of the Sanhedrin to change their time-table, so that it will harmonize with his (and the Father's) time-table. The enthusiasm of the crowds with respect to Jesus will hasten the crisis."

90. Dimont, *Jews, God and History*, 136, "This was the political atmosphere into which he stepped when he made his decision to come to Jerusalem. This was the time he had chosen to reveal publicly that he was the messiah. His destination was the Temple. His aim was the reform of some of its practices. From a political viewpoint, he had chosen the worst possible time to hasten Temple reforms."

the Old Church, Matt 21:18–22; Mark 11:12–14, 20–26; Israel's protracted confrontation against the Gospel provoked by traditional rivalry made the transition to Pentecost difficult beyond words. This age-long enmity the Christ quantified in the scope of his condemnatory power of speech: the tree died, withering away, bereft of hope. For another and similar parable, Luke 13:6–9.

The following day, once more on Temple grounds in the unavoidable presence of conflict, with a sense of urgency the ready chief priests and elders of the people challenged the operational authority of the Son of God/ Son of man with rebellious questioning. Mark 11:27–33; Luke 20:1–8; Matt 21:23–27, "Jesus answered them, 'I also will ask you a question; and if you tell me the answer, then I also will tell you by what authority I do these things. The baptism of John, whence was it? From heaven or from men?" That exacting test blunted this unambiguous wave of Pharisaic malice, racking up another collapse of expectations.

Jesus' teaching authority troubled the Jews; aroused by animosity, they resorted to a penchant for demonization, John 7:14–24. The members of the Church and the murderous leaders were less than impressed, unwilling to believe him from the heart. "You have a demon! Who is seeking to kill you?" That revolutionary convulsion excited hopelessly wanton winds for selecting and picking up raw evidence to hasten the Crucifixion.

The Lord and Savior, moving inflexibly ahead, overmatched the stultifying want of faithfulness by catalyst parables, of two sons, of wicked servants, and of a marriage feast. Once more, thereby, he exacerbated in the Church the assertive power of the dividing-line, again rattling in its moral center that troubled generation of irreconcilable hostility.

Dismissive chief priests and incorrigible Pharisees who half-absorbed particularly the endangering parable of the wicked servants, Matt 21:33–43; Mark 12:1–12; Luke 20:9–18, nevertheless felt its corrective impact. Mark 12:12; Luke 20:19–20; Matt 21:45–46, "When the chief priests and the Pharisees heard his parables, they perceived that he was speaking about them. But when they tried to arrest him, they feared the multitudes, because they held him to be a prophet." Simply, Jesus' time had not yet come. All the while, his bitter opponents spurned one elementary point the Lord of the Church often made: he placed them on the dark side of the dividing-line.

The Pharisees, sensing scornful winds of public pressure against them as well as the divine hollowing out of the Oral Law, pivoted for another taunting cycle of malice. Therefore, they took counsel (again) how to entrap him in his unbounded teaching. With collaborative Herodians,[91] that is, Sadducees, these Pharisees, unctuous now, initiated the appalling spectacle with hitherto unsuccessful flattery. A soothing question, seemingly. From Mark 12:13-17; Luke 20:19-26; Matt 22:15-16, "Teacher, we know that you are true, and teach the way of God truthfully, and care for no man; for you do not regard the position of man. Tell us, then, what you think. Is it lawful to pay taxes to Caesar, or not?"[92] The Lord gave his well-known reply, muting this revolutionary tidal force, "Why put me to the test, you hypocrites? Show me the money for the tax." Failing derisorily once more, both Pharisees and Herodians drooped off,[93] foiled, beaten, and still dense with disturbing currents of unbelief.[94]

The same day, Sadducees, faltering power seekers, launched a paining wave of malice wherewith they, once more, mocked the actuality of the

91. Hendriksen, *Matthew*, 800, "What a strange combination: *a.* Pharisees, who were—or made believe that they were—very concerned about keeping God's law, and *b.* partisans of the Herod family, who cared very little about the divine commandments. These two groups united against Jesus. Each has its own reason for wishing to get rid of the prophet from Nazareth."

92. Major, et al., *The Mission and Message of Jesus*, 148, "The Zealots regarded as unpatriotic the payment of tribute to Caesar and declared it to be unlawful for a Jew to pay it. There were many Jews who dared not refuse payment of the tribute who yet secretly sympathised with the Zealots. Even pious heads wondered at times whether the Zealots might not be right. Pharisees and Herodians (Mk. alone has the latter here) come to Jesus to resolve their doubts. Their action is basely hypocritical: their whole purpose is to entrap Him, and secure if possible, as Lk. points out, His arrest by the Roman governor (20:20). Had Jesus declared that it was unlawful to give tribute, He would have been at once arrested by the Roman authorities. Had He declared that it was lawful, He would thereby have seemed to many, not only to have forfeited any claim to be the Messiah, but even to be regarded as a brave, loyal, patriotic Jew."

93. Hendriksen, *Matthew*, 802, "Thus these 'spies' (Luke 20:20) veil their real intention, which was to trap Jesus in a statement which he was expected to make. They hide their purpose under a cloak of flattering compliments."

94. Bowker, *Jesus and the Pharisees*, 43, "The greater problem of Jesus was that he insisted on the issue of the importance of what he was saying (and doing) by coming to Jerusalem and teaching repeatedly in the Temple.

But even then, what was problematic about the *content of* the teaching of Jesus? Not necessarily the same things for all Jews: for example, Jesus' acceptance of belief in resurrection would be welcome to the Hakamim, but not to the Sadducees (Mk. xii.18). What was particularly welcome to the Pharisaioi was his claim (as much in actions as in word) that the action of God in the world of his creation came to be made possible simply by the expectation, or faith, that it will be so, not necessarily by making that faith visible through the acceptance and observance of Torah, both written and interpreted."

resurrection of the dead.[95] Matt 22:23–33; Mark 12:18–27; Luke 20:27–40. Hereby they also ridiculed the historic law pertaining to Levirate marriage, Deut 25:5–10, hopefully seeking to catch Jesus within menacing nets of faithlessness. The listening crowd sized up this commanding Sadducee defeat, which rippled down into their parallel universe, startling negative emotions on all levels. This punitive humiliation ate into, not to good measure, the ruling classes' way of life.

In this hard-hitting defeat of their opponents in the political hub of Jerusalem, the Sanhedrin, the Pharisees with rosy expectations and an inflated sense of Thora-identity espied a carefully chosen opening for more covert savagery, this time with respect to the greatest commandment. Matt 22:34–40; Mark 12:28–34; Luke 10:25–28. "The question asked by this law-expert was one that could be expected from him and from the men he represented. The rabbis, devoted to hair-splitting legalism, carried on lengthy debates about the commandments, arguing whether any particular one was great or small, heavy or light. . . . they often debated the question, 'Which—of the 613 commandments, 248 of them positive, 365 negative— was 'the great,' here in the sense of a superlative, 'the greatest,' one."[96] In the 613, the seventh called for love of God and only the twenty-sixth for love of neighbor. Whatever the utility of this provocative arrangement, still they debated the relation of the greater to the lesser[97] of these two commandments. However, they found that Jesus knew the Hebrew Bible; for he gave the irreproachable biblical answer. This unfailing interpretation with

95. Epstein, *Judaism*, 97, "Because the Pharisees recognized God as the God of all mankind, they held fast to the doctrine of the individual's relation and responsibility to God, and consequently believed in the survival of the individual soul and in retribution in the hereafter; whereas the Sadducees, with their nationalistic conception of religion, rejected all these essentially individualistic and eschatological notions as mere fantasies of the Pharisees."

96. Hendriksen, *Matthew*, 808–9.

97. Hertzberg, *Judaism*, 109 (quoting from *Shulkhan Arukh, Yoreh Deah 252*), ". . . you shall love your neighbor as yourself; I am the Lord . . .' [Lev. 19:18].

'I am the Lord. This explains two things. First, since the souls that are as they should be, are all a part of God, and since the soul of one man and the soul of his neighbor are both carved out of the same throne of Splendour, therefore 'love for your neighbor as for yourself' is meant literally, for he is as you. Since I, God, am He who created your soul and the soul of your neighbor, he is as you. And, second, if your love for your neighbor is as the love for yourself, this is considered love for Me, because 'I am the Lord.' Since your love for him is like the love for yourself, even for him who is an infinitesimal part of Me—how much more will you love Me! For the love of your neighbor will be considered as if I, God, had myself received it.'"

respect to the love commandment displayed the unloving foundation of Pharisaism; Pharisees as well as Sadducees, given the *necessity*, easily dispensed with any of the commandments, which they allegedly held high. In fact, they taught an indiscriminate monotheism never revealed in the Old Testament and also a hatred for enemies, Matt 5:43.

Turning, Jesus queried the now harried Pharisees. Mark 12:35–37; Luke 20:41–44; Matt 22:41–46, "What do you think of the Christ? Whose son is he?" In the Pharisees' shock of silence,[98] the Lord and Savior taught assembling crowds and the Twelve concerning the heterodox Pharisaic leaven. Matt 23:1–12; Mark 12:38–40; Luke 20:45–47. The whole of this teaching, the entire Olivet discourse, he concluded with a solicitous lament over Jerusalem. Then he broke forth with Matthew's apocalypse, the parables of the ten virgins and the talents, concluding in the public domain with an instruction on the last judgment.

Luke, 11:37–52, recorded a teaching episode similar to Matthew's apocalypse; the conclusion to this suitable characterization of Pharisaism captured the spirit of discontent against the Son of God/Son of man too. According to the Third Gospel, also this time the Pharisees launched another wave of malice. Luke 11:53–54, "As he went away from there, the scribes and Pharisees began to press him hard, and to provoke him to speak of many things, lying in wait for him, to catch at something he might say." In the dark hours and days leading up to the Cross, the Christ's enemies in thankless toil looked for undiscoverable human flaws in their assessment of the Law-giver and Gospel-maker.

As the ground tilted precipitously against Pharisees[99] and Sadducees[100] alike, in fact, against the Old Church, Jesus had completed his ministry,[101]

---

98. Hendriksen, *Matthew*, 812–13, "Also in this final confrontation between Jesus and his enemies, who had tried to trip him up, Jesus had vanquished these foes so completely that rebuttal had become impossible. In fact, no one even dared to quiz him any more."

99. Epstein, *Judaism*, 105 (protectively), "The Pharisees were always on the side of peace, and though they looked for the coming of the Messiah to restore Israel and set up the Kingdom of God, they held that it could not be brought about by violence, but only through righteousness of conduct and loyalty to the Torah."

100. Kirsch, *We Christians and Jews*, 57, ". . . they were useful to the Romans by providing a show of Jewish self-rule in Palestine, and the Romans rewarded their collaboration by keeping them in office and in possession of their wealth and of their access to wealth. Therefore the Sadducees had good reason to fear any Messianic movement, even one with the best prospects for success."

101. Dimont, Jews, *God and History*, 135 (protectively), "Nothing he preached,

except the Crucifixion and the Resurrection. John 10:17–18. Waves of obstructive malice shaped and sharpened by the Oral Law had struck hard, consciously accelerating passions for deicide. Still, day by day, the Lord of life, incarnate, strode to his confrontational destination, unstoppably merciful.[102]

Roman Malice

1. Since Caesarian authority tolerated no opposition, its war-prone rulers struck with sharply flashing short swords to eliminate every perceived political and military threat to the Empire. At times, according to this animating principle the Herods of rough strengths worked independently against the Christ, at times, in collusion with the Pharisees and/or Sadducees. Of course, in terms of military heft, uncontestable Rome exercised its authority from outside the Church,[103] which made its pushing against the covenant community no less deadly for terrorizing the people into submission.

For framing the macro-historical habitat of Jesus' ministry, Luke, 2:1, recounted names of ruling political authorities. "In those days a decree went out from Caesar Augustus that all the world should be enrolled. This was the first enrollment, when Quirinius was governor of Syria." Caesar Augustus (63 BC–14 AD), that is, Gaius Octavius, ruled the enormous

---

taught, or said was in contradiction to what other Jewish prophets, rabbis, or sects said or taught. Jesus was not in danger from the Jews. He was in danger from the Romans, for it was no longer safe to teach justice in a land ruled by terror."

102. Rivkin, *A Hidden Revolution*, 100–101, "The Pharisees for John are, along with the chief priests, the leaders of the Jews. They want Jesus put out of the way because he was so successful with the people. This is vividly portrayed in John's account of Jesus' entry into Jerusalem."

John 12:12–19.

103. Dodd, *The Meaning of Paul for Today*, 49, "The Empire was founded on violence: Rome 'made a solitude and called it peace.' It transcended national boundaries, but it ruled by an upper class of the privileged and showed its contempt for the poor by giving them 'bread and circuses.' Its blossoming might be the fine flower of humane culture, but its roots were in the degradation of slavery."

Butler Bass, *A People's History of Christianity*, 25, "The ancient Mediterranean world that Rome once ruled was a vast, culturally diverse set of societies, unrelated by languages, economics, religions, and histories, all forced into political unity by a brutal military. Vast numbers of people who inhabited the Roman Empire resented or hated Roman rule and experienced few, if any, benefits from its social and economic structures. The empire was not in any modern way even vaguely democratic or inclusive; instead, it was a rigidly hierarchical and status-based world of haves and have-nots, of masters and slaves."

Empire and for taxation purposes decreed this census, proceeding thereby with cold indifference to the memorable fulfillment of prophetically and historically sensitive Micah 5:2.

To clamp down on the Christ, the first Herod[104] (74 BC–4 BC) with cunning myopics commanded seasoned legionaries to slay Bethlehem sons two years old and under. Matt 2:16–18. This controversial Roman-appointed king of the Jews perceived the King of the Jews a threat to his political monarchy and, longer-range, to the Empire.

Displaying a firm grasp on historical currents then, Luke listed other Roman authorities, 3:1–3, Tiberius Caesar, who ruled the Empire throughout AD 14–37; Pontius Pilate,[105] who ruled from Jerusalem throughout AD 26–36; Archelaus,[106] Herod the Great's son, who ruled from Jerusalem throughout 4 BC–AD 6; Herod Antipas (Herod the Tetrarch) who ruled from Jerusalem throughout AD 6–39; and Philip, Tetrarch of Abilene, who ruled throughout 4 BC–AD 34.

Later, inflammatory Herod Antipas, tetrarch,[107] beheaded the Baptizer,[108] thereby eliminating a vocal critic of his marital sins. The last Old Testament prophet undermined the Herodian authority over restless and revolution-minded covenant people, and had to go. In a mean-spirited

---

104. Major, et al., *The Mission and Message of Jesus,* 234, "The King to whom Mt. refers is Herod the Great, who was sovereign under the Roman imperial rule, of the whole of Palestine and died in the spring of 4 B.C. His character as depicted here by Mt. is true to life. He was cruel, crafty, capable, passionate, and intensely suspicious. There is no record outside Mt. of his massacre of young children in Bethlehem and its neighbourhood, but various murders and massacres were committed by him, and a man who could execute a beloved and beautiful wife and two of his sons because he suspected them of treason would not be likely to hesitate about a slaughter of provincial infants."

105. Hendriksen, *Matthew,* 941, "Pontius Pilate was the fifth governor of the southern half of Palestine. He was 'governor' in the sense of being *procurator,* ruling over an imperial province, and as such directly responsible to the emperor. Although he had been endowed with civil, criminal, and military jurisdiction, he was under the authority of the legate of Syria."

106. Matt 2:22.

107. Hendriksen, *Matthew,* 585, "A 'tetrarch' was originally a ruler of the fourth part of a region, but later the term was used to indicate any prince or governor less in rank than a king (Herod the Great) or an ethnarch (Archelaus)."

108. Dimont, *Jews, God and History,* 135, "John met his death at the hands of the Idumean king, Herod Antipas, appointed ruler of Galilee by the Romans, because he openly denounced the marriage of Antipas to his niece as illegal and incestuous."
Lev 18:6, 16, 20:21.
Flavius, *Antiquities,* XVIII.v.4.

way, this Herod contributed to the waves of malice against the Son of God/ Son of man, Matt 14:1–12; Mark 6:14–21; Luke 9:7–9, without bypassing Luke 3:18–20. "When, after John's cruel death, Herod becomes convinced that Jesus is 'John the Baptist, raised from the dead,' Jesus, too, will withdraw himself *to some extent* from that king's immediate attention (Matt. 14:1, 2, 13)."[109] However, not even a Herod altered the day and hour of the Crucifixion.

Luke, 13:1–5, condensed in a brief account an illustration of Pilate's cruelty, the wanton murder of a number of Galileans, no doubt within Temple precincts, whose blood he mingled with that day's sacrifices.[110] Whatever the governor's motivation to kill in a privileged place of safety for all, his brutal grip on physical violence demonstrated cheapness of Jewish life. He forced subject peoples, violently, to submit to the Caesar's iron might.[111]

Luke also recounted a potential attack upon Jesus by Herod Antipas. Luke 13:31, "At that very hour some Pharisees came, and said to [Jesus], 'Get away from here, for Herod wants to kill you.'" Whatever the wild interior of collusion between destabilizing church leaders and hard-driving tetrarch, that fox,[112] they meant to instill fear of death in the Crucifixion-bound Son of God/Son of man, to bend him, however slightly, away from his atoning

---

109. Hendriksen, *Matthew*, 240. Ibid., 360, ". . . for Herod Antipas, who often had been warned (Mark 6:20) but had disregarded all of these admonitions, Jesus had not a single word (Luke 23:9)."

110. Major, et al., *The Mission and Message of Jesus*, 281, "The massacre of Galileans by Pilate is peculiar to Lk. There is no reference to it in Josephus or any other author. It must have taken place in the Temple at Jerusalem during some religious festival. The Galilean Zealots were notoriously turbulent, and Pilate was ruthlessly cruel. Many massacres marked his administration."

111. Kirsch, *We Christians and Jews*, 47, ". . . even Rome found fault with Pilate for being needlessly provocative, that is, in ordering Roman imperial standards into the city of Jerusalem and in dealing with rising unrest by means of increasing bloodletting."

Dimont, *Jews, God and History*, 139, ". . . Pilate's cruelty and rapacity became so notorious that the Emperor Tiberius had to remove him because he brought dishonor to Rome."

Epstein, *Judaism*, 106, ". . . the procurators who governed Judea abused their power and did everything to render the lot of their Jewish subjects miserable and bitter. Most notorious among these procurators was Pilatus. His administration (26 C.E—36 C.E.) was characterized by corruption, violence, robberies, and continuous executions without ever the form of a trial."

112. Hendriksen, *Matthew*, 161, "The opprobrious epithet 'that fox,' by the Lord applied to Herod Antipas (Luke 13:32), could have been used also to describe the latter's father, Herod the Great."

destination on Golgotha.[113] The merciless offensive from the Romans too converged with sharpening definition against the Lord and Savior.

Caesar's men, never far away, always observant,[114] daily fearful of ungovernable chaos precipitated by mass rioting, formed the fear-based political arena[115] within which associated Pharisees and Sadducees plotted to retain tempestuous authority over the Old Church. This military and political overmight added to the pounding waves of malice striking against the Christ, malice suspended only by the actual date set for the Crucifixion.

Matthew related cooperation between Pharisees and Sadducees regarding the plight of Roman taxation, source of bleak controversy. Matt 22:15–22; Mark 12:13–17; Luke 20:19–26. Luke, however, mentioned only "spies" sent out by wily teachers of the Oral Law and posturing chief priests. Nevertheless, Caesar's imperious impression on each shekel warned also Jesus, the Lord of heaven and earth, of the Roman omnipresence throughout the Land of Promise, a constant threat to crucify him prematurely.

2. Except for the murders of Bethlehem sons and the Baptizer, Roman malice moved against the Son of God/Son of man in a desultory manner, not really convinced that he posed a threat to the Empire. Pontius Pilate and Herod Antipas perceived Jesus more an irritation within explosive Palestinian ethnography, which general indifference changed to frightening depths at the immediate approach to the Crucifixion. Then, the Sanhedrin pushed and shoved Pilate for resolution in favor of its fierce denunciation

---

113. Major, et al., *The Mission and Message of Jesus,* 282, "The Pharisees have no desire to save Jesus from the fate which had befallen John the Baptist. They desire to frighten Him or discredit Him, but, above all, to get rid of Him. The reply of Jesus indicates the contempt in which He held Herod, the murderer of the Baptist. It also indicates that Jesus will act according to plan: not Herod's, but God's." Ibid., 568, "Here as in Lk. 13:1–5 we are left to speculate on the motives of those who brought the message to Jesus. It may be that these Pharisees were friendly disposed and wished to give warning of a real danger which threatened Jesus, and so save Him from the fate which had overtaken John the Baptist. There is evidence in Mk. 6:14ff., that Herod had his eye on Jesus, and it may have been a hostile eye. On the other hand there is the possibility that the warning was inspired by Herod himself or by his officers, and was a device to get Jesus out of Herod's territory without resorting to open expulsion."

114. Horsley, "Jesus Movements and the Renewal of Israel," 26, "In response to regular outbreaks of protest at festival time, the Roman governors made a habit of posting Roman soldiers on the porticoes of the Temple courtyard to intimidate Passover crowds. But that merely exacerbated the intensity of popular feeling."

115. Kirsch, *We Christians and Jews,* 57, "What they had to fear in Jesus' time was subsequently spelled out in historical events that developed in the war of A.D. 66–70."

of the Christ. ". . . most of their fellow-countrymen were eagerly looking forward to the coming of the Messiah and that the Messiah's coming was expected to bring an end to the Roman occupation. They therefore knew that the Romans would inevitably, in defense of their military and political position in the Middle East, take a most serious view of any Messianic movement and endeavor to crush it."[116] This Caesarian arrogance, militarily and politically, Jesus spelled out, withholding no injustice of exploitation. Mark 10:42–43; Matt 20:25–26, Jesus to the reluctant Twelve, "You know that the rulers of the Gentiles lord it over them, and their great men exercise authority over them. It shall not be so among you . . . ." This larger Roman military and political authority held the domineering Pharisees and over-bearing Sadducees within a cold embrace, wherein on fields of illusion and on groundswells of confidence they plotted with communal unity for the Lord's death.

Deathly Malice

For the Crucifixion, the compelling political powers operative in Palestine joined forces, Pharisees, Sadducees,[117] and militarily unmastered Romans; in effect, for this onslaught of malice hitting Christ, the power equation of overlapping circles collaborated to run the Lord and Savior onto the Cross as quickly as possible. With the Sadducees,[118] dominant in the Sanhedrin, they wanted him detained and dead, out of the way. Mark 14:1–2; Luke 22:1–2; Matt 26:3–4, ". . . the chief priests and the elders of the people gathered in the palace of the high priest, who was called Caiaphas, and took council together in order to arrest Jesus by stealth and kill him."[119] As

116. Ibid.

117. Kirsch, *We Christians and Jews*, 58–59, "Thus, . . . the Gospels indicate, Jesus was arrested by the temple police, under the authority of the high priest, and was brought to a hearing before the high priest and his aides and councilors (members of the Sanhedrin) who investigated his relation to the Messiahship (Mark 14:43, 53, 61–62)."

118. Simon, *Jewish Sects at the Time of Jesus*, 24, "In every respect, the Sadducees represented the past. They were conservatives in politics as well as in religion. With respect to the upsurge of messianic expectation the Sadducees manifested the hostility of the powers that be against any movement tending to subvert the established order. In this case, it was the Roman order. But this order guaranteed their own interests, and the Sadducees were in complete solidarity with the occupiers, since the Romans permitted them to practice their religion freely."

119. Klinghoffer, *Why the Jews Rejected Jesus*, 11–12, "From a straightforward contemplation of the text, it is not immediately clear what gets the Jews who object to Jesus

these church leaders planned and plotted, furies unleashed,[120] Jesus moved inexorably to the humiliating juncture of history for which he had come. Satan in this endless warring had done everything within his limited powers throughout divergent historical circumstances to prevent the Incarnation; now he wanted his death and burial: out of sight, out of mind, a mere memory scattered to mindless winds, ceasing to matter. Similarly, John 11:57.

Prior to Jesus' final Passover celebration, John 13:1–30, more than revolutionary Pharisees and Sadducees loomed out of restless mists. After the miraculous feeding of the five thousand, deluded many of Israel chose to preempt the Christ's mission. John 6:15, "Perceiving then that they were about to come and take him by force to make him king, Jesus withdrew again to the mountain by himself." By an improvised coronation, they envisioned a radiant ruler to close off the Roman occupation and inaugurate over a historical bridge of violence the dazzling age to come. He however faithfully worked and ministered within the Father's fundamentally eschatological timeframe only, not to lead a secular resistance movement to Roman rule, thereby betraying the Incarnation.

At the subsequent revelation of the bread from heaven, the bread of life, the Jews murmured, manifesting denial more stubborn than mere public resistance and fear of confusion. Because of this Pharisaic spirit, many of the crowds drew back, shocked and disappointed. For them Jesus was not the king to force open the Jewish time to come. While the Jews broke faith, awaiting an alien and chimerical experience of glory, the Christ ruled his kingdom since the beginning, continuing into eternity.

---

so worked up. If we try to read the Gospels together, imagining them as forming a single integrated story (to the extent possible, since they are marked by disagreements as to narrative detail), we find the Jews mounting an emotional staircase leading from initial warmth, to puzzlement and perplexity, to distress, to self-righteous annoyance, and finally to a murderous rage."

120. Dimont, *Jews, God and History*, 136, "The messiah the people were talking about was Jesus. This was the political atmosphere into which he stepped when he made his decision to come to Jerusalem. This was the time he had chosen to reveal publicly that he was the messiah. His destination was the Temple."

Rivkin, *A Hidden Revolution,* 104, "This, then, is the definition of the Pharisees that can be extracted from John: The Pharisees were a class of men held to be the religious authorities in the time of Jesus, controlling the synagogue and possessing sufficient power to bring about, in conjunction with the High Priests, the arrest of Jesus. It is a class of such influence over the Jews that even the miraculous signs of Jesus' divinity were disbelieved."

Preparatory to his death and burial, an unnamed member of the Church, under the disciples' haggling over monetary wastage, poured a precious ointment on Jesus' head. Her love for the Savior proved to be the last straw for Judas Iscariot, a thief, who incited the avaricious protestations, John 12:4. For filthy lucre, he then, making his fundamental break by night, betrayed the Christ to the governing church authorities, which at this time included Pharisees, all on edge with extra effort and strong consensus to execute the worst religious abuse in the disreputable history of the Church, which quick destruction required Roman connivance. Matt 26:14–16; Mark 14:10–11; Luke 22:3–6.

In John 16:1–33 the Lord and Savior prepared the Twelve (minus Judas Iscariot) for the consciousness of mission, first within the synagogual culture—work inextricably interwoven with persecution. The Spirit-moved apostle designated by this lay of the land one meaning of the world. Beyond that troubling world lay the Caesarean forces, enmitous to the core, the whole blanketed by Hellenism, all of which unwilling to cede even a smidgen of authority to the Christ.

At the institution of the Lord's Supper, Jesus dismissed Judas Iscariot, in fact, excommunicated him. Matt 26:20–25; Mark 14:17–21; Luke 22:14–23; John 13:21–30. Thus this son of perdition, John 17:12, 6:64, 70, served the manipulatory Satan by betraying the Lord and Savior to the governing church authorities, the entire Sanhedrin rallying to triumphal illusions. At the institution of the Supper, the Christ once more prophesied his death and resurrection. On that note, Jesus took the soon-to-be apostles to the Mount of Olives and the quiet of Gethsemane, where three times he voiced his tumultuous sorrow to the Father as well as with finality submitted his human nature to extreme humiliation, the hellish agony of the Crucifixion.

Precipitously, Judas' callow betrayal[121] and the Jews' grace-mocking plot gathered complicitous momentum, Matt 26:47–67; Mark 14:43–50; Luke 22:47–53; John 18:1–11. The Iscariot, by night[122] at the head of a for-

---

121. Kirsch, *We Christians and Jews*, 59, "Judas was described by the Gospels as contracting with the chief priests to 'betray' Jesus. What Judas had to sell was an insider's information as to where Jesus would be after dark, when he would no longer be surrounded by enthusiastic crowds of listeners. This was useful to persons who intended to arrest Jesus and wished to do so with the minimum of publicity and resistance."

122. Dimont, *Jews, God and History*, 135–36, "In the year 33 A.D. Jerusalem was crowded with pilgrims who had come from every part of the world to celebrate the Feast of Passover. Excitement ran high. A rebellion in the provinces had just been quelled. Rumors of another rebellion were rife."

bidding crowd with swords and clubs dispatched by decision-making chief priests and ranking elders of the people, sealed his betrayal with a fraternal kiss: for the mirthless price of thirty pieces of silver, Zech 11:12. John described the arresting party as officers delegated by the chief priests and Pharisees, an amorphous range of forces, which vigilante horde without force of arms captured the Christ easily, meeting no resistance, except from Peter's swordplay, and shackled him as a common criminal. In the sumptuous house/palace of Caiaphas,[123] the *prosecuting* teachers of the Oral Law and the elders scrambled fabricated testimony to make a case. Matt 26:59–64, "Now the chief priests and the whole council sought false testimony against Jesus that they might put him to death, but they found none, though many false witnesses came forward. At last, two came forward and said, 'This fellow said, "I am able to destroy the temple of God, and to build it in three days."' And the high priest stood up and said, "Have you no answer to make? What is it that these men testify against you?" But Jesus was silent. And the high priest said to him, "I adjure you by the living God, tell us if you are the Christ, the Son of God." Jesus said to him, 'You have said so. But I tell you, hereafter you will see the Son of man seated at the right hand of Power, and coming on the clouds of heaven.'" For the record, Jesus' "You have said so" stood out in Aramaic as a powerful affirmative, factually corroborated by Mark 14:62's "I am." This *yes*, however, in the ideologically stopped ears of the monotheist Sanhedrin rang and echoed blasphemously against the Third Commandment. Therefore, this informal council composed of Sadducees and Pharisees on a partisan pretext charged Jesus with breaking the Third, a sin worthy of the death penalty.[124] The Thora-proud ecclesial leaders, for sundering the covenant community from hearing, obeying, and worshiping the Lord of the Church, stripped away from the Sanhedrin's misbehaving heart every pretense at righteousness.[125] Matt 26:57–68; Mark 14:53–65; Luke 22:54–55, 63–71; John 18:12–24.

123. Major, et al., *The Mission and Message of Jesus*, 161–62, "The High Priest at this time was Joseph Caiaphas (A.D. 18–36), but his father-in-law, Annas (A.D. 6–15) was still alive, and he was the real, though not the official, head of the priesthood."

124. Kirsch, *We Christians and Jews*, 59, "Whether the chief priests really believed that it was blasphemous for Jesus to speak about his Messiahship and the coming Son of Man, as the Synoptic Gospels claim—and it is not clear how this could be construed as blasphemy—it is nevertheless the testimony of all four Gospels that the high priest and his councilors delivered Jesus to Pilate for the purpose of having him executed; also that the charge against Jesus before Pilate was the political charge of insurrection—'King of the Jews.'"

125. Simon, *Jewish Sects at the Time of Jesus*, 6, "The Sanhedrin was a court of justice

The church leaders with pent-up malice shrank back in a fit of revulsion at acknowledging Jesus the Christ. Cynically manipulating the then functioning Church Order, these men individually with mutual betrayal of covenant history pushed away the outward evidence of reprobation evident within them, the Sanhedrin's darkness of soul as well. Mark 15:1–5;[126] Luke 23:1; John 18:28; Matt 27:1–2, "When morning came, all the chief priests and the elders of the people took counsel against Jesus to put him to death; and they bound him and led him away and delivered him to Pilate the governor." They, the ruling powers, sought the death penalty from the Roman government.[127] Thus, with procedural abuses they drew the Caesar's authorities deeper into the tumults of conspiracy for eliminating the Son of God/Son of man, Lord and Savior. Church and State, inextricably bound up together and hopelessly intertwined by invisible chains, crammed into a short trial many intense, extra-judicial contradictions, the whole for Israel and the Roman Empire condemnation upon condemnation. As a result, darkening guilt weighed down the judges and all whom they represented.

The illegalities of this trial, compounding the darkness of soul within the Church, require at least one mention. "It has been emphasized . . . that the trial of Jesus was illegal on several technical grounds, such as the following: *a*. No trial for life was allowed during the night. Yet, Jesus was tried and condemned during the hours of 1–3 AM Friday, and executed on the Feast, which was forbidden. According to Pharisaic law, no hearings in a case involving capital punishment could even be initiated on the eve of a major festival like Passover. No conviction was allowed at night. To execute

---

whose function was to interpret and apply the law of Moses, rather than a council occupied with formulating doctrinal statements."

126. Major, et al., *The Mission and Message of Jesus*, 186, "The Sanhedrin were not allowed to pronounce a capital sentence after dark; they had therefore to wait for the dawn to do so. As soon as this was done, it being still very early, the whole Sanhedrin took Jesus before Pilate.

Here, the difference of twenty-four hours in the chronology of Jn. and the Synoptists accounts for Jn.'s statement that the Sanhedrin would not go into Pilate's palace lest they should be rendered unclean and so unable to keep the Passover. Consequently, in Jn. we have the curious scene of the trial of Jesus being conducted in two places at once. The trial concludes with Pilate pronouncing sentence when seated outside his palace on the pavement called in Aramaic, *Gabbatha*."

127. Hendriksen, *Matthew*, 941, "Jesus has to be led before Pilate because the Sanhedrin had no right, without Rome's approval, to carry out its decree (John 18:31)."

Epstein, *Judaism*, 106–7 (protectively), ". . . the Sanhedrin handed over Jesus to Pilatus, at whose order, Jesus, like many other Jews charged with sedition, was nailed to the cross by Rome."

a sentence on the day of one of the great feasts was contrary to the established regulations.[128] *b.* The arrest of Jesus was effected as a result of a bribe, namely, the blood-money which Judas received. *c.* Jesus was asked to incriminate himself. *d.* In cases of capital punishment, Jewish law did not permit the sentence to be pronounced until the day after the accused had been convicted."[129] Perversions of justice as these underscored the validity of Pontius Pilate's, Luke 23:4, "I find no crime in this man."[130]

At this time within the fast-moving crucifixion account, Matthew inserted Judas Iscariot's death outside the bounds of covenant community, by suicide. The Lord Jesus immortalized this guilt-laden man as the first publicly mentioned perpetrator of unfaithfulness in the Church during the Crucifixion-Resurrection week to face strict justice.

The Jews quickly seized dubious winds of opportunity, which Luke in a critical passage recounted, 23:1–2, "Then the whole company of them arose and brought [Jesus] before Pilate. And they began to accuse him, saying, 'We found this man perverting our nation, and forbidding us to give tribute to Caesar, and saying that he himself is Christ a king.'"[131] Faced by Jesus, Pontius Pilate, weighing the Jewish evidence,[132] immediately addressed the only Roman concern. Luke 23:3, "Are you the King of the Jews?" The

128. *Sanhedrin* IV.1.

129. Hendriksen, *Matthew*, 929.

130. Ibid., "In reality, the entire trial was a farce. It was a mis-trial. There was no intention at all of giving Jesus a fair hearing in order that it might be discovered, in strict conformity with the laws of evidence, whether or not the charges against him were just or unfounded."

Dimont, *Jews, God and History*, 138, "Any person familiar with Jewish judicial procedure in Biblical times will find it difficult to take the Gospel account literally. According to Jewish law at that time, no one could be arrested at night. It was illegal to hold court proceedings after sundown on the eve or the day of the Sabbath or festival." Etc.

131. Hendriksen, *Matthew*, 949, "When the members of that body make clear to Pilate that they desire nothing less than the prisoner's *death,* and when they then are made to understand that to secure their objective definite charges will have to be made against Jesus, they quickly present three of them: *a.* he perverts the nation; *b.* he forbids us to pay tribute to Caesar; and *c.* he claims that he himself is king (Luke 23:2)."

132. Major, et al., *The Mission and Message of Jesus*, 186, "The Synoptists' accounts of the trial by Pilate clearly indicate that Pilate was favourably impressed by Jesus and was most unwilling to sentence Him to death on the charge of treason; perceiving that on account of envy (Mk. 15:10) they had handed Jesus over as a prisoner." Ibid., 180, "According to the four Evangelists Jesus underwent four judicial trials before (1) Annas (Jn. 18:12–14, 1–24), (2) Caiaphas (Mk. and Lk. have 'the High Priest,' Mt. and Jn. have Caiaphas), (3) Pilate (Mk., Mt., Lk., Jn.), (4) Herod Antipas (Lk. 23:6–12)."

Son of man, *the* Judge, responded affirmatively, "You have said so."[133] All other charges hurled at the Lord and Savior of the Church by the Pharisees and Sadducees the governor ignored. One matter, of treason, only counted. For Pilate this answer counted as treason and insurrection, a threat to Roman solidarity and worthy a most excruciating death penalty. However, Jesus committed nothing remotely resembling sedition. Nevertheless, Pilate refused to declare and enforce the Man's innocence. Luke 23:13–17; John 18:28–32.[134]

Luke's account, 23:6–12, that Pilate sent Jesus to Herod Agrippa,[135] ruler/tetrarch of Galilee visiting in Jerusalem, calls for valid attention. On grounds that Jesus was born in bordering Galilee, Herod Agrippa, Pilate found, had shared responsibility for the outcome of this trial. Thereby the detestable governor attempted to alleviate pressure between condemning someone innocent of any crime and formless actualities of mass rioting. Herod Agrippa with his soldiers treated Jesus with contempt, mocking him. However, the tetrarch found no revolution in Jesus and returned him to Pilate, thereby also declaring Jesus innocent of any criminality against the Empire.[136] This double exposure to Roman justice intensified the upper hand by which authority figures Pilate and Herod spoke for Caesar and thus the Empire.

The governor, in cold fear of widespread disturbances and Caesarian disaffection, therefore, amidst outspoken tensions and leery of mass rioting, with a ritual hand washing declared Jesus' innocence and delivered

133. Bright, *The Kingdom of God*, 199, "It is significant that it is the unanimous witness of the Gospels that when Pilate asked him point-blank, 'Are you the King of the Jews?' his only answer was a blunt, 'You have said it' (Mark 15:2; Matt. 27:11; Luke 23:3; John 18:33–37)—which, if cryptic, was certainly no denial. Before the Sanhedrin his answer to the same question was a flat, 'I am' (Mark 14:62)."

134 Hendriksen, *Matthew*, 949, "Combining the Gospel accounts, one gains the impression that from the start almost to the finish, Pilate did everything in his power to get rid of this case. He had no love for the Jews."

135. Major, et al., *The Mission and Message of Jesus*, 187, "Lk. alone relates . . . that Pilate, learning that Jesus was a Galilean, sent Him for trial to Herod Antipas, who at that time was in Jerusalem, no doubt for the Paschal feast. The Herod family, although in many cases bad men, seem to have been scrupulous in the observance of Jewish religious customs. Lk.'s statements that Herod had never seen Jesus, and was delighted to have the opportunity to become acquainted with Him, hoping to see some notable miracles done by Him: that Pilate's act of courtesy led to the ending of a difference which had formerly existed between Pilate and Herod, seem to possess the quality of historic probability."

136. Hendriksen, *Matthew*, 463, "It was Pontius Pilate who sentenced Jesus to die on the cross, after he sent him to 'king' Herod Antipas (Matt. 27:26; Luke 23:6–12)."

him up to be crucified. Oblivious to the magnitude of the verdict, Roman jurisprudence expressed callous disregard for justice and truth;[137] only lasting elimination of competitors to the Empire's political structure and ruling authorities satisfied Pontius Pilate.[138]

During this justice-mangling trial, when faltering Pilate hesitated, the Jews turned the Third Commandment once more against Jesus, the Lawgiver. John 19:7, "We have a law, and by that law he ought to die, because he made himself the Son of God." Pilate, aware of Jesus' innocence but fearing an armed upheaval, relinquished his authority and allowed the church leaders to accept full responsibility for the Crucifixion. Matthew 27:25, "His blood be on us and on our children!" Herewith, as the first and with desperate yearning all of the covenant community at that time and forever accepted carefree responsibility of unknown depths for the crucifixion of her only Lord and Savior.

The Sanhedrin, seeing its victory slip away and desperate to eliminate the Head of the Church, displayed even more covenant unfaithfulness, clamoring for conviction. With desperate corruption of ideological roots uncovered, their shrill voices threatened insurrection. Therefore, the church leaders incited the people present to choose massively for Barabbas, Luke 23:19; this notorious revolutionary and murderer they wanted freed from Roman custody, not the Christ. The heavy-handed church leaders from out of the Pharisee/Sadducee world of meaning, false against the Old Testament history, intended nothing short of death for the Lord and Savior. Matt 27:15–23; Mark 15:6–15; Luke 23:18–25; John 18:38b–40. In all, the chief priests, elders, and rabbis pushed hard from out of the nadir of unbelief, subverting due process and fearless of the consequences in the face of the Judge; they preferred eternal damnation, a future easier to absorb than bowing in faithfulness before the Christ.

According to Matt 27:27–31; Mark 15:16–20; Luke 23:11; John 19:2–5, Pilate and his "Behold the man!" theatrics hastened the Lord Jesus—beaten, thorn-crowned, bloodied—to his final humiliation in degradation. The manipulated governor, though he found the Lord and Savior of the Church innocent of any crime, gave in to the Church's loaded and

---

137. John 18:38, Pilate's "What is truth?"

138. Dimont, *Jews, God and History*, 139 (protectively), "All the internal evidence points to a Roman atrocity, not a miscarriage of Jewish justice. Jews never in their history crucified anybody, nor ever demanded crucifixion for anyone."

lacerating language, "Crucify him, crucify him!" Uncharitable and vicious, they rushed to judgment.

The whole spectrum of judicial errors to the contrary, Jesus' unrelenting opponents clamored and pushed for condemnation; ". . . all [the] legal technicalities were but so many details. They do not touch the heart of the matter. The main point is nothing less than this: *it had been decided long ago that Jesus must be put to death* (see John 11:49–52). *And the motive behind this decision was envy.*"[139] Pilate, then, at the limits of his power and in a paroxysm of contempt, by court ruling released Jesus to the Church for the notoriously inhumane Roman execution method.[140] Matt 27:32–54; Mark 15:21–39; Luke 23:32–49; John 19:17–30. In effect, he too found the Lord of the Church guilty.

The four Gospels, Matt 27:32–44; Mark 15:21–32; Luke 23:332–43; John 19:17–24, grappled pointedly with the Crucifixion, a Roman torture death; each one, gripped by singular dedication, dwelled on this ultimate convergence of suffering as the amplification of God-forsakenness.

Suddenly, a strange turn of events occurred. On this catastrophic day and in the pandemonium of his defeat, the Satan wanted the slowly expiring Jesus off the Cross. Throughout the Old Testament dispensation, he had striven to prevent the Incarnation. After the Incarnation, he strove to kill the Lord and Savior. Once Church and State had crucified the Christ, the Enemy perceived the hitherto hidden springs of his eternal defeat, for Jesus achieved his purpose.[141] Gripped with satanic madness, church leaders with wasting efforts called upon the Son of God/Son of man to descend from the Cross. Matt 27:39–44, "Then two robbers were crucified with him,

---

139. Hendriksen, *Matthew*, 929.

Kirsch, *We Christians and Jews,* 46 (protectively), ". . . however reluctant Pontius Pilate is pictured in the Gospels as having been, he gave the order for Jesus' death."

Ibid., 6, "Stoning was specified in biblical law as the mandatory punishment for blasphemy (Lev. 24:10–16)." Deut 13:10; John 10:31.

140. Epstein, *Judaism,* 107 (protectively), "The Pharisees stood aloof from the whole affair. Their differences with Jesus were essentially religious. Never once did they reprove him for his messianic claims. In every case where they did rebuke him it was because of his disregard of their traditional interpretations of the laws of the Torah and the 'fences' erected round it. As such their difference had no bearing whatsoever on the political charge for which Jesus appeared before the High priest and his associates, and in which they could not intervene even if they would. Consequently not a single Pharisee is found to have participated in the trial, much less in the decision to hand over Jesus to the Romans."

141. Rev 12:1–6.

one on the right and one on the left. And those who passed by derided him, wagging their heads and saying, 'You who would destroy the temple and build it in three days, save yourself! If you are the Son of God, come down from the cross.' So also the chief priests, with the scribes and elders, mocked him, saying, 'He saved others; he cannot save himself. He is the King of Israel; let him come down now from the cross, and we will believe in him. He trusts in God; let God deliver him now, if he desires him; for he said, "I am the Son of God."' And the robbers who were crucified with him also reviled him in the same way." Under this combined pressure,[142] the Satan wanted Jesus off the Cross. In the dark mists of revolution, the Church made a wrenching decision with genuine contradiction: all wanted him dead and all wanted him off the Cross.

Throughout, Matthew, Mark, Luke, and John with steady progression published the absolute depths of unbelief to which the Satan drove the Church. Led by the Spirit, the Gospelers with the sense of belonging to the dominant way of history accomplished the eschatological purpose of the Gospel, or of the four Gospels.

Jesus according to or with respect to his human nature died, despicably, humiliated, between criminals, "numbered with the transgressors," Isa 53:12. Two robbers magnified the Christ's purpose in dying and death: to separate the Church, a reprobate on the one hand, a believer on the other. One, by grace, repented, Luke 23:39–43. Upon this eminently grace-full demonstration of the royal authority and the sovereign power of the Gospel, Jesus in the presence of calloused legionaries and mocking Pharisee/Sadducee leaders died, the King of the Jews = the Lord of the Church, his work of atonement complete. John 19:30, "It is finished." At that moment the inner curtain of the Temple was torn from top to bottom, exposing the emptiness in the Old Church's soul, for the Glory of Israel had departed. In the same instance, an earthquake rumbled through underground Jerusalem, tombs were opened, and a centurion exclaimed, Matt 27:54, "Truly this was the Son of God." Given the soldier's pagan pantheon, he may have meant, or said, "Truly, this was a son of God," whoever in this alternative ethos that deity may have been. Pointedly: in his dying and death, Jesus bore witness in nothing to caress in a pagan's imagination a god-belief at odds with the Gospel. As deep darkness settled, centering ominously over

---

142. Hendriksen, *Matthew*, 968, "The insults were coming from almost every side. Legionaries, bypassers, chief priests, scribes, elders, robbers, and multitudes of other spectators deride him."

Golgotha, the taunting hostility of the ecclesiastical crowd present petered out. Only the echoing exclamation of a Roman legionnaire lingered.

At the malicious instigation of the Sadducees and Pharisees, risk-obsessed Pilate sealed Jesus' sepulcher against the Resurrection. Matt 27:62–66. This obscurantist act of defeat and unchecked vanity mangled more the Enemy's reputation, his hostile takeover of the Church in shambles. Thus ended from within the Church and from without the persecution of the Person of Jesus Christ. Post-Pentecost Day, however, another phase of persecution began, now against the New Church, Rev 12:13–17.

On the third day, as prophesied, Jesus, the Son of God/Son of man, strode from the tomb, in terms of his human nature resurrected from the dead, the Firstborn of the dead, never to die again.[143] The Resurrection occurred away from the Sadducees, Pharisees, and Romans, and with the Crucifixion reformed the eternal foundation of the covenant.[144]

With the Resurrection and the Ascension, Matt 28:1–10; Mark 16:1–8; Luke 24:1–12; John 20:1–10; Acts 1:6–11, Christ Jesus, Lord and Savior, drew the Old Testament line of history into the New. He had defeated the Old Church with its Oral Law and blindsided the Roman Empire with its combatant legions, both steeped in unbelief, to create through covenant reformation the New Church. From the authoritative right hand of the Father, he governed heaven and earth for the final gathering of the Church in

---

143. Rivkin, *A Hidden Revolution*, 304, "It was here that the Christians parted company with their teachers. The Scribes-Pharisees could not acknowledge Jesus as having risen from the dead. Resurrection was not the issue, for it was the very core of Pharisaic teaching. Jesus' resurrection, however, was very much the issue. For Scribes-Pharisees, Jesus could not have been resurrected because during his lifetime he had challenged the Scribes-Pharisees with claims that they had firmly rejected. Jesus had not knuckled under to their authority. He persisted in teaching as though he were indeed the Son of man. He thus defied the very class that held the key to eternal life and resurrection. No one challenging their authority could possibly have been selected by God to be raised from the dead."

144. Dimont, *Jews, God and History*, 140 (casting aspersion), "With Jesus dead, Christianity seemed doomed. It was saved by the Jewish doctrine of resurrection. . . . News of this miracle quickly spread among the dispirited remnants of the followers of Jesus. All were convinced that he had risen from the dead. Not only Jesus, but Christianity had been resurrected."

Kirsch, *We Christians and Jews*, 5, "Estrangement began in the period immediately following the resurrection as the natural falling out of two religious communities, each of which saw itself as the people of God, *the people,* of the one and only God."

Epstein, *Judaism*, 138, "There is thus no place in Judaism for any notions of dying and reviving Gods such as are to be found in other religions." Christianity included.

the coming ages; hence, Jesus rules history to make his Kingdom explicit in every age therewith in the Spirit to magnify the Father.

MALICE IN CRISIS

Matthew more than Mark, Luke, and John renounced the Pharisaical crisis in the Church; therefore this retiring Gospeler intensively inveighed against its tight grip imposed on the covenant community. Out of the First Gospel, several concrete exposures:

Matthew 5–7/Luke 6:20–49

This lengthy collection of wisdom materials, similar in vibrancy to Proverbs and Ecclesiastes, consists of longer and shorter sayings, without however an immediately definable theme. One attempt at thematic definition focused on Matt 5:20, ". . . unless your righteousness exceeds that of the scribes and Pharisees, you will never enter the kingdom of heaven."[145] Yet since Matt 5:17–20 stands as a saying distinguishable from the preceding and the succeeding *logia*, sayings, of chapters 5–7, Matthew presented it as one of many high-intensity sections strung together for the intricate mix of this wisdom collection, the inner voice of which condemns covetousness.[146]

Proverbs' author by design positioned its definable theme early, "The fear of the LORD is the beginning of knowledge; fools despise wisdom and instruction."

Ecclesiastes' composer sensitively withheld his teachable moment until late in the document. Eccl 12:13–14, "The end of the matter; all has been heard. Fear God, and keep his commandments; for this is the whole duty of man. For God will bring every deed into judgment, with every secret thing, whether good or evil." Therewith the Spirit-driven author laid the curse of God upon the vanity of covetousness, the all too perceptible covetousness with which he wrestled.

---

145. Shearer, *The Sermon on the Mount*, 23, 27, 43; etc.

146. Kirsh, *We Christians and Jews*, 51 (a misunderstanding of Matt 5–7), "If the oral law as the Pharisees developed it is seen as *interpretation* of the law of God as given in the scriptures, it is not at all established that Jesus was opposed to oral law as such. On the contrary, it can be argued that Jesus himself founded his own tradition of 'oral law.' The Sermon on the Mount is full of instances in which Jesus took up items from the law of Moses and interpreted them."

Given the purpose of wisdom literature, primarily with respect to the vanity of covetousness, the fear of the Lord sharpens the awareness of accountability according to the Law before the Judge of heaven and earth. This awareness of, or alertness to condemnation upon all old appetites the Holy Spirit bequeathed typically to the wisdom literature in the Scriptures. Indeed, covetousness with its unceasing pressures *is* the root of all disobedience.

Although without a directly expressed thematic statement, Matt 5–7 and Luke 6:20–49 opened wide the sin devastating the church, thereby stirring up awareness of the fear of the Lord: answerability in the unavoidable court of the Christ.[147] These soul-searching instructions in wisdom, each *logion* in its own way but with similar intent, laid bare the deep-reaching and cloying tentacles of covetousness—the discriminatory exposure of jealousy, envy, lust, craving, and addiction, even desire, inclination, bent, penchant, predilection, propensity, liking, fondness, hankering, ambition; etc. With this concentration of wisdom sayings, Matt 5–7, Jesus condemned in the Church the root sin.

The Christ entered into his church to probe the heart of every member and uncover even the most radical of sins. Therefore, each saying never consisted of good advice, or moral guidance, but of a call in an age of crisis to repentance and real amendment. Thereto he ministered to ruin the unbridled fancies and root causes of self-love, covetousness' mark of self-identification.

Matthew 5:17–20

Forthrightly, Jesus validated the Law, the historic Ten, the far-flung rule for life and gratitude from the beginning and for all times, even eternity.

> "Think not that I have come to abolish the law and the prophets; I have come not to abolish them but to fulfil them. For truly I say to you, till heaven and earth pass away, not an iota, not a dot, will pass from the law until all is accomplished. Whoever then relaxes one of the least of these commandments and teaches men so, shall be called least in the kingdom of heaven; but he who does them and teaches them shall be called great in the kingdom of heaven."

---

147. He does, of course, hear, listen to, excuses for covetousness, Mat 25:41–46.

The Pharisees relaxed not only the least commandments; in fact, they fenced all off against living in righteousness, and taught Christ's Israel accordingly. Moreover, with high confidence they reserved for themselves first place in what they perceived with breathless speculation to be the kingdom in the time to come, while the Lord Jesus confined them firmly outside the Kingdom. Covetously, they of insatiable appetite strove for an unachievable accomplishment.

The Head of the Church intended to confirm the Decalogue and have his own follow in the way of gratitude, thereby securing the primary basis and essential quality of dominion in the covenant community as well as the Kingdom, always within each generation.

All in all, the Pharisees had fenced off the Decalogue from life and gratitude in favor of the much-touted Tradition of the Elders, which surrogate legal system had captured the heart of the Church. Based on the Oral Law, the alienating Pharisees promoted an alternative righteousness, one achievable by means of human endeavor. Herewith they as well as followers displayed a voracious covetousness: craving a bogus righteousness to attain the life to come based on a man-made legal currency.

Angry at the exposure of this circumambient darkness of heart, the Pharisees, and in kinship with them the Sadducees, refused to see themselves as the Christ did; they lived inside a central fallacy and wished no beam of the Light to penetrate the unbelief they harbored. All had hearts set on the easier way of the Oral Law to gain righteousness and therefore, whatever the delayed cost and the deferred pain, fought the Lord of the covenant community to the death; within their cloak of religiosity they pressed the point of confrontation.

According to the Decalogue, the public words of the First Commandment set the tone and the spirit indigenous to the life and gratitude of dominion, "You shall have no other gods before me." Before Christ Jesus, that is. In summary of the Ten, the Tenth called for intense scrutiny of the obedience to the whole of the Decalogue, to avoid merely superficial and powerless evidence of the Faith. Hence, the Tenth screened heart obedience: the whole of the Decalogue,[148] or nothing, only pagan marvels of legalism.

---

148. A note on the Tenth, Exod 20:17, "You shall not covet your neighbor's house; you shall not covet your neighbor's wife, or his manservant, or his maidservant, or his ox, or his ass, or anything that is your neighbor's." A house represented property, income, and stability, which allowed a man the means to marry and support a wife and children. This commandment's structure, first house, then wife, raised covenant hopes with respect to the third promise, of space. Deut 5:21 reversed the house/wife order.

The Jews, however, had broken with the First, substituting an ethical monotheism at variance with the Trinity. Moreover, by means of the Oral Law, they had subverted every commandment, giving voice to unauthorized powers of covetousness. As a result, battered and insecure, they circled about within the confines of the Tradition of the Elders, spinning deeper into incalculable voids of self-righteousness. Christ Jesus, in opposition, summoned all Israel to repentance, "For I tell you, unless your righteousness exceeds that of the scribes and Pharisees, you will never enter the kingdom of heaven." In the moral low of the Oral Law, the Pharisees refused to repent and live in the grace of Christ Jesus.

Matthew 5:43–45

The commandment to hate enemies at one time belonged to the fabric of the Oral Law, a definite strategy against Hellenization, Romanization, and whoever else harmed the Hasidean/Pharisaic movement, specifically, Sadduceism. At the same time, this grainy hate isolated the Pharisaic movement to achieve freedom of worship, an uninterrupted, fenced-off quiet to work out the Tradition of the Elders. The collective history of this unsettling truth, however, deeply corrupted the covenant community, and spun a ubiquitous commonplace to refute the actuality of Lev 19:18. Such calculated violence to this love commandment also swept up in waves of violence against the Head of the Church in periodically buffeting outbursts. Obviously, this hate-commandment[149] in the passage of time opened up legitimacy for every lust at revenge, the craving to get even, and exercise the

---

149. Kee, *Jesus in History*, 59, "Jewish scholars in particular have been at pains to point out that there is no passage in the Jewish Scriptures—or in the rabbinic tradition—that summons Israel to hate its enemies (Matt. 5:42)."

Epstein, *Judaism*, 148–49, "Respect for the human person forbids also hatred. This Biblical command (Lev. 19. 17) as understood by Talmudic teachers is of universal significance 'Whoever hateth any man hateth Him who spoke and the world came into existence' (Sifre Zuta Numbers 18)—*any* man, that is, whether Jew or non-Jew."

Ibid., 154, "The command to love one's fellow-man with all its implications is all-embracing, extending to all men, of whatever race or creed. Unmistakable in this connexion is the Biblical injunction 'to love the stranger as thyself' (Lev. 19. 34). In the words 'as thyself' is enunciated the great principle of human equality: the non-Jewish stranger is *as* thyself."

Schechter, *Studies in Judaism*, 65 (an escape route), "The words of the Scriptures might be at first glance (or first hearing) conceived to have this or that meaning, but if we consider the context or the way in which the sentences are worded, we must arrive at a different conclusion. This parallel may perhaps throw some light on the expression . . .,

degrading predilection for self-love. Self-love, of course, gratifies the hostile environment and unchecked vanity of unrighteousness before Christ Jesus. Jesus, however, mandated neighbor love in its heart function,[150] "But I say to you, Love your enemies and pray for those who persecute you, so that you may be sons of your Father who is in heaven; for he makes his sun rise on the evil and on the good, and sends rain on the just and on the unjust. For if you love those who love you, what reward have you?" This love sovereignly retrieved Lev 19:18 from Pharisaic (and Sadduceic) substitutes for godliness; the Lawgiver revealed in a time of extreme covetousness, by flatly rejecting in the Church the closed circle of dominating self-love, the potency of neighbor love for tomorrow's people.

The hate commandment Jesus cited, found nowhere in the Old Testament, the officially sanctioned Mishnah erased from memory,[151] its fragility of life in tatters. Only Matt 5:43 proves its existence. Here, to counteract the violence of hatred by the authors of this primitive *mishnayot,* Jesus asserted the first formation of the Summary of the Law. Matt 22:34–40; Mark 12:28–34; Luke 10:25–29. This love of neighbor as oneself included even a Herod the Great, a Caesar, a Herod Antipas, a Pontius Pilate, Roman troops, Sadducees, Samaritans, Gentiles, etc.[152] Pervasive neighbor love actually reformed the New Church.

'you have heard that it was said . . . but I say unto you,' a phrase frequent in the Sermon on the Mount. After the declaration made by Jesus of his attachment to the Torah, it is not likely that he would quote passages from it showing its inferiority. The only way to get over the difficulty is to assume that Jesus used some such phrase as the one just quoted, . . ., 'I might hear,' or 'one might hear,' that is to say, 'one might be mistaken in pressing the literal sense of the verses in question too closely.'"

150. Ibid., 65, "But the formula being a strictly Rabbinic idiom, it was not rendered quite accurately by the Greek translator. Hence the apparent contradiction between Matt. 3: 17, 20, and the matter following upon these verses. I only wish to add that in Rabbinic literature it is sometimes God himself who undertakes such rectifications."

151. Major, et al., *The Mission and Message of Jesus,* 453, "There would have been nothing surprising if any Jew had inferred from Lev. 19:18 that his duty was to love his fellow-Jews and hate his Roman enemies. But Jewish literature is ransacked in vain for evidence that such a conclusion is explicitly drawn. 'Thou shalt love thy neighbour and hate thine enemy' cannot be found."

152. Baeck, *Judaism,* (in a post-Pharisaic age), 211–12, "To place oneself in the position of our neighbor, to understand his hope and his yearning, to grasp the needs of his heart is the presupposition of all neighborly love, the outcome of our 'knowledge' of his soul. The innermost being of neighborly love is therefore contained in the principle Hillel called the essence of the Law, from which all else follows: 'Do not do unto others as you would not be done by.'"

Matthew 6:19-21

This commandment opposed, first, the Pharisaic fondness and appetite for treasures on earth and, then, commanded in the ongoing church reliance on the second covenant promise in terms of the necessities of life. Matt 6:24. However, the Pharisees (in immediate competition with the Sadducees) exercised ambition for wealth, greed at odds with covenant living. Despite self-evaluations to the contrary, Pharisees coveted the riches of the earth. In Luke 16:14, Jesus clearly stated that they were lovers of mammon. Luke 12:13-21, 16:19, 18:18-30; Matt 19:16-22; Mark 10:17-22. As the Judge of his people, Christ Jesus condemned this avarice and revealed right usage of capital, to the last denarius.

Overall, relative to Matt 5-7, the Lord Jesus omnipotently and thoroughly exposed the deep and broad ranges of covetousness intoxicating Pharisaism,[153] that is, the Church at that time. Constantly and persistently throughout this large collection of sayings he revealed the power and the extent of the Tenth Commandment in order to cleanse the Church of every lust and compel obedience also to Commandments One-Nine.[154] He hereby judged with authority his own and found all wanting with respect to the righteousness once bestown on Abraham, Genesis 15:6, utterly condemnable; with excommunicative discipline he revealed the covenant community in the short historical stretch leading up to the Crucifixion.

Matthew 15:1-9/Mark 7:1-8

The Pharisaic Corban-invocation Cross-bound Jesus pointed out as a particularly cheerless ejaculation of covetousness.[155]

153. Klinghoffer, *Why the Jews Rejected Jesus*, 59, "There could be only one reason for this: Jesus did not see himself as a link in the chain of tradition. This was a repudiation of the very heart of rabbinic faith. Without tradition, either the cryptic text of the Pentateuch was locked forever, its true meaning indiscernible, or it was open to all to guess as their intellect or whim directed them—a free-for-all of scriptural interpretation where the Torah means whatever the reader wants it to mean."

154. Shearer, *The Sermon on the Mount*, 40, "The Pharisees were purely selfish in their religion, and they sought their own glory, as [Jesus] shows in Chapter vi. 1-6)."

155. Simcox, *The First Gospel*, 166, "In the course of the exchange, several different issues are aired, though they are all related. There is first the issue of ritual washing of hands before eating. The disciples of Jesus do not conform to it. The critics do not accuse them of breaking the Mosaic law by their failure, for such washing is not prescribed in the law as such. Rather it is a pious custom, evidently of recent origin, yet a part of

In this account, two lasting systems of commandments clashed, the Pharisaic endorsed in the Tradition of the Elders and the Christ's given in Exod 20:1–17; of the two, the Mosaic ethical code remained valid forever. Pharisees and scribes from Jerusalem, however, on the offensive, walked with aggressive mien to Jesus at Gennesaret on the Sea of Galilee/Sea of Kinnereth, and condescendingly attacked the eating Twelve for failing to engage in a ritual hand washing.[156] (Mark explained the context more fully.) These non-commissioned judges asked Jesus with explicit accusation, "Why do your disciples transgress the tradition of the elders? For they do not wash their hands when they eat."[157] This ritual hand washing no law of Moses commanded; the LORD God had not revealed one such to the first commissioned leader of Israel.[158] In fact, this manipulative law was a novelty over time firmly knotted into the Oral Law.[159] To arrive from Jerusalem to make such ferment based on the Oral Tradition demonstrated the grasp this legal system had on Pharisaic hearts and minds, as well as the highly skilled surveillance with which they operated.

Covetous for powers of control over Israel, through the Twelve these *church leaders* bluntly sought and asserted domination over the accessible Jesus. In short, they called the Son of man to account.

'the tradition of the elders' and therefore to be followed by anybody who wants to be regarded as a good Jew. Jesus will not be put on the defensive, so he offers no defense of his disciples' laxity in the matter of handwashing. Instead, he accuses the critics of a far more serious breach—not of the tradition of the elders, but of the very law of God. They have, in fact, invented a tradition which actually would relieve a man of the duty of obeying God's law."

156. Bronner, *Sects and Separatism During the Second Jewish Commonwealth*, 17, ". . . laws dealing with the consumption of ritual clean food . . . played a very important and significant role in the religious life of the various sects during the Second Temple."

157. Kirsh, *We Christians and Jews*, 49, "When Jesus' disciples plucked grained as they walked on the Sabbath, 'threshed' it in their hands, and ate it, it was Pharisees who challenged Jesus' permissiveness (Mark 2:24). The disciples were seen as in violation of the Pharisees' strict interpretation of the biblical prohibition of work on the Sabbath."

158. Klinghoffer, *Why the Jews Rejected Jesus*, 58, "Again, the written Torah said nothing about the obligation to ritually wash one's hands before eating bread. This commandment was likewise entirely a matter of tradition, the intent being to elevate in holiness the act of eating above the crude animal need to feed the body. Here once more Jesus belittled 'the tradition of the elders,' as Mark phrases it in his Gospel. Jesus goes on the attack against the Pharisees, who question his followers' neglect of hand washing: 'You leave the commandments of God and hold fast the tradition of men.'"

159. Simon, *Jewish Sects at the Time of Jesus*, 6, "The rabbis who during this period increasingly assumed the role of spiritual leaders of the Chosen People, also devoted themselves to the interpretation of the Torah's stipulations."

According to Matthew, without given the immediate occasion for his response in terms of the Fifth Commandment, Jesus as the Head of the Church, prudent and deliberate, rose to the counter-offensive.[160] "He answered them, 'And why do you transgress the commandment of God for the sake of your tradition? For God commanded, "Honor your father and your mother," and "He who speaks evil of father or mother, let him surely die."[161] But you say, 'If any one tells his father or his mother, What you would have gained from me is given to God, he need not honor his father.' So, for the sake of your tradition, you have made void the word of God." This Corban-invocation, Mark 7:11, with its oath value effectively stripped a grown-up from the sense of rectitude and responsibility for observing the Fifth Commandment.[162] Blinded by covetousness, such a son pretentiously wrote off any financial assistance his (elderly, destitute) parents might have required.[163] Therefore, as the eschatological judge, Jesus condemned this Jerusalem delegation with their followers as hypocrites.

> "Well did Isaiah prophesy of you, when he said:
>
> 'This people honors me with their lips, but their heart is far from me;
>
> in vain do they worship me, teaching as doctrines the precepts of men.'"[164]

160. Sanders, *Judaism,* 422, "The New Testament confirms the importance that the Pharisees attached to 'tradition' by having Jesus criticize them on that very point. It even names two of these tradition: handwashing, which is not a biblical requirement (Mark 7.1–8), and the practice of declaring property or goods *korban* (Mark 7.11). A man could declare something *korban,* 'an offering', dedicated to God, but maintain the use of it during his own life. Jesus is said to rebuke the Pharisees for abusing this device by using it to shelter goods or money from other claims while retaining it for their own use (Mark 7.12f.)."

161. Exod 21:17.

162. Kirsh, *We Christians and Jews,* 50, "What may need to made clearer for Christians is that such Pharisee positions were arrived at and taught in good faith. In the case of the Corban rule, the Pharisees were no doubt defending the sanctify of vows made to God."

This anti-Fifth Commandment the Pharisees emplaced at least post-124 BC (NEB), 2 Mac. 3:8–13.

163. Rabbinic Judaism modified this covetous abuse of the Fifth. Hertzberg, *Judaism,* 98 (quoting the *Pesikta 23*), ". . . when it comes to honoring your parents, whether you are a man of substance or not, you are obligated to 'honor your father and your mother' [Ex. 20:12]—even if you have to beg from door to door."

164. Major, et al., *The Mission and Message of Jesus,* 98, "In criticism of the emphasis placed by the scribes on the Tradition of the Elders, Jesus cites Is. 29:13, in which the prophet complains of the verbal honour given to God by those whose hearts are far from Him."

Though they had the full backing of the Oral Law and the widespread approval of peers, Jesus placed the Pharisees and their slippery words squarely in the glare of condemnation.[165]

Matthew 23:1–36

To many of the Church and particularly to the Twelve, Jesus Christ spelled out the Matt 16:11 scorn for the soul-eating leaven of the scribes and the Pharisees,[166] who adversely controlled the heart and mind of the covenant people by sitting on Moses' seat,[167] the elevated chair in each synagogue. This collective noun referred to the synagogual seating arrangement, in which the synagogue's leader sat in front of and above the gathered worshipers,

---

165. Ibid., 99, "The Jewish Mishna, which preserves the Tradition of the Elders, was codified a good deal later than the Ministry of Jesus, but it may reflect Rabbinical teaching which was contemporary with Him. The Mishna is in agreement with the teaching of Jesus: that no vows or dedications could release a man from the obligations to support his parents. There may, however, have been some scribes, contemporary with Jesus, who taught that Corban vows and dedications could release a man from his filial obligations. Also it is possible that Christian criticism of such Jewish casuistry may account for the Mishna's teaching on this point."

166. Rivkin, *A Hidden Revolution*, 124, "Our definition drawn from the New Testament may now be concisely stated: The Pharisees were a scholar class committed to the authority of the Written Law and the *paradosis,* who enjoyed such prestige and who exercised such power that to all appearances they sat securely on Moses' seat."

167. Ferguson, *Backgrounds of Early Christianity*, 474, "Most synagogues had a platform where there would have been a reading stand; other features were benches lining the walls and a chief seat ('Moses' seat'; Matt. 23:2) for the person presiding."

Hendriksen, *Matthew*, 821, "Not only did every synagogue probably have a special seat, called 'Moses' chair,' assigned to the most famous scribe of the town or village where the synagogue was located, but in a sense the scribes and Pharisees as a body could be described as occupying that chair."

Rivkin, *A Hidden Revolution*, 252, "The Scribes-Pharisees had seated themselves on the cathedra of Moses, and in doing so, they spun off a mutation so powerful that to this day this revolutionary form of Judaism, and not the unmediated Judaism of the Pentateuch, is regarded by all Jews as 'traditional' Judaism."

This is entirely different from Exod 18:13.

Ibid., 231–32, "Underlying all these discontinuities separating the Mishnah system from the Pentateuchal system is the fact that a scholar class is sitting in Moses' seat even though Moses had never bestowed upon a scholar class any authority over God's Law. Such authority had been vouchsafed prophets and priests, but not scholars. Yet nowhere in the Mishnah do we find the *halakhah* expounded by either a prophetic or a priestly class."

in fact, the seat of judgment for internal controls with respect to Oral Law compliance.

For upholding remnants of the Commandments in the Tradition of the Elders, Jesus commanded all listening, ". . . so practice and observe whatever they tell you." "What Jesus must have meant . . . was that whenever the scribes and the Pharisees faithfully interpreted 'Moses,' their instructions should be obeyed."[168] In contrast to legitimate teaching, the Lord commanded multiple listeners, specifically the Twelve, not to do according to Pharisaic deeds, ". . . but not what they do; for they preach, but do not practice." In the Church Jesus ordered all not to follow them in their amassing hatred for the Messiah, for instance, or in persecuting believers in Christ, or in opposing the reformation of the Church, or in advocating a kingdom at odds with the Kingdom, or in covetousness relative to wealth. Though these domineering leaders taught the resurrection of the body, the coming of the kingdom in the time to come, and the achievement of self-righteousness, their actual works reached no further than overextended trust in the Tradition of the Elders. As well, Jesus commanded his followers to refrain from doing all Pharisaic works he condemned in vss 4–23.

Pharisees bound heavy burdens, hard to bear, on fellow-Israelite shoulders, that is, works to gain the resurrection of the body, to earn self-righteousness, and achieve entrance into the pharisaically perceived kingdom. However, were these great-in-their-own-eyes leaders willing to lift a finger to assist followers to gain the Pharisaic goals? Rather, than waste time to help strugglers under unbearable burdens for achieving self-righteousness, these leading men wanted visibility, with manipulation of perception attracting attention for and by their piety. Matt 6:1–6. They widened phylacteries on arms and foreheads as well as lengthened fringes on outer garments[169] for showing off pompous religiosity. These reminders of the divine law, the phylacteries and fringes, served in Pharisee heads an opposite purpose: to tell others how conscientious and religious practitioners of the Oral law they actually were. Therefore, these rebels in the Church loved places of honor at feasts and in synagogues to exude grandiose vanity and ostentation. All the while, they craved for formal salutations in public places, on streets, and in market places, demanding recognition, if not veneration, for decorative spirituality.

---

168. Hendriksen, *Matthew,* 821.

169. Num 15:37–41; Deut 22:12.

Carrying this religiosity to another extreme, Pharisees craved the titular "rabbi"[170] (= my lord, loosely, my teacher, or father/protector), a yearning for rank incommensurate with the Kingdom. Therefore, Jesus called specifically the Twelve never to covet the rabbi-title,[171] because they had one Teacher, the Christ, and before him they were equal in status, none superior in significance. Neither were they to call any one father, that is, protector, therewith replacing the Father in heaven. Neither bestowed the Christ freedom on the Twelve, or in the Church on any one else to be called master, in the sense of domineering over others as the Pharisees did. Christ himself was the only leader, the Master. In the Kingdom, service in Christ Jesus generated greatness, the last to be first. All exalting themselves faced severe public humbling, trailing off into a sideline of history, at that time: the Greco-Roman, the Pharisaic, or the Sadduceic, to confront the tidings of the Daniel 2 Judgment Day. All who humbled themselves Christ promised to raise up in glory, which prophetic vision sensitized the covenant sign of life.

Thereupon Christ pronounced seven free-from-excess woes, designated denunciations, upon Pharisees and scribes, with acute disparagement of the covetous preoccupations[172] thus condemned. "The woes on the Pharisees (Luke 11:39–52 = Matt. 23:25–36, with some additions and shifts in order) begin with an attack on the hypocrisy with which the Jewish laws of cleanliness are observed."[173] These strong-armed leaders of the Church

170. Magonet, *The Explorer's Guide to Judaism*, 123, ". . . 'rabbi', the title that marks them as scholar, teacher, judge, and spiritual leader of the people."

171. Sandmel, *The Genius of Paul*, 43, "The rabbi was a religious personality in a broad sense; he was not, as today, a functionary. The rabbi was a layman whose eminence and prestige depended on his scholarship in the Bible and his attendant ability to decide uncertain cases which touched on Biblical law but which were not explicitly mentioned in it."

172. Major, et al., *The Mission and Message of Jesus*, 390, "'That their piety is a sham is proved by the fact that alone with their extreme conscientiousness in trifles goes a remarkable indifference in the really vital matters, 'judgement and the love of God.' 'Judgement' is here, as often in the Old Testament, the quality which fits one to be a judge, i.e. a keen sense of right and wrong, an inward rectitude, an unshakeable determination to uphold what is right and true and good. The love of God is the essence of true religion."

173. Kee, *Jesus in History*, 79. Ibid., "After exposing the discrepancy between the Pharisees' outer show of piety and inner lack of devotion, Jesus attacks directly those who have not only failed to hear God's message through the prophets but also shared in murdering these men sent by God. The two specific murders mentioned in Luke 11:51, those of Abel and Zechariah, are probably intended to encompass the whole span of the history of Israel, from the first murder recorded in the first book of the Hebrew Bible,

had in their cultural silo approached and superseded, due to their assumed command position in the community of the covenant, debilitating Roman tyranny. Matt 20:25; Mark 10:42; Luke 22:25. In this dying movement, while in search for stability, power-directed, they lorded it over Christ's own in a manner commensurate with pagan tyrants, another adaptation from a militaristic cultural history, its crisis complete.

A probing question: Were Pharisees and scribes as covetous and befouled redemptively as targeted in the Gospels?

- Josephus, a Pharisee, found the entire faction consisted of upright people, and the Sadducees, that other Jewish reality, the troubling and actual culturally unrefined element among Jewish people. ". . . the Pharisees are friendly to one another, and are for the exercise of concord and regard for the public. But the behaviour of the Sadducees one towards another is in some degrees wild; and their conversation with those that are of their own party is as barbarous as if they were strangers to them."[174] From within this theatre of moral valuation, the hardline gatekeepers to the Oral Law neither planned nor propagated enmity, especially not toward the Christ.

  Others in the Oral Law tradition, modern rabbinic Judaism also of Pharisee descend, responded to the question equally appreciative of Pharisaism as Josephus did.

- "The Pharisees represented the middle ground of Jewish religious thinking. They were exceedingly tolerant in their religious views, totally different from the New Testament picture of them as narrow-minded bigots."[175]

- "It is an unfair caricature to picture the Pharisees as heartless pedants."[176]

- "The Pharisees were always on the side of peace, and though they looked for the coming of the Messiah to restore Israel and set up the Kingdom of God, they held that it could not be brought about by violence, but only through righteousness of conduct and loyalty to Torah."[177]

Genesis, to the last murder in the last book of the canon, II Chronicles." (The Hebrew Bible concluded with 2 Chronicles.)

174. Flavius, *Wars*, II.viii.14.

175. Dimont, *Jews, God and History*, 98.

176. Kee, *Jesus in History*, 59.

177. Epstein, *Judaism*, 105.

- "For [Judaism's] invincibility and deathlessness the Jewish people are indebted mainly to the Pharisees. They it was who generated among the people a spirit that proved mightier than the sword, and a loyalty that has stood the test of centuries."[178]

- "The Pharisees were indeed the party eminently suitable for coping with the needs of the times. For some time the Pharisees had been moving away from the national unit and the territorial state in the direction of individualism and universalism—the only foundations on which a reconstruction of Jewish life was now possible. The God of the Pharisees was not limited to Palestine."[179]

- "They had developed the institution of the Synagogue with its elaborate liturgy, which could now take the place of the Temple for prayer and worship. Furthermore, the conception of the oral Law enabled them to reconcile development and change with loyalty to tradition, and to undertake the far-reaching adjustments in Jewish life which the new conditions demanded."[180]

- ". . . the Pharisees clearly operated in good faith. No society can function without some provision for updating its laws. Times change."[181]

- "The Pharisees saw themselves—or at any rate their teachers—as the successors to the men of the Great Assembly. As they saw it, even when they innovated, they were doing nothing more than to make explicit was what already implicit in the tradition."[182]

---

178. Ibid., 111.

179. Ibid., 112.

180. Ibid.

181. Kirsch, *We Christians and Jews*, 52.

Major, et al., *The Mission and Message of Jesus*, 344, "In his *Rabbinic Literature and Gospel Teachings*, pp. 103f., Dr. C.G. Montefiore says: 'I would not cavil with the view that Jesus is to be regarded as the first great Jewish teacher to frame such a sentence as: "Love your enemies, do good to them who hate you, bless them that curse you, and pray for them who ill-treat you" (Lk. 6:27, 28). Yet how much more telling his injunction would have been if we had had *a single story* about his doing good to, and praying for, a single Rabbi or Pharisee! One grain of practice is worth a pound of theory . . . But no such deed is ascribed to Jesus in the Gospels. Towards his enemies, towards those who did not believe in him, whether individuals, groups, or cities (Matt. 11:20–24), only denunciation and bitter words! The injunctions are beautiful, but how much more beautiful would have been a *fulfilment* of those injunctions by Jesus himself."

182. Kirsch, *We Christians and Jews*, 52.

- "The Oral Law strives to apply the teachings of the Bible to all the events of existence; to provide religious and moral standards for all of life's activities; and to realize the Bible's teachings in the whole Jewish community."[183]

- "Christian critics of Judaism have supposed that the laws form a burden, turn people into robots, and define piety as a form of book-keeping ('I give so you give')."[184]

The above Judaic valuations, revisionist messages of defiance, differ radically from Christ's in the Gospels, draw attention to the biblically revealed collision of truth makers, the Lord Jesus or the Pharisees. Other views, in a Protestant tradition, raise or lower the stress levels concerning Pharisaism.

- "Today we realize that the picture drawn by the Gospel writers, sometimes exaggerated to the point of caricature, had retained only the most questionable traits and the most conspicuous faults of the sect. The picture is not completely false, in the sense that there were undoubtedly hypocrites and those who pretended to be religious among the Pharisees."[185]

- "Yet we may wholeheartedly accept the rehabilitation of the Pharisees, who were God-fearing men with views which closely approximated standard Christian theological positions with respect to the attributes of God, the question of predestination and free will, and the problem of the after-life."[186]

- "The fact that before Jesus pronounces 'woes' upon his bitter opponents, who are planning to kill him, he first has something good to say about their teaching should increase reverence and love for him. Also, it should be borne in mind that not all scribes and Pharisees were necessarily hostile to Jesus."[187]

183. Baeck, *The Essence of Judaism*, 23.
Simcox, *The First Gospel*, 166–67, "They had invented, or embraced, a tradition which provided for any selfish, hard-hearted man an escape hatch from God's clear commandments to honor and provide for parents." Ibid., 167, "If the 'religious' man can fill his time sufficiently with pious little practices, this will take his mind off the great commandments of God. By making his life harder in this way, he makes it vastly easier."

184. Neusner, *Judaism*, 175.

185. Simon, *Jewish Sects at the Time of Jesus*, 30.

186. Albright, *From the Stone Age to Christianity*, 390--391.

187. Hendriksen, *Matthew*, 821.

- "After the closing of the Old Testament canon there sprung up the last great heresy of the ages—Pharisaism—which assimilated into itself well-nigh all the heresies of ages past."[188]

These valuations eyeing the original people of the Oral Law simply epitomize the full gamut of post-Pharisaic appreciation, or the lack thereof. Through the inscripturation of the Tradition of the Elders into the Mishnah, Pharisaism transmuted into the Rabbinism, the more measured forerunner of modern Judaism. In the process, however, the rabbis introduced countless changes; they absolved the unbending Pharisees of crudities, therewith to counter the breadth of exposure, first, to Christianity and, second, to Mohammedanism. For instance: "Thus, the Corban rule that was in effect in Jesus' day was modified by the time the oral law was codified in the Mishnah (c. A.D. 200) in such a way as to safeguard the rights of parents."[189] Similarly, the remedying modification process drained away the commandment to hate enemies. In comparison to Pharisaism, Judaism brought about a paradigmatic revolution, which made the Oral Law less hostile, more amenable to prevent or temper persecutory pressures from Christianity and Mohammedanism. Erasures of the Corban rule, the hate commandment, and its sense of superiority made Pharisaism less troubling and repulsive, and to that extent presented the Gospels skewed and deceitful with respect to Pharisaism.

The question that now confronts all Gospel readers/students: was the Christ, the Judge of heaven and earth, a common liar, a hardened perverter of the historical givens, who excoriated Pharisaism unjustly? Always the Matt 16:16; Mark 8:29; Luke 9:20 query, "But who do you say I am?" demanded and demands timely answer, even pushing for a propositional response.

Within the bigger energies of that mutating political framework, the monopolizing Pharisees for the larger role and the outmaneuvered Sadducees for the lesser controlled and conditioned the Church, dictating her belief and life.[190] Both precarious movements of this dark, deeply religious period within the Church, each with its own heterodox drift, each with

---

188. Shearer, *The Sermon on the Mount*, 15.

189. Kirsch, *We Christians and Jews*, 50–51.

190. Albright, *From the Stone Age to Christianity*, 353, "For two full centuries, from cir. 130 B.C. to 70 A.D., Jewish religious life was characterized by this party conflict, in which the Pharisees gained ground steadily at the expense of their more aristocratic brethren."

its different imperatives, presented themselves and each other as blatant enemies of the Scripture-unifying Gen 3:14–19 covenant hope; more, they opposed vociferously and viciously Christ Jesus, Sovereign, as well as recalibrated the vital signs of the covenant, the promises and the obligations.

> ". . . the Judiac systems in Second Temple Times yielded two ways of life. The priest described society as organized through lines of structure emanating from the Temple. His caste stood at the top of a social scale in which all things were properly organized, each with its correct name and proper place. The inherent sanctity of Israel, the people, came down through genealogy to its richest embodiment in him, the priest. Food set aside for his rations at God's command possessed that same sanctity; so too did the table at which he ate his food. To the priest the sacred society of Israel produced history as an account of what happed in, and (alas) on occasion to, the Temple. To the scribe or sage, the life of society demanded wise regulation. Relationships among people required guidance by the laws embodied in the Torah, which were best interpreted by the sage.[191] Accordingly, the task of Israel was to construct a way of life in accordance with the revealed rules of the Torah. The sage, master of the rules, stood at the head of this society. As for prophecy's insistence that the fate of the nation depended upon the faith and moral condition of society, history testified to the external context and inner condition of Israel, viewed as a whole. Both sage and priest saw Israel from the aspect of eternity. But the nation lived out its life in the history of this world, among other peoples coveting the very same Land, within the politics of empires."[192]

In the sectarian Pharisee/Sadducee excess of daring against the Son of God/Son of man, leaders on those other courses with overvalued mind and shortsighted spirit flaunted the Lord and Savior of the Church. Through revolutionary fires intensified by petty arrogance, they shut eyes and ears to the actual erring of the rabbinical tradition. "However much the Jewish religion exposed itself to alien influences, it never changed its essential character, nor abandoned itself to those influences."[193] By repressive rule,

191. Bickerman, *From Ezra to the Last of the Maccabees*, 69, ". . . the Jewish scribe becomes a legitimate interpreter of the Divine Law."

192. Neusner, *Judaism*, 61. Ibid., "The Messiah's kingship would resolve the issues of Israel's subordinated relationship to other nations and empires, establishing once and for all time the correct context for priest and sage alike."

193. Baeck, *The Essence of Judaism*, 18. Ibid., "For this contention there is no better evidence than the fact that Judaism has preserved its monotheism stern and pure."

together these formidable adversaries determined to drag the Church forever into the dissonance of perpetually divine condemnation, far from the post-Pentecost freedom in the way of the Christ, Acts 15:6–21.

Thus far the Oral Law in its historical malice, the measure of its crisis full.

Chapter 3

The Oral Law in its Eclipse

RELENTLESS PHARISEES WITH CUMULATIVE Sadducee complicity carried forward with high confidence, indeed, with fierce concentration,
the purpose of the Oral Law: to destroy the Christ forever; his death by crucifixion and burial in a sealed sepulcher seemingly propped up this satanic
aim. Given the catastrophic moment of that animosity, the Crucifixion,
the Oral Law slipped into its eclipse, apparent by the inscripturation process into the Mishnah, from there evolving into rabbinic Judaism. This
evolutionary shift demonstrated a highly controversial paradigmatic alteration, much more involved than an absent-minded domestication of
the Tradition of the Elders. Further, with uncompromising persecution of
the Christ, after the Resurrection the Pharisee people moved against the
Church. 1) Acts 9:1–2, specifically Paul's persecutory maneuvers. 2) Rev
12:17, ". . . the dragon was angry at the woman, and went off to make
war on the rest of her offspring, on those who keep the commandments of
God and bear testimony to Jesus." Nevertheless, the Lord Jesus, ascended
and glorious, stirred the Church up and onwards linearly and eschatologically according to the covenant line begun in Genesis.[1] In early reactions to
the eclipse, one, whenever representatives of Christ, initially apostles, approached the peoples of the Synagogue or the Temple, the Jews collectively
reacted in a violent manner strong enough to invoke ever-present Roman

1. Dodd, *The Meaning of Paul For Today*, 13, "More and more it becomes clear that
no accommodation is possible. There is a clear issue: on the one hand the Way of the
Nazarene, with His startling assertions and denials; on the other hand all that the piety of
the time prized as the essentials of a revealed religion."

soldiery. This Paul discovered, Acts 21:27–36. And, two, the Jews, after the destruction of the Temple, amalgamated in the Synagogue, fighting to supersede the Church, until 312 AD, when Emperor (Flavius Valerius Aurelius) Constantine ensured toleration for Christianity. In the meantime, the Mishnah swallowed the laws of the *paradosis* and prescribed the way of Rabbinism into its historic eclipse.

Temple Violence

The first clash scowling Sadducees initiated. On a Sabbath soon after Pentecost, Apostles Peter and John on Temple precincts healed a paraplegic, then taught without equivocation the suddenly assembling Jewish crowds the deeper root and providential design of this miracle. Acts 4:13–17. However, the immediately awake-to-danger priests, captain of the Temple, and Sadducees, rattled leaders, in a moment of clarity solidified for a surge of conflict, taking the two apostles prisoner. Adroit Temple guardians wanted to collapse the proclamation of the resurrected Jesus, squelch the nascent church, and fight for inflexible reins of power, recently almost lost. Concluding this first post-Pentecost assault against the Christ, they put down the apostles with an austere warning. Acts 4:18–21, "So they called [Peter and John] and charged them not to speak or teach at all in the name of Jesus. . . . And when they had further threatened them, they let them go, finding no way to punish them, because of the people; for all men praised God for what had happened." The two apostles, mandated to proclaim the resurrected Christ in the Church, refused to mind the finger-wagging signals emanating from cynical Temple chiefs.

In the face of more undisputable apostolic signs and wonders, Acts 5:12–16, (Luke named only Peter) many Jewish people gathered also from towns surrounding Jerusalem: to the volatile chagrin of the high priest interacting with the party of the Sadducees. This time they arrested and whisked away the Twelve, locking them under tight surveillance in the common prison. However, an intriguing angel of the Lord Jesus extricated his men with the influential command, Acts 5:20, "Go and stand in the temple and speak to the people all the words of this Life." For this fighting spirit Jesus had called and commissioned the Twelve, amidst shifting political patterns on the one foundation to build the New Church and expand the Kingdom.

As the sovereign Lord of all creation and omnipotent Head of the Church, from the time of Solomon's construction of the first Temple Jesus owned this prime real estate. He willed that the apostles from and in this transitional place of teaching and judging, 1 Kings 8:31–32; 2 Chron 6:22–23, summon all Christ's chosen into the ongoing covenant community and, second, expose the infidelity as well as enmity of the Temple guardians; with respect to these ruling classes through a sequence of divine interventions he planned the end of the time-limited Temple, Matt 24:1–2. The venerable Temple had become a living mausoleum, whereas Christ projected irresistible patterns of growth for the future of the Church. Acts 19:20.

Because the Apostles again, rightfully, proclaimed the Gospel and Christ's rule on Temple grounds, the captain of the guard moved with alacrity, aware of public opinion. Acts 5:26, ". . . the captain with the officers went and brought them, but without violence, for they were afraid of being stoned by the people." Inside, however, because the apostles denigrated the authority of the High Priest, Annas with the fire of anger imposed the weight of his defunct office[2] (within human-scale limits the Romans allowed). Acts 5:28, "We strictly charged you not to teach in this name, yet here you have filled Jerusalem with your teaching and you intend to bring this man's blood upon us." Apparently, he ignored Matt 27:25, "His blood be on us and on our children." Peter, however, answered Annas and company with flat rejection, Acts 5:29–32, "We must obey God rather than men. The God of our fathers raised Jesus whom you killed by hanging him on a tree. God exalted him at his right hand as Leader and Savior, to give repentance to Israel and forgiveness of sins. And we are witnesses of these things, and so is the Holy Spirit whom God has given to those who obey him." Thus Peter and the other apostles stood, firm and unflinching, over against the vexed High Priest and the rancorous party of the Sadducees, in fact, the entire Sanhedrin, one to eclipse the other.[3]

To prove his unchristlike high priestly authority, full-of-malice Annas had the Twelve beaten, scourged; moreover, out of spite he charged them again not to speak in the name of Jesus and released the apostles from custody. Acts 5:41–42, "Then they left the presence of the council, rejoicing

---

2. In the Crucifixion-Ascension history, Christ Jesus as the King and the Prophet also took on the priestly office with respect to his people. Heb 4:14; etc.

3. An overstatement: Dimont, *Jews, God and History*, 139–40, "In fact the Jews came out in defense of the Christians, as evidenced in the New Testament itself. Acts 5:34–39 states that the Pharisee Rabbi Rabban Gamaliel openly opposed the Roman persecution of the Christians."

that they were counted worthy to suffer dishonor for the name. And every day in the temple and at home they did not cease teaching and preaching Jesus as the Christ." This, with tireless devotion, in precise answer to the council, the Sanhedrin.

Three attacks, state-sponsored violence, on the lordship of Jesus and the leadership of the Church within Temple precincts recorded the entrenched animosity against the Christ. With tangled revenge. Too late.

Later, burning and agitating with a surge of convulsive violence, Pharisees (from the synagogue of the Freedmen, from Cyrenia, Alexandria, Cilicia, and Asia) took Evangelist Stephen in custody on false charges, each a poisonous nonsense. Within the Sanhedrin,[4] Sadducees and Pharisees heard Stephen's apology,[5] without listening. Acts 7:54p, ". . . they were enraged, and they ground their teeth against him." Moved by fierce angers at odds with the resurrected Jesus, the tumultuaries of the Sanhedrin rushed to murder. Acts 7:58, "Then they cast [Stephen] out of the city and stoned him; and witnesses laid down their garments at the feet of a young man named Saul." Acts 22:20. Thus, Pharisees and Sadducees killed a messenger of the glorified and regnant Christ.

Suddenly, Sanhedrinic rage seized also the Jewish populace. Acts 8:1–3. With an outpouring of persecutory rapacity targeting godly members of the New Church in Jerusalem, daredevils compelled many of Christ to migrate elsewhere, seeking safe havens in Judea and Samaria. In

---

4. Pollock, *The Apostle*, 7, "The state being a theocracy, in which religious and national leaders were identical, the seventy-one members of the Sanhedrin were equally judges, senators and spiritual masters. The court was supreme in all religious decisions and in what little self-government the Romans allowed."

Major, et al., *The Mission and Message of Jesus*, 180, "It is generally assumed that the Sanhedrin, during the period that Judea was under the government of the Roman procurators, had no power to inflict capital sentences. On the other hand, the trial of Stephen and the infliction of the legal capital sentence—death by stoning—seems to conflict with this conclusion."

5. Simon, *Jewish Sects at the Time of Jesus*, 99–100, "The speech is essentially a vehement diatribe against the Jewish people (that is, official Judaism), which is eternally rebellious against the divine will. Stephen especially condemns the temple, which Solomon built in defiance of God's will: 'However, the Most High does not live in houses made by men'" (7:48, NEB). The meaning of such a statement becomes clear if it is remembered that in the usage of Hellenistic Judaism the word *cheiropoietos* ('made by man's hand') is more or less the technical designation for idols. In the Septuagint this term is often used to translate the Hebrew word *elil*, which means 'idol.' To reject the temple because it was made by human hands is thus to rank it with idolatry."

This idolatry, of course, applied more specifically to the Second Temple, Herod the Great's architecture.

the meantime, Acts 8:3, ". . . Saul was ravaging the church, and entering house after house, he dragged off men and women and committed them to prison." Through savage ruthlessness of persecution under the punitive aegis of the Sanhedrin, Pharisees and Sadducees promoted intense hatred for the Christ, searching out not only leaders but also other members of the Church to eradicate the majestic lordship of the holy and glorious Jesus.[6]

For incarcerating more of the Christ, Paul with formal letters of intro-duction and commission to Damascene synagogues pursued disciples who had fled Jerusalem. Acts 9:2p, ". . . so that if he found any belonging to the Way, men or women, he might bring them bound to Jerusalem." However, the sovereign Lord Jesus arrested Saul with an unexpected as well as unin-vited conversion, and commanded him otherwise. Instead of persecuting Jesus further, the Lord commissioned the man on that fateful day as the apostle to the Gentiles. This divine intervention in the decaying stages of Temple authority further forespelled its denouement.

Paul, after a stay in Arabia, Gal 1:17, taught in the synagogues of Damascus, proclaiming Jesus, but he in a time of emergency confounded murder-minded Jews, slipping away by dark of night in a basket let down from the city wall.[7] Acts 9:23–24; 2 Cor 11:32–33.

According to the Acts, post-Ascension, the Roman occupiers re-mained at a distance, after the Crucifixion no longer interested by Jewish intrigue. With the death of the King of the Jews, they had slapped down one more in a string of insurrections and turned to other temptations of power in conjunction with occupation.

Only, when Herod Agrippa I needed to ingratiate himself with the Jews, he, Acts 12:1, ". . . laid violent hands upon some who belonged to the church." To demonstrate Rome's brute force, he killed James, which pleased the Jews, and proceeded to arrest Peter, whom an angel of the Lord mysteriously released from a perilous place. In the Acts, this painful ordeal projected the first intrusion of Roman tyranny in the New Church. For a time thereafter, in Luke's narrative, Sadducee resistance to the Christ settled into background, but not that of the Pharisees.

---

6. Dodd, *The Meaning of Paul for Today*, 23, "The young Paul saw here a vocation which commanded his ardent devotion. He would be the instrument of the God of his fathers in putting down this pestilent and blasphemous heresy."

7. Sandmel, *The Genius of Paul*, 5, "Outside scholarly information, though justly con-troversial, fixes this date as roughly 35 A.D. No other reference in Paul's Epistles alludes to a securely known date or datable event. Even if it is correct that in 35 Paul escaped from Aretas' governor, we do not know what his age was at that time."

In the gifted construction of the Book of the Acts, Luke documented the Temple's last biblically recorded efforts, from this one place to overcome the Christ's church-reforming works.

Pharisee Violence

1. Because of Saul/Paul's first apostolic journeying,[8] the decisive attention of the Acts fell away from the Sanhedrin as well as Temple to rest on wild fires of synagogual opposition. The first revolutionary issue of this interference struck at Paul and Barnabas in Antioch of Pisidia, a Galatian city in central Asia Minor; rage of murder boiled up in the synagogue's unbelievers, on account of which Paul consciously moved into his office as apostle to the Gentiles.[9] Acts 13:44–46, "The next sabbath almost the whole city gathered together to hear the word of God. But when the Jews saw the multitudes, they were filled with jealousy, and contradicted what was spoken by Paul, and reviled him. And Paul and Barnabas spoke out boldly, saying, 'It was necessary that the word of God should be spoken first to you. Since you thrust it from you, and judge yourselves unworthy of eternal life, behold, we turn to the Gentiles." Acts 13:47, "For so the Lord has commanded us, saying,

> 'I have set you to be a light for the Gentiles,
> that you may bring salvation to the uttermost parts of the earth.'"[10]

Through this key section in the Acts, Luke revealed a hard-to-dispute turning point: unbelieving Jews venturing boldly and disastrously onto an off-ramp of history. Pharisaism, then, pedantically walked away into condemnation. As the Lord Jesus single-handedly and sovereignly intended, they rejected the Gospel. At the same time, amazing, the elect in that careless synagogue responded by believing Paul and Barnabas, hungry for the continuously vibrant apostolic word. Acts 13:48–50, "And when the

---

8. Dodd, *The Meaning of Paul for Today*, 24, "It meant that the new religion had broken through the narrow limits of a mere Jewish sect, and set out to claim the world."

9. Ibid., 55, "From that time he had to count 'perils from false brethren' among the difficulties of his work."

10. Isa 42:6, 49:6.

Horsley, "Unearthing a People's History, 2, "The principal distinction made among people was between Jews, among whom the new religion had its background, and the Gentiles, among whom the religion flourished and expanded."

Gentiles heard [the prophetic word], they were glad and glorified the word of God; and as many as were ordained to eternal life believed. And the word of the Lord spread throughout all the region. But the Jews incited the devout women of high standing and the leading men of the city, and stirred up persecution against Paul and Barnabas, and drove them out of their district." Also amidst obdurate Pharisees[11] the Lord Jesus drew the eschatological line of covenant history farther. In Pisidian Antioch, this historical precedent, despite thrown up obstacles, caught the ears of many, pressuring action for and against the Gospel.

Mobile Paul and company traveled to Iconium, beginning a motivated work, again in the local Jewish synagogue. Acts 14:2, "But the unbelieving Jews stirred up the Gentiles and poisoned their minds against the brethren." This surge of conflict generated physical violence. Acts 14:5–6, "When an attempt was made by both Gentiles and Jews, with their rulers, to molest them and to stone them, they learned of it and fled to Lystra and Derbe, cities of Lycaonia, and to the surrounding country; and there they preached the gospel." In the enduring mission to the Gentiles the apostolic heralds, suffering in the name of the Lord Jesus, learned in labyrinths of risk the troubled moods as well as the running intensities of persecution, preparation for worse.

At Lystra worse occurred. Acts 14:19–20, "But Jews came there from Antioch and Iconium; and having persuaded the people, they stoned Paul and dragged him out of the city, supposing that he was dead." Playing to public opinion, the Pharisees shook off restraints to limit damages to the synagogue; with the hard currency of hatred and basic prejudices of the Oral Law, they opened closed patterns beneath the surface of unbelief.

Implacably, irritated unbelievers in the neighborhood of Christ's men resented the Gospel and the proclamation of the Kingdom. Therefore, on the return journey to Antioch of Syria, the staging place, the apostolic party looping back walked past the numerically diminished and unsafe synagogues of Derbe, Lystra, Iconium, and Antioch of Pisidia, underpinning therewith an inescapable conclusion: solely by the word the Lord Jesus founded the Church.

11. Dodd, *The Meaning of Paul for Today*, 45, ". . . even the Jew whose personal life and conduct had little resemblance to the high ethical ideals of the Old Testament felt an exaltation of spirit as he thought that his nation alone of all peoples of the earth possessed the inmost secret of things. The rest of mankind was there for Israel's sake—to serve Israel or to chastise Israel as might be Jehovah's inscrutable purpose, but in any case to be subjugated or blotted out in the end, when God should finally declare His judgment."

Members of the Jerusalem congregation, however, took exception to believers from among the Gentiles who, without circumcision, remained at best half-Christians.[12] Acts 15:1–5. Such divisive attacks against the Gospel and the coming of the Kingdom surfaced from within the Church. Those of the *paradosis* served under the yoke of the Oral Law, Acts 15:10, unless and until the Christ broke them into the freedom of his rule.

The sovereign Christ through the apostles, sobered souls, made distinction between the Church and the Jewish opposition, now mainly Pharisee-controlled synagogues on the ground. He settled the ongoing covenant community in every place along the living highroad of history, always eschatologically centered.

2. During the second apostolic journeying, Christ's men travelled under compulsion of the Spirit westward; at Thessalonica in the local synagogue, the apostles taught from the Old Testament that Jesus is the Christ. Acts 17:5–9, "But the Jews were jealous, and taking some wicked fellows of the rabble, they gathered a crowd, set the city in an uproar, and attacked the house of Jason, seeking to bring them out to the people. And when they could not find them, they dragged Jason and some of the brethren before the city authorities, crying, 'These men who have turned the world upside down have come here also, and Jason has received them; and they are all acting against the decrees of Caesar, saying that there is another king, Jesus.' And the people and the city authorities were disturbed when they heard this. And when they had taken security from Jason and the rest, they let them go." To escape more of the now violently smoldering political and religious turmoil, the provident Thessalonian disciples sent Paul and Silas to Beroea, to find rest from persecution. Acts 17:13, "But when the Jews of Thessalonica learned that the word of God was proclaimed by Paul at Beroea also, they came there too, stirring up and inciting the crowds." At each such rejection, the Lord Jesus out of divine resolve and with unlimited

---

12. Pollock, *The Apostle,* 76, "The implications of such an argument went far wider than the issue at Antioch which remained in the context of Jewish obligations. Paul saw that the Christian Pharisees' contention was totally at variance with a truth he had understood since Damascus and would expound fully in his letters later on: that self-righteousness, however expressed, is the rival and not the complement of grace."

Klinghoffer, *Why the Jews Rejected Jesus,* 7, "At a council meeting of elders held in Jerusalem in the year 49, Paul made his case for dropping Jewish law as a requirement for Christians. After much debate, James agreed—and the direction of Christian history was set." The Council, of course, retained the Decalogue for gratitude.

dominion uncompromisingly wrote off synagogual claims with respect to the Kingdom.

In the Corinthian synagogue, Acts 18:5–6, ". . . Paul was occupied with preaching, testifying to the Jews that the Christ was Jesus. And when they opposed and reviled him, he shook out his garments and said to them, 'Your blood be upon your heads! I am innocent. From now on I will go to the Gentiles.'" That is, in that defining crisis the Gentiles in the Corinthian Church and elsewhere. With converted Gentiles as charter members, Paul laid at this historical reference point the notable foundation of the Church in that Roman colony,[13] which, however, evoked murdering animosity. Acts 18:12–17,

> . . . when Gallio was proconsul of Achaia, the Jews made a united attack upon Paul and brought him before the tribunal, saying, 'This man is persuading men to worship God contrary to the law.' But when Paul was about to open his mouth, Gallio said to the Jews, 'If it were a matter of wrongdoing or vicious crime, I should have reason to bear with you, O Jews; but since it is a matter of questions about words and names and your own law, see to it yourselves; I refuse to be a judge of these things.' And he drove them from the tribunal. And they all seized Sosthenes, the ruler of the synagogue, and beat him in front of the tribunal. But Gallio paid no attention to this.

Consequent to this hard bounce in public rage, Paul had stiffer troubles in the Corinthian Church.[14] However, again, also at this crossroads of people, the Church moved on, leaving the failing synagogue behind, also its Grecian, or Gentile, members collectively lost in another kingdom. Overall, during this second journeying, Paul and company experienced less hostility and persecution, primarily because they worked in the churches instead of in synagogues and on market places. Vagaries of resistance in the Corinthian Church to the word, however, festered further complex swirls of painful unrest.

---

13. Horsley, "Unearthing a People's History," 13, "Because it was a hub of shipping, Corinth became a cultural melting pot after its colonization by Roman veterans and freedpersons, who presumably spoke Latin."

14. Ball, *The Life and Journeys of Paul,* 185, "Paul's enemies doubted his claim to apostleship and even criticized his speech and personal appearance, but his friends were genuinely awakened to shame and repentance."

3. During the third journey, in Ephesus, at hearing the Gospel hard discontent energized Jews. Acts 19:8–9, "And [Paul] entered the synagogue and for three months spoke boldly, arguing and pleading about the kingdom of God; but when some were stubborn and disbelieved, speaking evil of the Way before the congregation, he withdrew from them, taking the disciples with him, and argued daily in the hall of Tyrannus." Here, too, as everywhere then, virulent tides of opinion against the Gospel twisted unbelievers to impair the proclamation of the word; thereby they crossed over into unforeseen consequences. Enemies of Jesus Christ never fared well.

When itinerant Jewish exorcists, specifically seven sons of a Jewish high priest, Sceva, sought to duplicate Paul's healing miracles, a demon overpowered them. Acts 19:11–20. This brief encounter with a priest, a reminder of Sadducee hatred, even in a population center far away from the Temple, alerted Paul and company to ongoing potentials of persecution.

Throughout and despite often painful and disappointing conflicts, nevertheless Acts 19:20, "So the word of the Lord grew and prevailed mightily."

Jerusalem-bound, Paul survived a plot generated by Macedonian Jews, Acts 20:3. Throughout the known world then, the incompatibility of the Church and the Synagogue settled in, clashes of Pharisees against the Christ diminishing.

Thereafter, the Lord Jesus granted the Apostle to the Gentiles a time of rest from persecution and violence, that is, until his final arrest.[15]

In the gifted construction of the Book of the Acts, Luke documented the Synagogue's last biblically recorded efforts, from many places, to overcome the Christ's church-reforming works.

Roman Violence

In crowded Jerusalem for the 57 AD Pentecost celebration, Pharisees, Sadducees, and Romans joined hands to stop the most visible Apostle of the Christ. Acts 21:27–36. Jews from Asia to settle old scores stirred up violence, accusing Paul of defiling the Temple and attempted in a street brawl to kill him, Acts 21:28. The riot-ready Roman military commander,

---

15. Keck and Furnish, *Interpreting Biblical Texts*, 12, "It is not uncommon for Paul to bear the brunt of animus against Christianity itself—on the assumption that it is he who ruined what Jesus began."

however, seized Paul and restored order, superficially. Though this tribune of the cohort indulged Paul to make an apology, the blood-thirsty Jews refused to listen. Acts 22:22, "Away with such a fellow from the earth! For he ought not to live." Within unsavory Roman barracks, Paul scarcely restrained the tribune from scourging him, a Roman citizen. Once arrested, despite self-absorbed Sadducee and Pharisee pressures for vigilante justice, Roman legal methodology took over.[16]

The Council, that is, the Sanhedrin, composed of Pharisees and Sadducees, also declined to hear the Apostle to the Gentiles, Acts 23:1–10. The High Priest that year, Ananias, struck him on the mouth, a rough way to demand silence. Paul stopped the burgeoning animosity and imminent murder by sowing dissension between Pharisee and Sadducee with respect to the resurrection of the dead. Acts 23:10, "And when the dissension became violent, the tribune, afraid that Paul would be torn in pieces by them, commanded the soldiers to go down and take him by force from among them and bring him into the barracks." More than ever, Temple authorities and Pharisees on the disobedience side of the dividing-line resorted to brute uprisings against the Lord Jesus.

A Jewish plot, with complicity of the chief priests and elders, failed when the tribune sent Paul by night under military escort to Caesarea, to the governor, Felix. Later, before him, Ananias supported by some elders and a spokesman, Tertullus, with supercilious scorn arraigned their case against Paul. Specifically, Acts 24:5–6, ". . . we have found this man a pestilent fellow, an agitator among all the Jews throughout the world, and a ringleader of the sect of the Nazarenes. He even tried to profane the temple, but we seized him." Against this calculated injustice, Paul made his defense, but Felix, ensconced in dreaming for a money bribe, procrastinated to await the arrival of Lysias the tribune, before handing down his decision.

The Jews pressed their case with the next governor, (Antonius) Festus, seeking Paul's transference to Jerusalem, and on the way kill him.[17] Festus heard Paul, Acts 25:8, but preferred to do the Jews a favor and planned a confrontation. Paul, however, seeing only suicidal death by agreeing, appealed to Caesar, from which in the Roman legal genius there was no recourse. Eventually, by means of this lesser of two evils, Paul nevertheless

16. Fulfilling Acts 21:11p, "So shall the Jews at Jerusalem bind the man who owns this girdle and deliver him into the hands of the Gentiles."

17. Klinghoffer, *Why the Jews Rejected Jesus*, 107, "The urgency of the Jews' distress, their anger at him, can be explained by reflecting on the Jewish belief that when Jews turn away from God's commandments, the whole community will suffer."

arrived in Rome: through the cooperation of Pharisees, Sadducees, and Romans, the Lord answering one of his prayers in an unanticipated manner.[18] In Rome he met with a delegation of the area synagogue, most of whom disbelieved the Apostle. To them he spoke the concluding condemnation in the Book of the Acts. Thus Acts 28:25–28, quoting Isa 6:9–10,

> "The Holy Spirit was right in saying to your fathers through Isaiah the prophet:
> 'Go to this people, and say, You shall indeed hear but never understand,
> and you shall indeed see but never perceive.
> For this people's heart has grown dull, and their ears are heavy of hearing,
> and their eyes they have closed;
> lest they should perceive with their eyes,
> and hear with their heart,
> and turn for me to heal them.'
> Let it be known to you then that this salvation of God has been sent to the Gentiles;
> they will listen."

Over the history recounted in the Book of the Acts, in city after city, Sadduceism and Pharisaism stumbled into darkening eclipse, preparing for the paradigmatic alteration that congealed the Oral Law into the Mishnah. The bending away from covenant history consolidated the disputatious Tradition of the Fathers, the *paradosis,* into the Mishnah, Tosefta, and later the even more massive Talmudic literature, which moved Judaism further and further from Christianity, its proponents determined to believe and live in the Jewish manner.

Thus far the Oral Law to its historical eclipse.

A discomfiting question: What was and is the conflicted relationship between Judaism and Christianity?

For some, Christianity constituted a sect within, or derivative from Judaism. Acts 24:5, 24:14, 28:22. Without necessarily implying partisan dysfunction, or base motives, the distinction may have pointed to a group pattern rather than an ideological formulation. "To [the] three sects,[19] a fourth was added in the third decade of the first century A.D., namely, the

---

18. Rom 15:31, ". . . that I may be delivered from the unbelievers in Judea . . . ."
19 The Pharisees, Sadducees, and the Zealots.

Christian sect."[20] With respect to Pharisaic-Talmudic tradition, this sect-identity fastened itself within Judaism's psychical immensity. "Thus arose in that century the Judaeo-Christian sect which in time tore itself away from Judaism to found the Christian Church."[21] Such sectarian language legitimized early Jewish multiple identities, while making the Christ a schismatic and the covenant community a feckless spoiler of broadminded unity.

For some, Pharisaism constituted the parent religion and Christianity a regrettable, if not intractable, offspring. "[Early Christian writers] succeeded to a task in which the LXX translators had been pioneers. Jewish Christianity, like the parent religion, Judaism itself, was a Semitic faith maintaining and propagating itself in the Hellenistic world."[22] This progenitor idea also hardened into a continuous fixation.[23] For instance, " . . . the ambivalence about Judaism within Christianity itself, inheriting, and seeking at the same time to deny, the tradition from which it emerged."[24] Again, ". . . though the Jewish people are the direct continuation of biblical Israel, others feel that they have inherited that role, either alongside the Jewish people or as a replacement for them."[25] In this manner, the parent-child formulation maintained a lingering

---

20. Dimont, *Jews, God and History*, 99. Ibid., 140; etc.

Magonet, *The Explorer's Guide to Judaism*, 122, ". . . it must be pointed out here that, although the Pharisees are frequently attacked in the Gospels, it would seem that Jesus belonged to their number, as is evident from the many teachings held in common."

21. Epstein, *Judaism,* 107. Ibid., 111–12.

In a similar vein: John R. Coats, *Original Sinners,* 88, "The seed of Abraham became '*the* formative influence on Christianity . . . .'"

22. Barrett, *The New Testament Background,* 209.

Kee, *Jesus in History,* 108, following Rudolph Bultmann, "As a historical person, Jesus should be thought of within the sphere of late Judaism and not as the inaugurator of Christian faith." Bultmann, *Primitive Christianity,* 86–93.

23. Marrow, *Paul, His Letters and His Theology,* 85, "It is to be expected that, since the first Christians were 'Jews by birth' (Gal 2:15), one of the first problems to beset the nascent faith had to do with its relation to the parent stock, Judaism."

Rivkin, *A Hidden Revolution,* 26, "The Pharisees are thus firmly embedded in the sacred texts of Christianity. They appear in all four Gospels as dangerous opponents of Jesus Christ. They appear in Acts in connection with both Peter and Paul. In his Epistle to the Philippians (3:5, cf. Gal. 1:13–14), Paul affirms that he had been a Pharisee and a persecutor of the Church before his transformation. The New Testament thus ties the birth of Christianity umbilically to the Pharisees and their teachings."

24. Magonet, *The Explorer's Guide to Judaism,* 5, 17, Christianity and Islam in different ways inherited the biblical tradition, that is, the Pharisaic, Jewish.

25. Ibid., 27; ibid., 237.

linkage between all of the Oral Law and Christianity.[26] This relationship, however popular and well-meant in history-of-religion worlds, disseminated a connection repeated with consistent impetus. " . . . it was the Pharisees who carried on the Old Testament tradition and who marked out the delicate but fundamental line which orthodox Christianity was to take."[27] This parent-religion idea carried over into another, . . .

. . . a mother-daughter relationship. For some Christianity became along with Mohammedanism one of Judaism's offspring.[28] "But there is another consequence to the concept of the 'oneness' of God that has had a profound effect on Jewish thought, and indeed the thought of its 'daughter' religions Christianity and Islam."[29] The Jewish claim for originality pushed specifically now Christianity into a secondary position, a condescension. Later, during the Middle Ages, this condescension settled in deep. "Occasionally a philosophical theologian within Jewry . . . has posited a missionary role among the Gentiles for the daughter religions which have sprung from the Bible, but throughout the ages all Israel has stood fast in the faith that the Torah is the inheritance of the congregation of Jacob."[30] This familial bond placed post-Pharisee Judaism in a dominant theatre of influence: an aggrieved matriarch with wayward daughters.

26. Baeck, *Judaism*, 77, ". . . to embrace all humanity. The same is also true of Christianity and Mohammedanism which are world religions insofar as they are derived from Judaism." Ibid., 80.

27. Albright, *From the Stone Age to Christianity*, 354.

28. Finkel, *The Pharisees and the Teacher of Nazareth*, 11, ". . . the growing pains of a new daughter religion known as Christianity."
Deissmann, *Paul*, 124, "The Gospel of Jesus connected the beginnings of our religion most closely with its mother-religion, Judaism."

29. Magonet, *The Explorer's Guide to Judaism*, 23. Ibid., 162, "Both are in some sense daughter religions of Judaism, the former having seen itself as the authentic successor." Etc.
Epstein, *Judaism*, 144, ". . . Judaism withdrew from the missionary field and was satisfied to leave the task of spreading the religion of humanity to her daughter faiths."

30. Hertzberg, *Judaism*, 16–17.
Neusner, *Scriptures of the Oral Torah*, 17, "Historians of Judaism take as dogma the view that Christianity never made any difference to Judaism. Faith of a 'people that dwells apart,' Judaism went its splendid, solitary way, exploring paths untouched by Christians. Christianity—people hold—was born in the matrix of Judaism, but Judaism . . . officially ignored the new 'daughter' religion and followed its majestic course in aristocratic isolation. But the Judaism expressed by the writings of the sages of the Land of Israel in the fourth century—the age of Constantine—not only responded to issues raised for Israel by the political triumph of Christianity but did so in a way that, intellectually at least, made possible the entire future history of Judaism in Europe and beyond."

With these blood analogies, the parent-religion linkage and the mother-daughter relationship, the Jews sought to gain/earn/buy evasion from persecution. Once Christianity became a preferred religion and later when Mohammedanism dominated the Mediterranean Basin, Judaism pushed a self-protective comparison model: to wit, normal daughters never carry on blood feuds against a mother. To eliminate political suppression, the Jews again and again appealed to the common origin, the Hebrew Bible, seeking thereby historical legitimacy during successive eras in which rival powers contested the rightful existence of the international Jewish nation.

Searching for Christianity's origin moved others beyond any parental model. ". . . in 1947, an electrifying event occurred. Manuscripts dating back to 100 and 200 B.C. bearing a striking resemblance to the Christian creed were discovered. The so-called 'Dead Sea Scrolls' had been found, and with them the mystery of the origin of early Christianity may have been solved."[31] According to this speculative drift of opinion, Christianity had existed at least two hundred years before Christianity when Jesus, "its greatest and noblest spokesman,"[32] became, not its originator but its illustrious marketer. In this Dead-Sea-Scrolls matrix, curiously, speculators sought a firmer toehold for the Christian origin. "It is not even accurate to say that Christianity eventually broke away from Judaism. It is more accurate to say that, out of that matrix of biblical Judaism and that maelstrom of late Second-Temple Judaism, two great traditions eventually emerged: early Christianity and rabbinic Judaism. Each claimed exclusive continuity with the past, but in truth, each was as great a leap and as valid a development from that common ancestry as was the other. They are not child and parent; they are children of the same mother."[33]

Others found Paul the originator of Christianity and the active force behind the abrupt break with Judaism. Whereas, allegedly, Jesus still fitted a Pharisee profile, not so the Apostle. ". . . within a few decades the Christian church under the influence of Paul was altering its conception of Jesus in a way that meant that he was no longer thought of as merely human, and implied that he was in fact a second God—a belief which was a denial of the unity of God as Jews understood the term. Once this development had

---

31. Dimont, *Jews, God and History*, 130.

32. Ibid., 133. Ibid., "The Christians were not anxious to impute to Jewish rabbis the total origin of their religion, feeling it enough that Jesus was Jewish. Neither were the Jews anxious to assume credit for the complete authorship of Christianity, feeling that they had contributed enough by providing the central figure in the Christian religion."

33. Crossan, *The Birth of Christianity*, xxxiii.

taken place accommodation of Jewish Christians within Judaism was no longer possible and the final rift between the two became inevitable."[34] This conviction confirmed that Christianity betrayed Judaism and moved into a pagan orbit. "The great schism between Christians and Jews did not occur until after 50 A.D., when the Christian sect was taken to the pagans and made a world religion. This was both the decision and the accomplishment of one man, another Jew, the real builder of the Christian church."[35] Paul. In some respects, the break was complete early on, yet a fusion between the two lingered, until 132–35 AD.[36] "In the third rebellion against Rome, when the Christians were unable to accept bar Kochba as their messiah, they declared that their kingdom was of the other world, and withdrew themselves completely from Judaism and everything Jewish. The alienation process was completed."[37] Judaism[38] and Christianity, according to this model, moved forever onto separate ways.[39]

Of course, the adversarial ways of the Pharisees and the Christ never moved synchronously: that undoing the prophets had foretold. "So reaction against the Pharisees had to come. With Jesus this reaction assumed the only form it could effectively take, that of a sweeping religious reformation, in some respects following the lines of the prophetic movement some nine centuries previously, . . . Again and again Jesus insisted that He came to fulfil the Torah and the Prophets, not to destroy them. In order to fulfil them, however, He rejected the increasing mass of secondary regulations and restrictions, to some extent following precedents set by the Samaritans, the Sadducees, and the Essenes, but adopting a consistently spiritual

34. Epstein, *Judaism*, 107. Ibid., 119, "In order to escape Hadrian's common proscription of the Torah and to gain some temporary advantages, the Jewish Christians did not hesitate to renounce all the religious practices they had observed for about a century and, cutting themselves adrift from their own people, finally joined the mass of pagans who under the influence of Paul had during the intervening period been attracted to Christianity."

35. Dimont, *Jews, God and History*, 140. Ibid., 144, "Christianity was no longer a Jewish sect, for Paul had abandoned the Mosaic tradition."

36. Rebellion One, under Nero and Vespasian: AD 66–74. Rebellion Two, under Trajan: AD 115–17. Rebellion Three, under Hadrian: AD 132–35.

37. Dimont, *Jews, God and History*, 152–53.

38. Horsley, "Jesus Movements and the Renewal of Israel," 25, "The old construct of a monolithic Judaism glosses over the fundamental division and multiple conflicts that persisted for centuries in Judean and Galilean history."

39. Bright, *The Kingdom of God*, 196, "Judaism and Christianity early became two distinct, if closely related, religions."

attitude to ritual which was foreign to any of these groups."[40] However, any such mediating model hardly conforms to the reality the Spirit revealed in the New Testament. The impossibility of reconciliation rose under the weight of unruly events.

Whatever the mediating models and reconciling intentions, every circle of care carving Christianity out of Pharisaism, or Judaism, confronts (with restraint of language) a shaming downfall: *No, No, NO!* Any tampering with the Old Testament prophetic vision dislocates the historical progress under Jesus Christ's lordship,[41] each crossing a line for a guilt's reward, with its own adrenalin hit.

Christianity is the development of the first covenant reformation, Gen 3:14–19, over Noah, Abraham, Moses, and David. Yahweh himself, the Lord Jesus in the fullness of the time, finally reformed the promises and the

---

40. Albright, *From the Stone Age to Christianity*, 391–92.

Sanders, *Judaism*, 400, ". . . competing apologetic positions—(1) the Pharisees ran Judaism and were full of love for one and all; (2) the Pharisees ran Judaism and were awful—are influenced by the need to explain Christianity's break with Judaism. Jewish scholars have generally seen Jesus as a good Jew who had a few serious theological or legal debates with his contemporaries. Christianity was founded by Paul, not Jesus. It was Paul who exalted Jesus to such a degree that Christians broke with Jewish monotheism. That is, Jewish scholars have generally seen the break as *credal* and as being based on the doctrine that Jesus was divine."

Simon, *Jewish Sects at the Time of Jesus*, 135–36, ". . . it was with a Judaism (after A.D. 70) identified with Pharisaism that Christianity consummated its break. The revolutionary preaching of St. Paul and the developments of Christology in a direction contrary to traditional monotheism had increasingly transformed the at least relative tolerance enjoyed by the nascent church in Israel into hostility and hatred. From that time on a rather intransigent orthodoxy began to develop and harden into rabbinical Judaism."

41. Neusner, *Scriptures of the Oral Torah*, 23, "People really did differ about the same issues. These issues—the meaning of history, the identity of the Messiah, and the definition of Israel, or of God's instrument for embodying in a social group God's will—would define the foundations of the dispute from then on. So we find for the first time a genuine confrontation: people differed about a shared agendum in exactly the same terms."

Dodd, *The Meaning of Paul for Today*, 14, "The risen Christ is Victor indeed over death; but He is not Victor over the Pharisees. For all the raptures of the disciples, the great system of Pharisaic Judaism stands, as imposing, as self-sufficient, as ever. The tragic conflict is not yet resolved."

obligations. In this way,[42] Christianity "arose with Jesus of Nazareth."[43] The Christ shaped covenant history.

Hence, the Pharisaic drift, from which arose a world-class religion: normative rabbinic Judaism[44] sagging into a continual bending away from the eschatological covenant line. Begun in the post-Ezra era, the Hasidim-Pharisees founded another religion,[45] one at enmity with Yahweh, the Lord Jesus Christ. Specifically, the Pharisees continued this paradigmatic shift in direction, which public fissure Apostle Paul specified in Acts 13:44–47, 18:5–11, 28:23–28. At that time, the Apostle to the Gentiles purposefully turned from the Synagogue for the continuing Church.

---

42. Simon, *Jewish Sects at the Time of Jesus*, 133, ". . . orthodox Christianity did not proceed from just any form of historic Judaism. No, it is seen as proceeding from that true religion as old as humanity itself, represented and practiced by Adam, Noah, the patriarchs, and the prophets."

43. Albright, *From the Stone Age to Christianity*, 401.

44. Burrus, "Shifting the Focus of History," 16, "Judaism in the first centuries was a widely respected ancient *ethnos;* notable for its exclusivity, it also accommodated aspects of cultural adaptation and mission activity. The emergence of Christianity is therefore an extension of the adaptive development of Jewish identity in late antiquity. Outside observers initially understood early Christians as part of the Jewish *ethnos,* as did many Christians themselves."

45. Bronner, *Sects and Separatism During the Second Jewish Commonwealth*, 85, "With the destruction of the Temple, Pharisaism emerged triumphant, while all its opponents disappeared. Pharisaism continued to shape the character of Judaism, and the life and thought of the Jew for all times. It is true that Pharisaic Judaism stamped the Jewish religion with a legalistic tendency for all times, and made 'separation' one of its major characteristics. Yet, this was imperative."

Finkelstein, *The Pharisees*, xxi, "Pharisaism became Talmudism, Talmudism became Medieval Rabbinism, and Medieval Rabbinism became Modern Rabbinism. But throughout these changes of name, inevitable adaption of custom, and adjustment of Law, the spirit of the ancient Pharisee survives unaltered."

Chapter 4

The Oral Law in its Design

*L*AW THROUGHOUT NEW TESTAMENT literature depicts adaptive applications—the Old Testament as an encompassing whole, the Decalogue as
a lively unit, or the Oral Law as a deviant system, along with several special
meanings. *Law*, therefore, came with multiple sightlines, at times running
off into divergent directions, law is good, law is bad.[1] This is true, notably with respect to Pauline literature, specifically Galatians (*c.* AD 52) and
Romans (*c.* AD 58), documents written before the Matthew, Mark, Luke,
and John Gospels. The Apostle to the Gentiles died a martyr's death *c.* AD
60,[2] before which date, obviously, he wrote his provoking pastoral letters
to Spirit-adorned Churches. For the eschatologically-poised congregations
Paul addressed readily understood these weighty 'law' distinctives; listening members had heard him open the Hebrew Bible and speak to marked
effect. This was true with respect to the Galatian Churches, in Christ the
first he founded, Acts 13:13—14:23.[3] Different, the Roman congregation

1. Deissmann, *Paul,* 99, "The harsh expressions against the Law, which [Paul] occasionally uses, are outweighed by other passages, in which he strives to do justice to
the Law. Indeed he not infrequently continued to use the Law as authority quite in the
manner of his fathers."

Sandmel, *The Genius of Paul,* 32, "Where other Greek Jews found the Law an intellectual, and therefore a remote or theoretical problem, Paul found a deep personal difficulty,
not *about* the Law, but in his own observance of it. Had Paul not found this personal
difficulty, he would not have been led to a virtual abrogation of the Law."

2. Crossan, *The Birth of Christianity,* 15, "[Paul] was executed at Rome, in the faraway
capital of the empire, around 60 A.D."

3. Keck and Furnish, *Interpreting Biblical Texts,* 33, "Paul's letters are the oldest texts

consisted of many, Rom 16:1–23, whom he had met during his travels in Asia Minor and on Europe's eastern fringes, in Grecian lands. Never did the Lord Jesus abrogate the Law of Moses, or do away with the Decalogue.

Legal Identities

Because of arresting normative values for law, misunderstandings developed. At times, the apostle stressed the importance of the Decalogue; at times, through active misunderstanding, antinomians by common consent clutched purposefully at the *law is bad* theme. However, clearly, first readers of the Paul's Letters grasped the *law* and *law* distinctions, but hesitation and confusion deceived many of the Church since. Several timeworn instances prove the pressures of this revolutionizing spirit. "Paul's attitude to the historic Law of Moses is curiously contradictory on the surface. On the one hand it reflects for him that inexorable moral order which is in the nature of things. The nature of things is the will of God, and the law which reflects it must be of God, and therefore holy, spiritual, just and good. On the other hand he detests this law as the supreme instrument of slavery . . . ."[4] Confusion between these disconnected poles interrupted Spirit-guided reading notably in Pauline literature on the Law. However, to injure the darkness of distorted impressions within, an explanation of law designations clarifies controversy between two impressive legal systems.[5]

Depiction of these two clashing systems of law—one to life for gratitude, one to death for self-righteousness—in the ongoing covenant community, opens up the alarmingly effective design of the Oral Law.[6]

---

in the New Testament, First Thessalonians antedating the oldest Gospel, Mark, by almost two decades."

4. Dodd, *The Meaning of Paul for Today*, 71.

5. Keck and Furnish, *Interpreting Biblical Texts*, 42, "One's judgment about Paul's cultural heritage will also influence the way one reads and interprets his letters. That Paul was born into a Jewish family is beyond dispute, and we have his own testimony that until his conversion to Christianity he had been an earnest practitioner of the Jewish Law (Rom 11:1; 2 Cor 11:22; Gal 1:13–14; Phil 3:4–6; cf. Rom 9:1–3). While all students of Paul can agree on this much, there is substantial disagreements about the extent to which Paul, even before his conversion and dedication to a Gentile mission, had been acculturated to hellenistic society."

6. Fonrobert, "Jewish Christians, Judaizers, and Christian Anti-Judaism," 234, "According to that traditional narrative, the rabbis subsequently rarely felt compelled to engage their Christian rivals. They simply ignored the Christian rise to imperial power and devoted themselves to the task at hand, namely, the interpretation of the biblical laws and

The Larger Identity *(Italics for Oral Law references)*

At times the Law referred to the Old Testament in its entirety, the law and the prophets.[7] Gal 3:10, "For all who rely on *works of the law* are under a curse; for it is written, 'Cursed be every one who does not abide by all things written in the book of the law, and do them." Gal 4:21, "Tell me, you who desire to be *under law*,[8] do you not hear the law?" Rom 2:14, "When Gentiles who have not *the law* do by nature what *the law* requires, they are a law to themselves, even though they do not have the law." Rom 3:21, "But now the righteousness of God has been manifested apart from *the law*, although the law and the prophets bear witness to it." Rom 10:4, "For Christ is the end of *the law*, that every one who has faith may be justified." First readers of Paul's Letters were thoroughly familiar with this law designation. Heb 7:5, 8:4, 9:19, 10:1, 8; etc. Constant contact with this ground rule aspires to appreciate the capacious New Testament in its legal outlook.

The Sharper Identity *(Italics for Oral Law references)*

1. Predominantly, throughout New Testament literature, but specifically Paul's, primary reference to the Decalogue lays down its positive fervor; the Lord God gave the Ten to spell out the only way of gratitude for salvation. In the Old Testament as well as the New, despite the tally of years and centuries, this transmissibility of the Decalogue's purpose the Christ grounded in constancy, whatever political upheavals, boundary reallocations, and (external or internal) heretical attacks. Gal 2:15–16, "We ourselves, who are Jews by birth and not Gentile sinners, yet who know that a man is not justified by *works of the law* but through faith in Jesus Christ, even we have believed in Christ Jesus, in order to be justified by faith in Christ, and not

---

the development of the legal trajectory from Moses to Hillel and beyond. Christian writers, in the other hand, often did engage Judaism, considered to be their mother religion, later morphed into a competitive sibling. When they did so, the terms were typically supersessionist, spiteful, and otherwise derogatory: Judaism was viewed by ancient Christians as an antiquated religion at best, one whose true promise had been fulfilled in Christianity."

7. Matt 5:17, 7:12, 11:13, 22:40; Luke *16:16, 24:44;* Acts 24:14; etc.

Marrow, Paul, His Letters and His Theology, 209, ". . . Paul sees in 'the law and the prophets' our principal and only way to understanding what we mean when we confess our faith in the 'gospel concerning his Son' (Rom 1:3)."

8. Kittel, *Theological Dictionary of the New Testament,* Vol. IV, 1070, ". . . this must not be taken as an occasion to revive the issue whether there is a distinction between the use of *nomos* without the article and its use with the article."

by works of the law, because *by works of the law* shall no one be justified."[9] Gal 2:21, ". . . for if justification were through *the law,* then Christ died to no purpose." Gal 3:2, ". . . Did you receive the Spirit *by works of the law,* or by hearing with faith?" Gal 5:1, "For freedom Christ has set us free; stand fast therefore, and do not submit again to *a yoke of slavery.*" Gal 5:14, "For the whole law is fulfilled in one word, 'You shall love your neighbor as yourself.'" Gal 6:2, "Bear one another's burdens, and so fulfill the law of Christ." Etc. Never had Yahweh through the long Old Testament dispensation populated the Law, or keeping the Law, with powers to justify; its structural integrity laid open the only habitable way of gratitude.[10] Blatantly clear, however, Pharisaic betrayal of history in the Galatian Churches dislodged the Law from its deep roots of righteousness in Christ Jesus before the Father in favor of the Oral Law's shameless exploitation of self-righteousness.

The Letter to the Romans carried a similar warning against a stultifying process to pervert the international stature of the Decalogue. Rom 2:12, "All who have sinned without the law will also perish without the law, and all who have sinned *under the law* will be judged by the law." James 1:22–25; Rom 2:13, "For it is not the hearers of *the law* who are righteous before God, but the doers of the law who will be justified." Rom 2:15, "They show that what *the law* requires is written on their hearts, while their conscience also bears witness and their conflicting thoughts accuse or perhaps excuse them." In Rom 2:17–24 various phrases punctuate the same open-ended character with respect to the Ten, the Law ensures the primary means of living before God. Similarly, the next paragraph, Rom 2:25–29. The Lord God in thunderous Sinai revelation intensified and for ever established the fundamental importance of the Decalogue, that which the apostle carried into the depths of his normative ministry.

With consistency, then, Paul bared the confirmed endurance of the Law. Rom 3:19–20, "Now we know that whatever the law says it speaks to

---

9. Marrow, *Paul, His Letters and His Theology,* 95, "Paul's opponents in Galatia seem to have been of this variety of Jewish Christians. They offered Christians an 'added plus' to their all-sufficient faith in the gospel."

10. Keck and Furnish, *Interpreting Biblical Texts,* 78, "Nowhere else does Paul write so negatively about the Law. Here he does so because he sees in the Galatian situation something the Galatians themselves do not see—that it cannot be the intent of the Christ-event to produce a situation in which the relation to God depends upon fulfilling a structure of obligations; for both Jews and Gentiles—each group in its own way—had been in that situation before. In the nonpolemical situation of Romans, Paul can write that God's aim in sending the Son was 'that the just requirement of the law might be fulfilled in us, who walk . . . according to the Spirit.' (Rom 8:4)."

those who are *under the law*, so that every mouth may be stopped, and the whole world may be held accountable to God. For no human being will be justified in his sight *by works of the law*, since through the law comes knowledge of sin." Rom 3:21, 28, 31, 4:14, 15, 16, 7:4, 5, 7, 8, 9, 12, 14. Rom 7:16, "Now if I do what I do not want, I agree that the law is good." Rom 8:3–4, "For God has done what the law, weakened by the flesh, could not do: sending his own Son in the likeness of sinful flesh and for sin, he condemned sin in the flesh, in order that the just requirement of the law might be fulfilled in us, who walk not according to the flesh but according to the Spirit." Rom 9:4, "They are Israelites, and to them belong the sonship, the glory, the covenants, the giving of the law, the worship, and the promises." Rom 13:8, ". . . for he who loves his neighbor has fulfilled the law." Rom 13:10, ". . . love is the fulfilling of the law." Throughout luminous Romans, too, Paul measured out the high standard of living by way of the Decalogue.[11]

Elsewhere also, in other Letters, the Ten Commandments compose the only life acceptable in Jesus Christ before the Father. First Tim 1:6–7, "Certain persons by swerving from [a good conscience and sincere faith] have wandered away into vain discussions, desiring to be teachers of *the law*, without understanding either what they are saying or the things about which they make assertions." First Tim 1:8–9, "Now we know that the law is good, if any one uses it lawfully, understanding this, that the law is not laid down for the just . . . ." Heb 7:11, "Now if perfection had been attainable through the Levitical priesthood (for under it the people received the law), what further need would there have been for another priest to arise after the order of Melchizedek, rather than one named after the order of Aaron?" Heb 8:10, "This is the covenant that I will make with the house of Israel after those days, says the Lord: I will put my laws into their minds, and write them on their hearts, and I will be their God, and they shall be my people." Heb 10:16, 10:28, "A man who has violated the law of Moses dies without mercy at the testimony of two or three witnesses." James 1:25, "But he who looks into the perfect law, the law of liberty, and perseveres, being no hearer that forgets but a doer that acts, he shall be blessed in his doing." James 2:8–9, "If you really fulfil the royal law, according to the scripture, 'You shall love your neighbor as yourself,' you do well. But if you show partiality, you

---

11. Marrow, *Paul, His Letters and His Theology*, 110, "The temptation to be one's own master, to 'self-lordship,' 'not by transgressing the Law, but by fulfilling it according to [one's] own interpretation (. . .), has proven too strong to resist."

commit sin, and are convicted by the law as transgressors." James 2:10–12, "For whoever keeps the whole law but fails in one point has become guilty of all of it. For he who said, 'Do not commit adultery,' said also, 'Do not kill.' If you do not commit adultery but do kill, you have become a transgressor of the law. So speak and so act as those who are to be judged under the law of liberty." James 4:11, "Do not speak evil against one another, brethren. He that speaks evil against a brother or judges his brother, speaks evil against the law and judges the law." Second Pet 2:21, "For it would have been better for them never to have known the way of righteousness than after knowing it to turn back from the holy commandment delivered to them." First John 2:3, "And by this we may be sure that we know him, if we keep his commandments." First John 2:4, 3:22–24, 5:2, 3. Etc. Consistently and persistently throughout the New Testament, the Spirit of the Father and the Son exhibited the Decalogue as a positive good, the way for all upright in Christ to walk.[12]

2. In contrast, for a secondary activity, the Lawgiver singled out the Commandments to expose sin and the covetousness of sinfulness. Gal 2:19, "For I through the law died to *the law*, that I might live to God." (By high exposure to the Law, Paul died with respect to earning a righteousness and a salvation dependent on the Oral Law.) Gal 3:5, "Does he who supplies the Spirit to you and works miracles among you do so *by works of the law*, or by hearing with faith?" Gal 3:10, "For all who rely on *works of the law* are under a curse; for it is written, 'Cursed be every one who does not abide by all things written in the book of the law, and do them.'" Gal 3:11–12, "Now it is evident that no man is justified before God by *the law*; for 'He who through faith is righteous shall live'; but *the law* does not rest on faith, for 'he who does them shall live by them.'" Gal 3:13, "Christ redeemed us from the curse of *the law*, having become a curse for us—for it is written, 'Cursed be every one who hangs on a tree.'" Gal 3:17–18, "This is what I mean: the law, which came four hundred and thirty years afterward, does not annul a covenant previously ratified by God, so as to make the promise void. For if the inheritance is by *the law*, it is no longer by promise; but God gave it to Abraham by a promise." Gal 3:19p, "Why then the law? It was added because of transgression, till the offspring should come to whom the

---

12. Keck and Furnish, *Interpreting Biblical Texts*, 75, ". . . this divine freedom to initiate a new rectified relation to God is consonant with the real meaning of Scripture ('the law and the prophets bear witness to it'). Thus Paul undertakes a fresh interpretation of Scripture, and of the call of Israel."

promise had been made." Gal 3:21–22, "Is the law then against the promises of God? Certainly not; for if *a law* had been given which could make alive, then righteousness would indeed be by *the law.* But the scripture consigned all things to sin, that what was promised to faith in Jesus Christ might be given to those who believe." Gal 5:19–24, 6:13, "For even those who receive circumcision do not themselves keep *the law*, but they desire to have you circumcised that they may glory in your flesh." Rom 3:20, "For no human being will be justified in his sight *by works of the law*, since through the law comes knowledge of sin." Rom 4:15, "For *the law* brings wrath, but where there is no law there is no transgression." Rom 5:20–21, "*Law* came in, to increase trespass; but where sin increased, grace abounded all the more, so that, as sin reigned in death, grace also might reign through righteousness to eternal life through Jesus Christ our Lord." Rom 7:5, "While we were living in the flesh, our sinful passions, aroused by *the law*, were at work in our members to bear fruit for death." Col 3:5–11; 1 Tim 1:8–11; Rev 21:8, 22:15; etc.

The Law, that is, the tenured Decalogue manifested double duty: 1) the capacity to lay open the evident way of gratitude, and 2) the facility to lay bare the sinfulness of breaking the Commandments, while the Tradition of the Elders led off into condemnation.

A Demeaning Identity

The Oral Law, however, interrupted the covenant way and deviously inserted an alien competitive measure and excessive force to subvert the Commandments and push attention into the covetousness of autosoterism for the Jewish way.[13] The 613 *mitzvot*, the *paradosis* of the Elders, the force of Judaism,[14] constructed on scribal authority a legal system competing in

13. Sanders, *Judaism*, 413–414, "A description of Pharisaism by Paul would be even more helpful, since we would discover what counted as Pharisaism in the Diaspora. The only direct information that Paul gives is that Pharisees were zealous for the law (implied in Gal. 1.14), which coincides perfectly with what we learn from Josephus, but it does not get us far."

Marrow, *Paul, His Letters and His Theology*, 30, "Circumcised on the eighth day, of the people of Israel, of the tribe of Benjamin, a Hebrew born of Hebrews; as to the law a Pharisee, as to zeal a persecutor of the church, as to righteousness under the law blameless (Phil 3:5–6; see Rom 11:1; 2 Cor 11:22)."

14. Horsley, "Unearthing a People's History," 23–24, "In the ancient world in which the Gospels originated, however, religion was not separated from the political-economic

the Church for supremacy over the Decalogue.[15] "The God of Israel gave his people a law to keep them close to him; [the Rabbis] made the law into a means of getting a hold on him, to 'boast of [their] relation to God (Rom 2:17)."[16] Every aspect of Judaism stressed for identifying the Oral Law of the Jews.

The Apostle to the Gentiles remorsefully recounted on occasion his Pharisaic past. Gal 1:13–14, "For you have heard of my former life in Judaism,[17] how I persecuted the church of God violently and tried to destroy it; and I advanced in Judaism beyond many of my own age among my people, so extremely zealous was I for the traditions of my fathers." Paul carried this burdensome memory to his death.

---

life. In fact, at the time of Jesus there was no such thing yet as a religion called Judaism, judging from our sources such as the Gospels, the Dead Sea scrolls, or the contemporary Judean historian, Josephus." Acts13:43; Gal 1:13.

15. Sandmel, *The Genius of Paul*, 28–29, "In the interpretative literature, we quite frequently encounter the view that [Paul's] nullification of the Law of Moses (*but not the Bible*) was the concession he made in order to gain converts among the pagans; to re-phrase this vulgarly, Paul was offering a reduced rate to entice customers."

16. Marrow, *Paul, His Letters and His Theology*, 106.

17. Rivkin, *A Hidden Revolution*, 78, "The Judaism Paul speaks of in Galatians must have been identical with the Judaism of Philippians, namely, that of the Pharisees. However, whereas Paul refers to it as the Law of the Pharisees in Philippians, he identifies it with the 'traditions of the fathers' (*to patrikon paradoseon*) in Galatians. And since the term *paradosis* is used by both Josephus (*Ant*. XIII:297, 408) and Mark (7:3, 5, 8, 9, 13) to designate the nonwritten Law, it is evident that Paul is reiterating that as to the Law he had been a Pharisee." Ibid., 123, "Paul's definition, as we have seen, is confirmed by the Synoptics. Mark, Matthew and Luke portray the Pharisees as that scholar class which championed the authority of the twofold Law, the Written Law and the *paradosis*. The definition drawn from them enlarges that derived from Paul, since it neither contradicts it or adds any data that would be incompatible with Paul's definition."

Sandmel, *The Genius of Paul*, 17, "The Jewish heritage of Paul was primarily the Old Testament. There is no reason to be skeptical of his statement that in his study of Judaism he had surpassed his fellow students of his own age."

Pollock, *The Apostle*, 6–7, "Under the fragile, gentle Gamaliel, a contrast with the leaders of the rival School of Shammai, Paul learned to dissect a text until scores of possible meanings were disclosed according to the considered opinion of generations of rabbis, who had obscured the original sense by layers of tradition to protect an Israelite from the least possible infringement of the Law; and, illogically, to help him avoid its inconveniences."

1. Paul,[18] writing before the Gospels according to Matthew, Mark, Luke, and John,[19] preferred different nomenclature relative to the Oral Law. Rather than adopting the Tradition of the Elders and the Oral Law, he wrote of the written code, pointing thereby to early attempts at preserving literally the memory-based Oral Law, before the final and authoritative inscripturation of the Mishnah. Rom 2:27, "Then those who are physically uncircumcised but keep the law will condemn you who have the written code and circumcision but break the law." Rom 7:6, "But now we are discharged from the law, dead to that which held us captive, so that we serve not under the old written code but in the new life of the Spirit." To substitute this written code for the Decalogue confuses. The Decalogue, as the lustrous way of gratitude, never held any one captive, but the Oral Law did. Gal 3:23–29.

Paul repeatedly throughout the Letters overrode the contestable functioning of the written code. Second Cor 3:5–6, "Not that we are competent of ourselves to claim anything as coming from us; our competence is from God, who has made us competent to be ministers of a new covenant, not in a written code but in the Spirit; for the written code kills, but the Spirit gives life." In this place of scorn, the apostle distinguished and separated the tablets of stone, 2 Cor 3:3, and the letters on stone, 2 Cor 3:7, from the written code, the *grammatos*, or *gramma*, an exegetical counsel constantly to be borne in mind. Nevertheless, for the Pharisees, on account of living for a righteousness based in the written code,[20] the Old Testament turned thereby into a dispensation of death, 2 Cor 3:7. Because the *paradosis* people had subverted the Old Testament history Paul pointed out that they had covered their faces, hence no longer able to see accurately. Second Cor

18. Dodd, *The Meaning of Paul for Today*, 73, "It was therefore of the utmost importance that one who knew from the inside the system which Jesus attacked should, through being compelled to confront his own exaggerated legalism with his Master's independence, point the way to the more fundamental implication of what Jesus had done. Paul found himself driven to reconsider, not this precept or that, but the whole nature of law as such; and it is a mark of his real greatness that he did so on the basis, not of theory merely, but of experience."

19. Rivkin, *A Hidden Revolution*, 76, "For these writers, the Pharisees were those Jews who had vexed Jesus during his lifetime and who had participated in bringing about his crucifixion. For them the Pharisees were objects of hostility."

20. Keck and Furnish, *Interpreting Biblical Texts*, 102, "[Paul] did insist that the synagogue did not rightly understand its own text (2 Cor 3:12–18), but from his angle, the Jews' problem was not neglect but unenlightened zeal (Rom 10:2–3)."

Marrow, *Paul, His Letters and His Theology*, 106, "It was . . . more difficult for Paul to draw Christians away from the seductions of the law than for the prophets to keep Israel free from alien gods."

3:15, "Yes, to this day whenever Moses is read a veil lies over their minds." That veil consisted of the Oral Law. Thus, they earned under law not life but death—an eternal existence abounding in divine wrath.

2. *Under the law* or *under law* refers first to the Pharisaic ethic. Gal 3:23, "Now before faith came, we were confined under the law, kept under restraint until faith should be revealed." For Paul and companions this *under the law* captured all caught up in Pharisaism.[21] The Oral Law as well as its earliest codified forms incarcerated all adherents within an appalling legal system. Rom 7:6. However, the Lord Jesus through the apostolic party working in Galatia had called many out of area synagogues to establish his congregations of the Church. Gal 4:4–5, "But when the time had fully come, God sent forth his Son, born of woman, born *under the law*, to redeem those who were *under the law* so that we might receive adoption as sons." Christ Jesus through the Incarnation and for voluntary servitude entered into the interiors of the Oral Law, the Church at the end of the Old Testament dispensation. The Tradition of the Elders, however, did not imprison him; rather, he worked salvation in the Church as he had done throughout the Old Testament dispensation, commissioning Adam, Noah, Abraham, Moses, and David. Gal 4:21, "Tell me, you who desire to be under law, do you not hear the law?" Gal 5:4, "You are severed from Christ, you who would be justified by *the law*; you have fallen away from grace." The Galatian Churches, suddenly as bewitched,[22] sought return to the Pharisaic legal system and, hence, bondage to an elaborately unbiblical law. Therefore, Gal 5:18, "But if you are led by the Spirit you are not *under the law*." Instead, in the freedom of Christ all Christian congregations as one walked in the way of the Commandments, Spirit-moved.

In Romans too, Paul, alive and acute berated captivity under the law, Rom 8:15, imprisonment wrought by the Oral Law. Rom 2:12, "All who have sinned without the law will also perish without the law, and all who have sinned *under the law* will be judged by the law." Rom 3:19, "Now we

21. A misunderstanding: Keck and Furnish, *Interpreting Biblical Texts*, 106, "The Law is not inherently 'against' the way of faith; rather, it is a transitional authority, similar to the *paidago*(set macron over o)*gos* who has charge of a child for a set period of time (Gal 3:15—4:11)."

22. Sandmel, *The Genius of Paul*, 112, "A 'Judaizer' is not a Jew, but rather a Christian who advocates and practices Jewish observances."

Marrow, *Paul, His Letters and His Theology*, 102, "They who had had a taste of the exhilarating freedom of the gospel were all too willing to 'submit again to a yoke of slavery' (Gal 5:1)."

know that whatever the law says it speaks to those who are *under the law*, so that every mouth may be stopped, and the whole world may be held accountable to God." Rom 3:21, 6:14, "For sin will have no dominion over you, since you are not under law but under grace." Rom 9:31–32, ". . . that Israel who pursued the righteousness which is based *on law* did not succeed in fulfilling that *law*. Why? Because they did not pursue it through faith, but as if it were based on works." Rom 10:5, "Moses writes that the man who practices the righteousness which is based *on the law* shall live by it." Lev 18:5. With provocative evidence and public pronouncement, the apostle served notice first to the Church at Rome.[23]

Elsewhere too, Paul used the *under the law* designation to distinguish the Oral Law. Phil 3:4–5, ". . . as to righteousness *under the law* blameless."[24] Phil 3:9, ". . . and be found in [Christ], not having a righteousness of my own, based *on law*, but that which is through faith in Christ, the righteousness from God that depends on faith." Col 2:16, 2:20–23; 1 Cor 9:20–21.

This *under the law* and *under law* terminology applied to the Tradition of the Elders and its Oral Law in its earliest codifications, the huge selfish bubble which held its believers embedded in a captivity wherein to exult on the illusive terrain of self-righteousness. Gal 2:4–5. However, as indicated above, specifically in Paul, a sentence and a paragraph may have reference to two different laws, the Oral Law and the Decalogue, or the Old Testament. In any case, the literary environment and a sharp eye clarify the visibility problem of any *law* word.

3. Because of fluidity in the Aramaic, *under the law* at times had a positive connotation, one of freedom. Heb 9:22, "Indeed, under the law almost everything is purified with blood, and without the shedding of blood there is no forgiveness of sins." James 2:12, "So speak and so act as those who are

23. Keck and Furnish, *Interpreting Biblical Texts*, 74, "If God's rectitude expresses itself 'apart from law' (Rom 3:21), then the Law's nexus of achievement/reward is not the base on which to understand God's intergrity (sic)." Law, then, as the Oral Law.

24. Rivkin, *A Hidden Revolution*, 77, "Paul, in striving to establish his right to reject the need for circumcision, spreads before the Philippians his Jewish credentials. He is determined to still the opposition by an impressive listing of his Jewish ties, . . . (no convert to Judaism he). And then to make crystal-clear his relationship to the Law, Paul affirms that he was a Pharisee, who could pride himself on this steadfast loyalty—'as to righteousness under the law blameless."

Marrow, *Paul, His Letters and His Theology*, 33, ". . . it is a passage that has been prey to the temptations of facile dismissal as mere hyperbole, just another rhetorical device to serve the manifestly polemical and apologetic ends of the letter to the Philippians (see Phil 3:2–3). But, to do Paul justice, one must take him at his word."

to be judged under the law of liberty." In Christ, the Law runs in its positive bedding.

4. On occasion, Paul referred to single commandments, an *entoles*. Rom 7:8, "But sin, finding opportunity in the commandment, wrought in me all kinds of covetousness." In this point of view, obviously, the Apostle specified the Tenth. In the world of the *nomos*, the Church, the instructive Tenth enforced its sweeping presence. Rom 7:7–12, 13. Similarly, Heb 7:18; 2 Pet 3:2; 1 John 2:7–11, 3:23, 4:21. Each reference keyed in an explicit commandment, not the Ten as a whole.[25]

5. Throughout the New Testament times, the Oral Law carried on both the Jewish Sabbath and the circumcision rite; each of these Old Testament distinctives the LORD God had enforced as covenant statutes. With respect to the Sabbath,[26] Exod 20:8–11; Deut 5:12–15, 34:28, and Exod 31:15–16, "Six days shall work be done, but the seventh day is a sabbath of solemn rest, holy to the LORD; whoever does any work on the sabbath day shall be put to death. Therefore the people of Israel shall keep the sabbath, observing the sabbath throughout their generations, as a perpetual covenant." Since the initiation of this covenant, Sabbath observances sharply distinguished Jews from neighbors. However, the sign of the covenant, circumcision, had deeper roots and more physicality, tracing its origin to Abraham. Gen 17:10–11, "This is my covenant, which you shall keep, between me and you and your descendants after you: Every male among you shall be circumcised. You shall be circumcised in the flesh of your foreskins, and it shall be a sign of the covenant between me and you." Rom 2:25–29, 3:30, 4:9–12; 1 Cor 7:17–24; etc.[27] Because of these commandments the Oral-Law enforcers carried on with the Sabbath and the circumcision rite, even though the Messiah had accomplished all the Law.

---

25. Marrow, *Paul, His Letters and His Theology*, 34, "Paul's polemic against the law and against legalism has accustomed us to see the material impossibility of fulfilling 'the law.'"

26. Klinghoffer, *Why the Jews Rejected Jesus*, 56, "Consider the Sabbath, that most distinctive of all Jewish institutions. The Hebrew scriptures offer only the scantiest idea of what constitutes a departure from the practice of Sabbath rest. Nowhere is the category of forbidden creative activities, reminding the Jew of God's creation of the world and mistranslated as 'work' (*melachah*), ever defined. Only the oral Torah does this, and in great detail."

Major, et al., *The Mission and Message of Jesus*, 481, "In the first century A.D. the observance of the Sabbath had become the hall-mark of Judaism. It was something by which every Jew, without distinction of age or sex, was shown to belong to the Chosen People."

27. This living symbol the Christ reformed into the baptismal sacrament. Col 2:8–15.

During the first decades of the New Testament Church, the Circumcision Party in the Jerusalem congregation badgered and buffeted apostles and elders to compel all of Christ from the Gentiles to keep the Sabbath Oral-Law style and undergo this brief surgical procedure. According to their terrible-when-slighted convictions, faith in Christ Jesus for righteousness required additional work, one beginning with circumcision and publicized with Sabbath traditions.[28]

Paul, early on, recognized the double standard in the factional Circumcision Party's faith in Christ for justification, the weightier element its added imposition of circumcision for works-righteousness. Gal 2:1–9,

> . . . after fourteen years I went up again to Jerusalem with Barnabas, taking Titus[29] along with me. I went up by revelation; and I laid before them (but privately before those who were of repute) the gospel which I preach among the Gentiles, lest somehow I should be running or had run in vain. But even Titus, who was with me, was not compelled to be circumcised, though he was a Greek. But because false brethren secretly brought in, who slipped in to spy out our freedom which we have in Christ Jesus, that they might bring us into bondage—to them we did not yield submission even for a moment, that the truth of the gospel might be preserved for you. And from those who were reputed to be something (what they were makes no difference to me; God shows no partiality)— those, I say, who were of repute added nothing to me; but on the contrary, when they saw that I had been entrusted with the gospel to the uncircumcised, just as Peter has been entrusted with the gospel to the circumcised (for he who worked through Peter for the mission to the circumcised worked through me also for the

28. Keck and Furnish, *Interpreting Biblical Texts*, 76, "Given the Galatian trend toward accepting circumcision, Paul insists that 'every man who receives circumcision . . . is bound to keep the whole law' (5:3). Law, however, is precisely that structure of the God/human relationship from which Christ has freed believers." The Oral law, that is!

Sanders, *Judaism*, 213, "Jewish families circumcised their sons. It is a slightly curious fact that even though Jews were not the only circumcised males in the Mediterranean world, nevertheless both insiders and outsiders regarded circumcision as distinctively Jewish."

Asch, *The Apostle*, 465, ". . . if the external circumcision of the body become the only gate through which there is entry into the Kingdom of Heaven; if only through the circumcision of the flesh one can become a son of Abraham, Isaac, and Jacob; then, I say, all our labour is in vain; for if justification is only through the Torah, then the Messiah died in vain."

29. Marrow, *Paul, His Letters and His Theology*, 86, "What Paul did was to take with him to Jerusalem a test case, Titus; and Titus 'though he was a Greek . . . was not compelled to be circumcised' (Gal 2:3)."

> Gentiles), and when they perceived the grace that was given to me, James and Cephas and John, who were reputed to be pillars, gave to me and Barnabas the right hand of fellowship, that we should go to the Gentiles and they to the circumcised.

Titus' uncircumcision became the test case. The apostles with James too believed for the New Testament dispensation the irrelevancy of circumcision with respect to righteousness in Christ Jesus. Only, false brethren demanded in addition to believing righteousness in the Savior the work of circumcision for salvation. Therefore, Paul to the Galatian Churches, Gal 5:3, "I testify again to every man who receives circumcision that he is bound to keep the whole law." Not the lenient Oral Law, but the unfenceable Decalogue in its entirety, to perfection, even as far as removal of covetousness from secretive depths of heart. This acute sense of justice for legal and ethical perfection with respect to the Ten controls the New Testament damnation upon the Tradition of the Elders. They from the Gentiles who fell victim to the Pharisee-minded Circumcision Party the Lord Jesus then compelled to keep the Law entire; circumcision locked them into the impossible, autosoterism, self-salvation, along with the Pharisees. This consuming fire for all under the Pharisaic legalics underscored throughout the New Testament canon every condemnation upon the Oral Law.

For and in the Church, however, the Christ had defeated and abrogated the way to Jewish righteousness. Gal 5:6, "For in Christ Jesus neither circumcision nor uncircumcision is of any avail, but faith working through love." Gal 6:12–15, "It is those who want to make a good showing in the flesh that would compel you to be circumcised, and only in order that they may not be persecuted for the cross of Christ. For even those who receive circumcision do not themselves keep the law, but they desire to have you circumcised that they may glory in your flesh. . . . For neither circumcision counts for anything, nor uncircumcision, but a new creation." Rather, Christ Jesus discharged his own from the Law pharisaically interpreted, never to add works in order to achieve salvation, while he upheld the Ten for expressive gratitude in salvation. In the Church, only enemies of the Cross reverse this order. Phil 3:18. First Cor 7:18–19, "Was any one at the time of his call already circumcised? Let him not seek to remove the marks of circumcision. Was any one at the time of his call uncircumcised? Let him not seek circumcision. For neither circumcision counts for anything nor uncircumcision, but keeping the commandments of God." As the rule of thankfulness! For all believers, the old of the Oral Law with its unending entitlement to righteousness passed away; the continually new gratitude conquered. Therefore, Phil 3:2–3, "Look out for the dogs, look out for the evil-workers, look out for those who mutilate the flesh.[30] For we are the true circumcision, who worship God in spirit, and glory in Christ Jesus, and put no confidence in the flesh." Phil 3:9, ". . . not having a righteousness of my own, based on [the Oral law], but that which is through faith in Christ, the righteousness from God that depends on faith."[31] Thus, the generosity[32] of the Lord Jesus broke through the confusion and conflict imposed by the Circumcision Party he himself had drawn into the Church.[33]

In various New Testament places, *law* stands out with special significance, as the ". . . against such there is no law," Gal 5:23. In the Scriptures, the Lord Jesus placed no prohibitions against the fruit of the Spirit, which comes from living the Commandments, no restrictions on the gratitude according to the Ten and, therefore, no barriers to the love commandment.

According to Rom 7:1–3, the law of marriage since Gen 2 encapsulates for the godly in life all commandments with respect to the institution of marriage, to which others also do well to listen.

In Rom 7:7–12, with respect to the depth and extent of the Faith, Paul found "another law at war with the law of my mind," "the law of sin," which law he perceived as a rule, an overriding proclivity to achieve all sorts of lusts. For a similar sense, but to achieve peace and order, 1 Cor 7:17p, "This is my rule in all the churches."[34]

---

30. To read with caution: Sandmel, *The Genius of Paul*, 30n, "See Romans 2:21–24 and 8–9 for examples of Paul's partisanship and unfairness; and for his questionable taste, see Gal. 5:12, which is to be translated 'I wish that those who unsettle you (about circumcision) would castrate themselves.' See also Philippians 3:2, where Paul, in speaking of circumcision, says: 'Look out for the dogs, look out for the evil-workers, look out for those who mutilate the flesh.'"

31. Marrow, *Paul, His Letters and His Theology*, 41, "In other words, what was radically altered was precisely Paul's view of salvation. The new understanding of salvation was so different that it rendered any prior understanding, not erroneous, but worthless, impotent, and helpless."

32. Ibid., 97–98, "The gospel of Jesus Christ in itself brought salvation to those who believed—and there was room neither for, nor possibility of, adding anything no matter how 'holy and spiritual and good.'"

33. Ibid., 103, "In the letter to the Galatians, Paul's argument for Christian freedom is, principally, an argument for freedom from the 'yoke of slavery' (Gal 5:1) of the law. His own conversion did really mean tearing down (Gal 2:18) the whole secure structure of the law which he had erected like some secure bulwark around himself."

34. Ibid., 93, "Paul speaks of the law as 'holy . . . spiritual . . . good,' and of the

These different senses of law mean more a rule than a legal entity as the Commandments. Again, the context influences and determines the *law* referents: the initial readers of the Letters were familiar with the terminology and made the distinctives quickly, for thus the apostle had taught for living intensely in the churches. Frankly, it is time for all the Church to catch up, learning to distinguish the biblical way from the Jewish way.

The Law with its springs of benediction is the standard for living and the measure of judgment.

In contrast, the Oral Law is the demeaning pharisaical standard for self-righteousness.[35]

Thus far the Oral Law in its historical design.

⁎

---

commandment as 'holy and just and good' (Rom 7:12, 14, 16). The requirements of the law are 'just' (Rom 8:4). It finds its ultimate fulfillment in love: [Rom 13:10]."

35. Sandmel, *The Genius of Paul*, 48, "Out of the misunderstanding of what Torah meant to rabbinic Jews, there emerged two reactions among Protestants, in particular since the 1870's: (1) the identification of Judaism with 'legalism' and (2) a supercilious and condescending attitude both to Judaism and to legalism itself. Out of some of this Protestant literature one would infer something which no Jew has ever experienced: that the Torah was a burden."

Conclusion One

IN ORDER TO MAINTAIN its self-righteousness in perpetuity, the Hasidic/ Pharisaic movement intended to block and bar the Lord Jesus. This, for instance, the parable of the wicked tenants clarified amidst abuse and death. Matt 21:33–43; Mark 12:1–12; Luke 20:9–18. With this parable, the Lord Jesus defined and condemned the Tradition of the Elders in its long-term plans.

Barrier to the Incarnation

1. The Pharisaic movement from its inception refined and expanded its legal system to block the Incarnation. These enemies of the Christ had developed a separate righteousness accomplished by fulfilling the jot and tittle of the rabbinic proscriptions and prescriptions. By means of this awesome legal system, which post-70 AD swallowed remaining Sadducees too, its movers and shakers by monotheism had broken the First Commandment, raising up with a monopolistic claim on the Church an alternative deity, an absentee god.[1] Rather than bow in the pain of repentance, they therefore wanted nothing to do with the Christ, the present God.

Jewish monotheism bred its own salvation, a judicious living of the Oral Law. Hence, Jews, strenuously, to the death, sought every means possible to prevent the Word from becoming flesh. They had their own god, similar to the nations, and their own system of righteousness, similar to the nations. With might and main, they barred the coming of the sovereign Son in the fullness of time.

1. Dodd, *The Meaning of Paul for Today*, 37.

2. With every means at its disposal, the Pharisaic movement from its beginning conspired against the Lord coming in the flesh, Jesus Christ. Before the Incarnation, they wanted nothing of Yahweh. Every day they rejected his messianic authority in favor of another, a fiery warrior to remove Roman imperialism from the Land of Promise and to institute the Kingdom, then disappear, they with savage ambition in solid command of the future.

For centuries before Christ, the Pharisees with the connivance of the Sadducees built a momentous barrier to the Incarnation and Jesus' eternal lordship.[2]

Barrier to the Crucifixion

1. Unable to prevent the Incarnation, the Jews proceeded with a vengeance to kill Jesus in Nazareth by casting him from a cliff top, Luke 4:29, and in Jerusalem by stoning, John 8:59, 10:31. By murder, they wanted an end to his lordship, shut away the prophetic word, and prevent him as the Priest from accomplishing the Crucifixion and, in fact, the reformation of the Church.

Because of Roman dominion, only the ruling governor/procurator/prefect imposed the death sentence. Purposefully, then, the Jews, Pharisees and Sadducees, pushed for death by crucifixion and eliminate the Christ; to kill him for common treason to Roman authority became the 'sensible' way, without calling down upon them the fury of vindictive Pontius Pilate for an illegally imposed death sentence.

2. By excising Jesus Christ from the Church, they perceived hope for their monotheism. At unsuspecting cost to themselves, they sealed off the revelation of the Son who came to make the Father known, and the Father with the Son to reveal the Holy Spirit. Hardened in religiosity, church leaders and other members denied the Old Testament prophetic revelation of the Son of God/Son of man. They made the Crucifixion the defining moment of Pharisaism.

Yet, to reestablish his Church and proclaim his dominion to a remnant, the Christ nevertheless took some of Old Israel to fulfill his covenant promise to Abraham, forming the new and eternal Israel. Matt 11:25–30; Luke 10:21–22.

---

2. Rivkin, *A Hidden Revolution*, 32, "The New Testament writers saw the Pharisees as the stumbling blocks, barring Jesus from reaching out to the people."

Barrier to the Mission

Post-Pentecost, as Jesus expanded the missionary reality of the Gospel beyond Israel among the Gentiles, synagogue leadership beginning in Pisidian Antioch, Acts 13:44–47, maligned and blasphemed the word of the Lord. Acts 18:5–6, 28:23–25. In the Jerusalem Church, the Circumcision Party, Acts 11:2, 15:1, and elsewhere, Titus 1:10, to the bitter end resisted the word of God. They wanted inside and outside the covenant community nothing of the coming of the Kingdom and the new creation. However much the Jews on the frontlines of resistance threw up barriers and blockades to the Christ and his apostles, the Church grew. Acts 28:28, "Let it be known to you then that this salvation of God has been sent to the Gentiles; they will listen." The Lord Jesus intended the Gospel as the light to the nations.

Christ through the apostles met the resistance of the Oral Law proponents inside the Church with an array of condemnations; the Lord Jesus was done with them and solidified the anti-church in the enmity of covetousness. Early on, with Paul leading, the Head of the Church made the glory of grace shine forth everywhere.

Thus, throughout the New Testament canon, the Christ exposed, condemned, and conquered the design of the Oral Law.

Straightforward, overall, Jesus and his Spirit-bound apostles revealed the course, the malice, the eclipse, and the design of the Tradition of the Elders, therewith to glorify the Father.

Conclusion Two

Various explanations for tensions between Christianity and Pharisaism/
Judaism enter any work on the locale in which the Spirit authored the New
Testament canon. Critical thinkers have always sought to understand this
religious milieu.

> "The obtuseness of Jesus' generation is indicated in his scathing
> observation that they can predict the next day's weather, but they
> cannot discern the infinitely more significant change that is taking
> place through Jesus: the inbreaking of the Kingdom of God (Luke
> 12:54–56). Preoccupied with workaday affairs, they are more con-
> cerned about the rain clouds blowing in off the Mediterranean and
> the searing winds from the desert to the southeast than they are
> about the breakup of the present order implicit in the words and
> works of Jesus."[1]

This argument Kee based on Pharisaic ignorance, inability to read the
signs of the times.

> "The Godfearers were a fruitful recruiting ground for Christian-
> ity, but their presence also testified to the appeal Judaism had for
> pagans, an appeal that did not end with the coming of Christi-
> anity, so Christianity was in a struggle with Judaism for their al-
> legiance. Much of the tension between Jews and Christians and
> the Christian polemical literature against the Jews (even when

1. Kee, *Jesus in History*, 80–81.
Finkelstein, *The Pharisees*, 99, "To avoid being lost in Canaanite superstition, Persian
insobriety, Egyptian licentiousness, and Roman ferocity, which had conquered Greece
itself, the Pharisee determined to hold on with almost superhuman strength to the traditions of his ancestors."

academic and not reflecting real contact) resulted from this sense of competition."[2]

This argument Ferguson based on missionary rivalry.

"Christianity and Judaism have lived side by side and in each other's presence for nineteen hundred years and throughout that span have continually contested as to which was the true heir of the covenant with the Father."[3]

This argument Kirsch based on legitimacy, ownership of the covenant.

"We are left with two religious communities that were actually very close to one another, that for a time actually shared one scripture, the Hebrew Bible, but that were driven apart by incompatible exclusivist claims. Each community saw itself as the true people of the biblical God, and saw its rival as the impostor."[4]

This argument Kirsch based on family enmity.

However, Christian/Jewish hostility the Bible's Author revealed preparatory to the reformation of the covenant with Abraham. Gen 12:1-3,

"Now the LORD said to Abram, 'Go from your country and your kindred and your father's house to the land that I will show you. And I will make of you a great nation, and I will bless you, and make your name great, so that you will be a blessing. I will bless those who bless you, and him who curses you I will curse: and by you all the families of the earth [shall be blessed].'"

The blessing or the cursing of the Seed of Abraham, Gal 3:16, whether from outside or inside the Church opens up the disparity between Christianity and Judaism, as once Ishmael discovered too late. All internal opposition to the Messiah the Old Testament prophets had condemned, the Baptizer as the last.

2. Ferguson, *Backgrounds of Early Christianity*, 573.
3. Kirsch, *We Christians and Jews*, 5.
4. Ibid.,15.

Apologetic Note

STARTING OUT, I INTENDED on a neutral exposition of the history and meaning of the Oral Law. Slowly, however, in writing and editing, I recognized with consternation a vehemence entering the manuscript notes. Upon reflection, that intensity of enmity against the design of the Oral Law stands, unapologetically without, however, hateful motives.

Bibliography

Achtemeier, Paul J. and Elizabeth. *The Old Testament Roots of Our Faith.* Philadelphia: Fortress, 1962.

Albright, William F. *From the Stone Age to Christianity: Monotheism and the Historical Process.* Garden City: Doubleday, 1957.

Asch, Sholem. *The Apostle.* Translated by Maurice Samuel. New York: G.P. Putnam's Sons, 1943.

Baeck, Leo. *The Essence of Judaism.* New York: Schocken, 1948/67.

Ball, Charles F. *The Life and Journeys of Paul.* Chicago: Moody, 1951/71.

Barrett, C.K. *The New Testament Background: Selected Documents.* New York: Harper & Brothers, 1956/61.

Bass, D. Butler. *A People's History of Christianity: The Other Side of the Story.* New York: HarperCollins, 2009.

Bickerman, Elias. *From Ezra to the Last of the Maccabees: Foundations of Postbiblical Judaism.* New York: Schocken, 1962.

Bowker, John. *Jesus and the Pharisees.* Cambridge: Cambridge at the University Press, 1973.

Bright, John. *The Kingdom of God: The Biblical Concept and Its Meaning for the Church.* New York: Abingdon, 1953.

Bronner, Leah. *Sects and Separatism During the Second Jewish Commonwealth.* New York: Bloch, 1967.

Bruce, F.F. *Jesus & Christian Origins Outside the New Testament.* Grand Rapids: Eerdmans, 1974/77.

Bultmann, Rudolph. *Primitive Christianity: In its Contemporary Setting.* Translated by R.H. Fuller. New York: World Publishing, 1956/70.

Burrus, Virginia, and Rebecca Lyman. "Shifting the Focus of History." Virginia Burrus, ed., *Late Ancient Christianity*, Vol. II. Denis J. Janz, Gen. Ed., *A People's History of Christianity.* Minneapolis: Fortress, 2005.

Charlesworth, James H. *Jesus within Judaism: New Light from Exciting Archaeological Discoveries.* New York: Doubleday, 1988.

Coats, John R. *Original Sinners: A New Interpretation of Genesis.* New York: Free Press, 2009.

Crossan, John Dominic. T*he Birth of Christianity: Discovering What Happened In the Years Immediately After the Execution of Jesus.* Harper/SanFrancisco, 1998.

Deissmann, Adolf. *Paul: A Study in Social and Religious History.* New York: Harper & Brothers, 1912/57.

Dimont, Max. *Jews, God and History.* New York: New American Library/Signet, 1962.

Dodd, C.H. *The Meaning of Paul for Today.* London: Collins/Fontana, 1920/60.

Donin, Hayim Halevy. *To Be a Jew: A Guide to Jewish Observance in Contemporary Life.* New York: Basic Books, 1972.

Epstein, Isidore. *Judaism: A Historical Presentation.* New York: Penguin, 1959/82.

Ferguson, Everett. *Backgrounds of Early Christianity.* 2nd edition. Grand Rapids: Eerdmans, 1993.

Finkel, Asher. T*he Pharisees and the Teacher of Nazareth: A Study of Their Background, Their Halachic and Midrashic Teachings, the Similarities and Differences.* Leiden/Keulen: E.J. Brill, 1964.

Finkelstein, Louis. *The Pharisees: the Sociological Background of their Faith.* I. Philadelphia: The Jewish Publication Society of America, 1938/46.

Flavius, Josephus. *The Wars of the Jews.* Translated by William Whiston. *Josephus: Complete Works.* Grand Rapids: Kregel, 1970.

————. *The Antiquities of the Jews.* Translated by William Whiston. *Josephus: Complete Works.* Grand Rapids: Kregel, 1970.

Fonrobert, Charlotte E., "Jewish Christians, Judaizers, And Christian Anti-Judaism," in Virginia Burrus, Ed., *Late Ancient Christianity*, Vol. II in Denis R. Janz. Gen. Ed., *People's History of Christianity.* Minneapolis: Fortress, 2005.

Freedman, Samuel G. *Jew vs. Jew: The Struggle for the Soul of American Jewry.* New York: Simon & Schuster, 2000.

Hendriksen, W. *New Testament Commentary: Exposition of the Gospel According to Matthew.* Thus far the Oral Law to its historical eclipse Grand Rapids: Baker, 1975.

————. *New Testament Commentary: Exposition of the Gospel According to Luke.* Grand Rapids: Baker, 1978/90.

Hertzberg, Arthur, ed. *Judaism.* New York: George Brazillier, 1962.

Horsley, Richard A., "Unearthing a People's History," and "Jesus Movements and the Renewal of Israel," in Richard A. Horsley, ed. *Christian Origins, Vol. I.* Denis R. Janz, Gen. Ed. Minneapolis: Fortress, 2005.

Keck, Leander F. and Victor P. Furnish. *Interpreting Biblical Texts: The Pauline Letters.* Nashville: Abingdon, 1984.

Kee, Howard Clark. *Jesus in History: An Approach to the Study of the Gospels.* New York: Harcourt, Brace & World, 1970.

Kendall, R.T., and David Rosen. *The Christian and the Pharisee: Two Outspoken Religious Leaders Debate the Road to Heaven.* New York: Warner, 2007.

Kirsh, Paul J. *We Christians and Jews.* Philadelphia: Fortress, 1975.

Kittel, Gerhard, ed. *Theological Dictionary of the New Testament. IV.* Grand Rapids: Eerdmans, 1967/69.

Klinghoffer, David. *Why the Jews Rejected Jesus: The Turning Point In Western History.* New York: Random/Doubleday, 2005.

Levine, Etan. *The Aramaic Version of the Bible.* New York: De Gruyter, 1988.

Magonet, Jonathan. *The Explorer's Guide to Judaism.* London: Hodder & Stoughton, 1998.

Major, H.D.A., T.W. Manson, and C.J. Wright. *The Mission and Message of Jesus: An Exposition of the Gospels in the Light of Modern Research.* London: Ivor Nicholson, 1937.

Marrow, Stanley B. *Paul, His Letters and His Theology: An Introduction to Paul's Epistles.* New York: Paulist Press, 1986.

May, Herbert Gordon. "Synagogues in Palestine," in *The Biblical Archaeologist Reader*, G. Ernest Wright and David Noel Freedman, eds. New York: Doubleday/Anchor, 1961.

S. Dean McBride, Jr. "The Yoke of Torah," in Ex Auditu: An International Journal of Theological Interpretation of Scripture, Vol. 11, 1-15, 1995.

Neusner, Jacob. *Scriptures of the Oral Torah: Sanctification and Salvation in the Sacred Books of Judaism.* New York: Harper & Row, 1987.

Neusner, Jacob. *Judaism: An Introduction.* New York: Penguin, 2002.

Pollock, John. *The Apostle: A Life of Paul.* Garden City: Doubleday, 1969.

Rich, Tracey R., "A List of the 613 Mitzvot (Commandments)" from Webmaster@JewFAQ. Org.

Rivkin, Ellis. *A Hidden Revolution.* Nashville: Abingdon, 1978.

Roth, Cecil. *A Short History of the Jewish People.* Hartford: Hartmore House, 1936/67.

Russell, D.S. *Between the Testaments.* Philadelphia: Fortress, 1960/65.

Sanders, E.P. *Judaism: Practice and Belief, 63 BCE–66CE.* Philadelphia: Fortress, 1992.

Sandmel, Samuel. *The Genius of Paul: A Study in History.* Philadelphia: Fortress, 1958/79.

Schechter, Solomon. *Studies in Judaism: Essays on Persons, Concepts, and Movements of Thought in Jewish Tradition.* New York: Atheneum – a Temple Book, 1970.

———. *Aspects of Rabbinic Theology: Major Concepts of the Talmud.* New York: Schocken, 1909/61.

Shearer, J.B. *The Sermon on the Mount: A Study.* Richmond, VA: Presbyterian Committee of Publication, 1906.

Simcox, Carroll E. *The First Gospel: Its Meaning and Message.* Greenwich, Connecticut: Seabury, 1963.

Simon, Marcel. *Jewish Sects at the Time of Jesus* Translated by James H. Farley. Philadelphia: Fortress, 1967.

Taylor, Robert D. and Ronald J. Ricci. "Three Biblical Models of Liberty And Some Representative Laws," in Ex Auditu: An International Journal of Theological Interpretation of Scripture, Vol. 11, 1995.